CORPORATION LAW

CORPORATION LAW

KENNETH S. FERBER, LL.M., Ph.D.

Adjunct Professor of Law

Stetson University

College of Law

Prentice
Hall

Upper Saddle River, New Jersey 07458

Library of Congress Cataloging-in-Publication Data

Ferber, Kenneth S.
    Corporation law / Kenneth S. Ferber.
        p.   cm.
    Includes index.
    ISBN 0-13-084017-3
    1. Corporation law—United States.   I. Title
KF1414.3.F47 2001
346.73'066—dc21

                              00-051046

Executive Editor: Elizabeth Sugg
Editorial Assistant: Anita Rhodes
Production Editor: Sharon Anderson, BookMasters, Inc.
Production Liaison: Eileen O'Sullivan
Director of Production and Manufacturing: Bruce Johnson
Managing Editor: Mary Carnis
Manufacturing Manager: Ed O'Dougherty
Design Director: Marianne Frasco
Cover Design Coordinator: Miguel Ortiz
Cover Design: Bruce Kenselaar
Composition: BookMasters, Inc.
Printing and Binding: Victor Graphics

Prentice-Hall International (UK) Limited, *London*
Prentice-Hall of Australia Pty. Limited, *Sydney*
Prentice-Hall Canada Inc., *Toronto*
Prentice-Hall Hispanoamericana, S. A., *Mexico*
Prentice-Hall of India Private Limited, *New Delhi*
Prentice-Hall of Japan, Inc., *Tokyo*
Prentice-Hall Singapore Pte. Ltd.
Editora Prentice-Hall do Brasil, Ltda., *Rio de Janeiro*

10 9 8 7 6 5 4 3 2 1
ISBN 0-13-084017-3

CONTENTS

Chapter 2
WHAT IS A CORPORATION?   17

Chapter 3
DECIDING WHETHER AND HOW TO INCORPORATE   27

Chapter 4
CORPORATION STRUCTURE   36

Chapter 5
DO YOU WANT A CLOSE CORPORATION?　　　　　　　　50

Chapter 6
DUTIES OF OFFICERS AND DIRECTORS   65

Chapter 7
RAISING CAPITAL   **88**

Chapter 10
SHAREHOLDER SUITS

Chapter 11
MERGERS, ACQUISITIONS, AND DISSOLUTIONS 155

Chapter 12
WHAT ARE INSIDER AND TENDER OFFERS?   170

Chapter 13
PUBLIC DISTRIBUTION OF SECURITIES   185

PREFACE

Everyone needs reference material for corporation law. This book was designed for novices, those without formal legal training, to acquaint them with the fundamentals of corporation law. The chapters flow in a normal order; they are easy to follow and understandable. Forms are provided in the appendix. Enough information and forms are included to well start one on the formation of a corporation. Most problems can be prevented or solved by a reading. Key terms, review questions, and essay questions appear at the end of each chapter as a reinforcement of the reading.

ACKNOWLEDGMENTS

The support and encouragement of my loving wife, Joan, and our children, Karen Sue and Kevin, and Rolex (my daughter's Persian cat) was most welcome.

My thanks to the American Bar Association, Section of Business Law, Committee on Corporate Laws, for allowing me to reprint parts of the Revised Model Business Corporation Act.

I am especially grateful to Prentice Hall for providing me this opportunity. My editor, Elizabeth Sugg, and Dana Leigh Meltzer, provided the support that made this effort a reality. My thanks to the entire Prentice Hall family for their support and aid.

YOUR CLIENT WANTS
TO GO INTO BUSINESS

OBJECTIVES

After completing this chapter, you will be able to:

1. Define the various ways to go into business ownership.
2. Know the advantages of each business vehicle.
3. Know the disadvantages of each business vehicle.
4. Choose the proper vehicle for the proper business objectives.
5. Know the procedure to form the proper business vehicle.

INTRODUCTION

An attorney is retained by a client who wants to go into business. There are several types of **business entities** (ways to go into business; corporation and partnership are two of the many choices). Legal secretaries and/or paralegals assist attorneys in interviewing clients, obtaining facts and information, preparing proper forms and agreements, performing legal research and recording documents. It is necessary to find out what **vehicle** (entity) the client has in mind. Then one must discuss the proper vehicle with the attorney. The attorney explains to the client the different ways to go into business, the advantages and disadvantages of each, and then comes to a decision with the client for the best vehicle to achieve the client's goal.

TYPES OF BUSINESS ENTITIES

- Sole Proprietorship
- General Partnership
- Limited Partnership
- Corporation
- Closed Corporation
- Limited Liability Company
- Limited Liability Partnership

Joint Ventures, Business Trusts, Professional Corporations, Nonprofit Corporations, and Public Corporations, are not the everyday work of a law firm and fall into more specialized areas.

SOLE PROPRIETORSHIP

A sole proprietorship is a business owned by one person. It is easy to form and generally can be done orally. Usually, no filings are necessary with state and/or municipal agencies. It is not a **legal entity.** This means you cannot sue or be sued, or purchase or sell property in the company name. You must sue, be sued, or purchase or sell property in the name of the **sole proprietor** (the person who is the owner of the business). For example, ABC Pizza is owned by Mary Smith. You must sue Mary Smith, **d/b/a** (doing business as) ABC Pizza.

John Jones wants to go into the plumbing business as a sole proprietor. He rents a store and places his name on the window. "John Jones—Plumber." He is now a sole proprietor. He receives all of the profits of the business. He runs the business, hires, fires, and makes all business decisions. If there are losses, he bears the losses. John Jones may have invested $500 to start his business. He is personally liable for all debts incurred by the business regardless of the amount.

The major **disadvantage** of sole proprietorships is unlimited personal liability. If the plumber is driving his car to a customer to repair plumbing and has an accident, injuring a person so that person will no longer be able to walk or work, he could be **personally liable** (at fault) for millions of dollars. If his car is insured for $100,000 liability, the insurance company will pay the first $100,000 and John Jones will be personally liable for the remainder. It does not matter how much is invested in the company, the sole proprietor has **unlimited** personal liability. If the plumber broke something in a customer's home, there would be personal liability. He may have charged $50 for the repair and on his way out accidentally knocked over and broke a $10,000 antique. He is personally liable for the value of the antique.

Taxes

Earnings are taxed as **ordinary income** (all the money made during the year); losses can be deducted from ordinary income. The sole proprietor does not pay a separate income tax on the business. A schedule showing the income or loss from the business is attached to the personal tax return of the sole proprietor.

Sale or Disposal

During the life of the sole proprietor, the business can be sold at any time, the same as any property can be sold. The sale, however, is sometimes difficult to make since the business is closely tied to the personality of the sole proprietor.

Death

When the sole proprietor dies, the business terminates. The **assets** (items owned by the business) can be sold by the **heir or heirs** [people designated by the **decedent** (party that died) to receive the property on death] of the deceased pursuant to order of the Probate or Surrogate Court in the **jurisdiction** (place) in which the decedent passed away.

Note: We are assuming that no state, county, city, town, or village license is required to be a plumber in the area where John Jones starts his business. You must check the local **statutes** and ordinances, and rules and regulations. Statutes are created by Congress on the federal level and State legislatures on the state level. Ordinances are created by county, city, town or village ruling bodies. Rules and regulations are made by administrative agencies. If already licensed, then proceed as above and commence business.

Note: Caution—If John Jones changes the sign to read "Dunedin Plumbing, John Jones Plumber" (Dunedin being the name of the city where John Jones wants to practice plumbing), he is using a fictitious business name. Whenever you have a fictitious name, you must register that name with the county, city, town, or village; check local **statutes** (laws). The certificate to file is usually just a notice with the name of the fictitious business, its address, and the name and address of the owner. Some states require you to place a small ad in the legal notices section of the local newspaper saying that you are carrying on a business under an assumed name at a certain location. Some states require the newspaper notice and a filing. The way to tell if a name is fictitious is simple. Just check your birth certificate. If the name on your business is not exactly as on your birth certificate, it is fictitious and requires either a filing, a notice, or both depending on your location.

Note: If the client is going to hire employees, he or she must have an Employer ID number from the U.S. Internal Revenue Service (IRS). The accountant or CPA for the sole proprietor will usually obtain one. Check with the CPA or accountant; if they are not going to obtain one, you can acquire one by calling the local IRS office. When you obtain the form, complete it and file it with the IRS. Some states require a State ID number as well. If so, contact the State Tax Department for the form and filing requirements.

Note: If your state has a sales tax and the client is selling an item that requires sales tax, a sales tax number is usually obtained by the accountant or CPA. If the client wants your law firm to do it, just call the sales tax department in your state, obtain the form for a tax number, complete it, file it, and you will be sent a number.

Note: If your client has employees, check your state requirements. Usually the client will have to obtain workers compensation insurance and unemployment insurance. Usually the accountant or CPA takes care of this. If you are going to do it, simply call a licensed insurance agent and the agent will take care of both insurance needs.

Advantages of a Sole Proprietorship

- Easy to form.
- Can be oral or written.
- Generally no filings necessary with state or municipal agencies.
- Owner receives all profits.

- Owner runs the business and makes all decisions.
- Owner hires and fires.
- No federal tax is paid on the earnings of the business. The earnings of the owner are taxed as ordinary income of the owner.
- Can be sold, given as a gift, or left to the heirs of the owner.

Disadvantages of a Sole Proprietorship

- Unlimited personal liability.
- On death of owner the business terminates. No continuity. The assets may be sold by the heirs of the deceased.
- May be difficult to raise capital.
- Very often have to spend long hours at the business.
- May be difficult to sell as it is a personal business between the owner and the customers.

GENERAL PARTNERSHIP

A general partnership involves two or more persons or entities who carry on a business for profit as co-owners. Persons are defined to include corporations, general partnerships, limited partnerships, sole proprietorships, joint ventures, and other entities (business vehicles, ways to go into business). Therefore, two corporations can join together as a general partnership. One corporation, one general partnership, one sole proprietorship, one limited partnership, or any combination or number of these entities can join together as a general partnership. The possibilities are endless as long as you have two or more carrying on a business for profit as co-owners.

Number of Persons and Investment Needed

The number of partners in a general partnership is **infinite** (unlimited). Anything of value can be used as an investment, as long as it is agreed on by all other partners. Money, knowledge, work, labor, promissory notes and other intangibles, real estate, or **personal property** (anything other than real property and real property is land or anything firmly affixed to the land that cannot be removed without damage to the land or item; everything else in the world is personal property). One partner can invest knowledge, another labor, and another money, or any combination of these or others can be used as a partner's investment.

Name of General Partnership

Any name can be used as the partnership name as long as the name does not require a license. If it does, you must have the license. You cannot call yourself certified public accountant, unless you are a licensed certified public accountant. You cannot call yourself anything that will indicate you are a government agency unless you are a government agency created by law.

Advantages of a General Partnership

The basic advantage of a general partnership is that it is easy to form, oral or in writing, and does not require any filing (unless it is a fictitious name—then proceed as discussed under sole proprietorship). A group of people or entities can agree orally that they want to be a general partnership and that is it, they are a general partnership. It is that simple and easy. It takes little or no cost to form. Another advantage is taxes. Each partner's earnings in the partnership are reported as ordinary income to the partner. The general partnership does not pay an income tax. Losses can be deducted on income tax returns against other gains from other business ventures. This could be a big advantage. A disadvantage taxwise would be if, for example, there were ten equal partners and the business earned $10,000 for the year, and all the partners agreed to keep the $10,000 in the partnership for expansion. However, each partner would have to report $1,000 (his or her share of earnings) on his or her income tax return as ordinary income, even though it was not taken out of the business.

Disadvantages of a General Partnership

Every general partner has unlimited personal liability similar to a sole proprietor, and every partner is liable for **all** of the debts of the partnership. This is called **joint and several liability.** For instance, the partnership owes Mr. Jones $5,000. This means the partnership owes Mr. Jones $5,000; together **(jointly)** the partners owe Mr. Jones $5,000; and **severally** (individually) each partner owes Mr. Jones $5,000. Mr. Jones **can only collect a total of $5,000.** However, if he cannot collect from the partnership, he can collect jointly from all partners or individually from any one partner. If one partner has to pay the $5,000 and there are five partners, then the partner paying the $5,000 has a right to be **indemnified** (receive payment) from the other four partners in the amount of $1,000 each. He accomplishes this through a lawsuit in equity, asking for an accounting. There are two different kinds of courts: a law court where you sue to collect dollars and a court of equity. If you do not have a remedy at law, then you go to a court of equity. A partner **cannot** sue the partnership. If you did, you would be suing yourself. Thus, since you have no remedy at law, you go into a court of equity and ask for an accounting and indemnification. Some states have only one court and the judge sits both as a court of equity and a court of law.

Oral General Partnership

First, in an oral general partnership, all partners have an equal vote regardless of their investment. If there are five partners and one invests $10 and each of the others invest $10,000, all of the five have an equal vote. Each of the five share equally in profits and losses regardless of their investment. You must also remember the Statute of Frauds. Any agreement concerning real estate or that cannot be completed within one year must be in writing. This pertains to general partnerships as well as other writings. The statute of frauds has nothing to do with fraud. It is a preventative statute, designed to prevent fraud by requiring certain transactions to be in writing. There are seven contracts (agreements) that must be in writing to comply with the statute.

- Any agreement that cannot be completed within one year. Therefore, if the object of the partnership cannot be completed within one year, it must be in writing.
- Any agreement concerning real property must be in writing. If a partner intends to use real property or a lease for real property instead of cash as a contribution to the partnership, then, that would have to be in writing.
- Anytime one offers a creditor to pay the debts of another, this must be in writing. Therefore, if one potential partner offers to pay a creditor of the partnership a sum of money to be considered as the investment of the partner, this must be in writing.

- Anytime a trustee, executor or administrator offers to pay a debt of the fund being administered out of the pocket of the trustee, executor or administrator, this must be in writing. Therefore, if a potential partner was owed monies from a trust and the trust did not have the funds to pay, but the trustee offered to pay the monies to the partnership in the name of the potential partner, out of his own funds, this would have to be in writing.
- Sale of goods (movable, tangible, personal property) over $500.00 must be in writing. If a partner was going to transfer certain personal property to the partnership as the investment of the partner, this would have to be in writing.
- Sale of securities, creating a security interest, or royalties over $5,000.00 must be in writing. If a partner as investment in the partnership was transferring royalties to the partnership over $5,000.00, this would have to be in writing.
- A contract concerning marriage, except the actual marriage contract must be in writing. This would not pertain to a partnership.

Agent of Partnership

Each partner is an **agent of the partnership** (has authority to act on behalf of the partnership). This means that any partner can **bind** (make liable) the partnership as long as the partner buys something for the partnership that the partnership can use. This is called **apparent authority.** An **example** might be the purchase of note pads or stationery. A sales person in a store is an agent for the store and has authority to sell you merchandise and take your payment on behalf of his or her principal, i.e., the owner.

Apparent Authority

Each partner as an agent has the **apparent authority to bind** (make liable) the partnership. Apparent authority means any partner can go into an office supply store and buy office supplies and charge it to the partnership. Similarly, if the partnership makes and sells pizzas, any partner would have apparent authority to buy an inexpensive vehicle to use for deliveries and charge it to the partnership as long as the supplies can be used by the partnership. The partner would not have apparent authority to buy a $300,000 Rolls Royce to deliver pizzas unless, for example, the pizza business was in a very exclusive and wealthy community. Apparent authority means obvious authority to buy what you are buying as an agent for the partnership. The burden of proving apparent authority is on the seller, so the seller must be sure the buyer has authority to bind the partnership.

Termination of Partnership on Death of a Partner

If one partner dies, the partnership terminates. The new Revised Uniform Partnership Act (**RUPA**) adopted by some states allows the surviving partner to purchase the interest of the deceased partner and continue the business. The value of the business could be established by an accountant and agreed to by all parties; if not, by the court. Check your state statutes to see which law applies.

Loyalty

No partner can sue the partnership. If a partner sued the partnership, the partner would be suing himself or herself and that would not be permitted. Every partner owes the partnership the duty of loyalty. This means you must do the best for the partnership at all times and cannot compete with the partnership without the consent of all partners. For example, if you are a partner in a pizza shop in Los Angeles, California, you cannot go into the pizza business yourself or participate in any way with any other party, corporation, or business anywhere in the world, without the consent of all of your partners in the Los Angeles shop. This is the duty of loyalty. You cannot compete with the partnership. If you want to open a pizza shop in New York, you must have consent because someday the Los Angeles partnership may want to expand to New York and you would be a competitor. Thus, you cannot compete without the consent of all partners.

Adding Partners or Selling a Partner's Interest

All partners must agree to a sale of the business or to the sale of the interest of one partner. **All** partners must agree to add a partner. You cannot add partners unless all present partners agree. If you have five partners (the number is not important) and four of the partners want Mr. Jones, a millionaire, to join the partnership because he is willing to invest $2,000,000 in the partnership and one partner does not want Mr. Jones in the partnership, Mr. Jones cannot become a partner. To add partners, **all** partners must agree. If one partner wants to sell an interest to Mr. Smith, and four of the partners agree to the sale but one does not, Mr. Smith cannot buy the interest.

Assignment of Interest

If a partner cannot sell his interest for failure to receive **unanimous** (all) consent of the partners, assignment of the interest to the partnership to another party is an option. This can be accomplished without consent of the partners. Assignment means that the **assignee** (party buying) has the right to receive all profits of the **assignor** (party selling). The assignor (seller) still attends partnership meetings and votes; the assignee (buyer) does not attend. Losses are the assignor's (seller's) responsibility. Profits go to the assignee (buyer).

Example: Ms. Anderson is one of six partners in the ABC book store. The partnership was not created in writing. It was created orally. Ms. Anderson asks all of the other five partners to consent to her selling her undivided one sixth interest in the book store to Mr. Frank. One partner withholds consent and Ms. Anderson is unable to sell her interest to Mr. Frank.

Ms. Anderson now assigns her interest in profits from the book store to Mr. Frank. Consent of partners is not required with an assignment. Ms. Anderson now receives money from Mr. Frank for his right to receive the profits from the partnership that belong to Ms. Anderson. Ms. Anderson is still a partner and can vote at partnership meetings. Ms. Anderson is liable for all losses of the partnership. Mr. Frank receives whatever profits would have been paid to Ms. Anderson.

Liability of New Partner

If the partnership has four equal partners (number not important) and owes $100,000 to creditors, and all partners allow one partner, Mr. A, to sell his interest to Mr. T, Mr. T, from that point on, is liable for any **new** debts of the partnership equally with his other three partners. Mr. T is **not** liable for any portion of the previous $100,000 owed. Mr. A has that **liability** (debt) with his former three partners.

Partnership Agreement

In the absence of a written agreement, the issues just discussed will be settled by the laws in most states or by the Uniform Partnership Act (UPA) or the Reformed Uniform Partnership Act (RUPA). A writing can modify the situation to a more desirable position. The writing would be called a partnership agreement, articles of partnership or a buy and sell agreement. Different parts of the country have different names, but the content of the writing is always the same. An agreement is a contract. In this contract the terms of the partnership would be outlined, the duties of each partner, if any, compensation, kind of investment each partner would make, cash, goods, real property, personal property or intangible, selling rights for each partner, voting rights, profit and loss distributions and rights upon the death of each partner and any other provisions pertaining to this particular transaction.

If the parties agree that a partnership interest may be sold, the interest should be offered first to the partnership. If the partnership does not exercise its right of purchase then, it is offered to the individual partners. If the individual partners decline to exercise their option of purchase then, the seller is free to offer the interest for sale to anyone in the general public without restrictions. This gives the partners an opportunity to control that interest and the hands that it may come into. If you just restrict the sale of an interest of a partner, it is tantamount to ceasing the interest of the partner and the court will not permit that and will force liquidation of the partnership or payment of a fair and just price, set by the court to the holder of the interest, without control by the other partners. By the method discussed above, the selling partner has three different ways of selling and only the order of sale is outlined and restricted.

Assets

The assets (properties) of the general partnership belong to the partnership, not to the partners. The partners merely have an interest in all of the assets owned by the partnership. Therefore, if you have five equal partners and five exactly equal stores, each partner **does not** own one store. Each partner owns one-fifth of each of the five stores.

Right to Sue and Be Sued

If the state has **legislation** allowing a partnership to buy and sell property in its own name and to sue and be sued in its own name, the company can do these things in the name of the partnership. Otherwise, it must buy, sell, sue, or be sued in the names of the partners doing business as the partnership. For instance, A, B, C, and D are equal partners in a general partnership named "The Group, a (name of state where the main office is) General Partnership." For example, "The Group, a New York General Partnership." If the State of New York did not have a statute allowing the partnership to sue or be sued in its own name, it would read as follows, "A, B, C, and D doing business as The Group, a New York General Partnership." If you sued as A, B, C, and D, d/b/a (doing business as) "The Group a New York General Partnership," you could obtain a judgment against A individually, B individually, C individually, D individually and "The Group" (partnership). This gives you an opportunity to collect from five places (A, B, C, D, and the partnership) rather than from just one if you sued just the partnership.

Note: Caution. Whenever you have a fictitious name, you must register that name with the county, city, town, or village; check local statutes (laws). The certificate to file is usually just a notice with the name of the fictitious business, its address, and the name and address of the owner. Some states require you to place a small ad in the legal notices section of a local newspaper saying that you are carrying on a business under an assumed name at a specific location. Some states require the newspaper notice and a filing. The way to tell if a name is fictitious is simple. Just check your birth certificate. If the name on your business is not exactly as on your birth certificate, it is fictitious and requires either a filing, notice, or both, depending on the area.

Note: If the partnership is going to hire employees, it must have an Employer ID number from the U.S. Internal Revenue Service (IRS). The client's accountant or CPA will usually obtain same. You can obtain one by calling the local IRS office. When you obtain the form, complete it and file it with the IRS.

Note: If your state has a sales tax and the client is selling an item that requires sales tax, this number is usually obtained by the accountant or CPA. If you desire to do it, just call the sales tax department in your state, obtain their form for a tax number, complete it, file it, and you will be sent a number.

Note: If your client has employees, check your state requirements. Usually the client will have to obtain workers compensation insurance and unemployment insurance. Again, usually the accountant or CPA takes care of this. If you are going to do it, simply call an insurance agent and he or she will take care of both insurance needs.

Advantages of a General Partnership

- Easy to form.
- Generally can be oral or in writing.
- Inexpensive to form.
- Earnings taxed as ordinary income to partners. No separate tax for the general partnership.
- Losses shared by each partner equally, unless there is a written agreement to the contrary, and then they are deducted from ordinary income.

Disadvantages of a General Partnership

- Unlimited personal liability for each partner.
- Equal vote and distribution of profits and losses unless a written agreement to the contrary.
- Each partner as an agent has apparent authority to bind the partnership.
- Partnership terminates on death of a partner unless an agreement exists to the contrary. (RUPA may change this, if your state adopted RUPA.)
- A partner cannot add a partner to the partnership unless all the partners agree, or a writing exists that permits the addition.
- A partner cannot sell his or her interest without consent of all partners, unless a writing exists to the contrary.
- Every partner owes loyalty to the partnership. A partner may not be able to open a similar business in another state without the consent of all the partners.
- Partnership assets belong to the partnership, not to the individual partners.

LIMITED PARTNERSHIP

A limited partnership consists of one or more general partners and one or more limited partners. The number is **infinite** (unlimited). The general partnership is informal; it can be formed orally or in writing and does not have to be recorded anyplace. The limited partnership is formal. It must be in writing. It must be recorded with the secretary of state, and it must have the information required by statute. The general partner or partners run the business. The general partners have unlimited personal liability and all the advantages and disadvantages of general partners.

Restricted Rights of Limited Partners

Limited partners do not have a say in running the business. Limited partners cannot work for the limited partnership. They have no vote. They can only invest money. General partners can invest money, knowledge, labor, and real or personal property. Limited partners' liability is generally limited to their investment. Whether limited partners receive a percentage of profits on a yearly or other basis, or just on the sale of assets, is stated in the limited partnership agreement. If limited partners work for the limited partnership, they will be considered general partners as far as creditors are concerned and limited partners as far as the other partners are concerned. If a limited partner's name is in the limited partnership, he or she will be considered a general partner as far as creditors are concerned, and a limited partner as far as the other partners are concerned.

Tax Advantages

Limited partners enjoy tax advantages. Thus, a limited partnership is usually referred to as a tax shelter. The limited partnership agreement can say that all interest paid on mortgages that the partnership has will belong to the limited partners, and they may deduct it on their personal tax forms. Real estate taxes, capital improvements, and other taxable deductions can be given to the limited partners to deduct on their personal tax forms. They are therefore buying tax deductions and the hope of future sharing in profits. The majority of the profits will go to the general partners although the capital will come from the limited partners. In return, the general partners have unlimited personal liability.

Ownership of Real Property and Ability to Sue and Be Sued in Its Name

A limited partnership can own and dispose of real property in its own name and sue and be sued in its own name, only if there is a statute allowing it. (Check your state statute.)

Uses of Limited Partnerships

Limited partnerships are usually used in the financing of real estate projects: malls, buildings, shopping centers, etc. They are also used to finance wildcat oil drilling, to locate oil, to purchase cattle, and to finance movies and Broadway plays. These are all areas of high risk.

　　Note: Caution. Since the limited partnership is formal and requires a written filing, the rules of a fictitious name do not apply. However, if the limited partnership sets up a **division** (separate business) that is not incorporated, in some states the rules apply as to fictitious name as follows (check your state statute). Whenever a limited partnership has a fictitious name it must register that name with the county, city, town, or village; check local statutes (laws). The certificate to file is usually just a notice with the name of the fictitious business, its address, and the name and address of the owner. Some states require a small ad in the legal notices section of a local newspaper that the limited partnership is carrying on a business under an assumed name at such and such a location. Some states require the newspaper notice and a filing. The way to tell if a name is fictitious is simple. Just check the owner(s) birth certificate. If the name of the business is not exactly as on the birth certificate(s), it is fictitious and requires either a filing, notice, or both depending on the area.

　　Note: If the limited partnership is going to hire employees, it must have an Employer ID number from the U.S. Internal Revenue Service (IRS). The accountant or CPA for the client will usually obtain same. An individual can obtain one by calling the local IRS office to obtain the form, completing it, and filing it with the IRS.

Note: If the state has a sales tax and the client is selling an item that requires sales tax, again this number is usually obtained by the accountant or CPA. To do it, just call the state sales tax department, obtain its form for a tax number, complete it, file it, and they will send you a number.

Note: If your client has employees, check your state requirements. Usually the client will have to obtain workers compensation insurance and unemployment insurance. Again, the accountant or CPA usually takes care of this. An individual can simply call an insurance agent and he or she will take care of both insurance needs.

Advantages of a Limited Partnership

- Limited partners are generally limited to the loss of their investment.
- Tax advantages for both general and limited partners are the ability to pass earnings and losses directly to the partners who add earnings to their ordinary income and deduct losses from their ordinary income.
- The interest of all parties is usually transferable.
- Under RUPA, death of a partner will not terminate the partnership. In some states death will terminate partnership.
- It is easy to raise additional capital by adding new partners.

Disadvantages of a Limited Partnership

- General partners have unlimited liability. In many states limited partners are at risk to add additional money to the partnership if needed.
- Limited partners cannot work in the business.
- Limited partners have no vote in the management of the business.
- Organizational expense can be quite high for lawyers and accountants.
- A limited partnership is formal and must be in writing, filed, and in compliance with the state statute.

CORPORATIONS

A corporation is a **legal entity** (business). It is an artificial person. A corporation can do anything a person can do. It can buy and sell real estate in its own name. A corporation can bring a lawsuit or be sued in its own name. It can do anything that a natural person can do. Corporations have many advantages and few disadvantages. It is easy to raise capital for, manage, buy an interest in, or sell an interest in a corporation. It has **perpetual life** (it can go on forever). The rest of this book is dedicated to corporations in much greater detail.

Note: Caution. Since a corporation is **formal** (requires a written filing), it does not have to record a fictitious name. However, if a corporation sets up a **division** (separate business) owned by the corporation that is not also incorporated, in some states (check your state statutes) the fictitious rules apply, as follows: Whenever a corporation has a fictitious name, it must register that name with the county, city, town, or village; check local statutes (laws). The certificate to file is usually just a notice with the name of the fictitious business, its address, and the name and address of the owner. Some states require placement of a small ad in the legal notices section of a local newspaper that a corporation is carrying on a business under an assumed name at such and such a location. Some states require the newspaper notice and a filing. The way to tell if a name is fictitious is simple. Just check the birth certificate(s) of the owner(s). If the name of the business is not exactly as on the birth certificate(s) of the owner(s), it is fictitious and requires either a filing, notice, or both depending on the area.

Note: If the corporation is going to hire employees it must have an Employer ID number from the U.S. Internal Revenue Service (IRS). The accountant or CPA for the client will usually obtain it. An individual can obtain one by calling the local IRS office to obtain the form, completing it, and filing it with the IRS.

Note: If the state has a sales tax and the client is selling an item that requires sales tax, a sales tax number is usually obtained by the accountant or CPA. If an individual desires to obtain one, just call the sales tax department in the state, obtain the form for a tax number, complete it, file it, and they will send a number.

Note: If your client has employees, check your state requirements. Usually the client will have to obtain workers compensation insurance and unemployment insurance. Usually the accountant or CPA takes care of this. If an individual is going to do it, simply call an insurance agent, and he or she will take care of both insurance needs.

LIMITED LIABILITY COMPANY (LLC)

While limited liability companies have existed for many years, for well over fifty years in Europe, they are comparatively new in the United States. In many states they are less than five years old. Some states do not allow them at all. In a few states they are close to twenty years old. While these are new, it means that there is not always certainty as to liabilities and rights of parties. This creates a type of gamble for the client. Many established conservative attorneys will wait until there has been sufficient litigation in all areas so that all possible contingencies are known and rights and liabilities have been established by the courts. This usually takes at least fifty years. Therefore, this writer suggests extreme caution when counseling concerning these vehicles. If your client sets up a limited liability company in state A and then does business in State B where they do not have limited liability companies, and the courts of State B rule on a dispute, the results can be severe and totally different than your client ever conceived.

Limited Liability Company Members

Owners of a limited liability company are known as members and are not individually liable for the obligations, debts, and liabilities of the organization.

Operating Agreement

A member owns an interest in the limited liability company and is a **party** (signer) to the contract known as the operating agreement, or member control agreement, limited liability company agreement, or regulations (the names are different in various states; the contents are more or less the same). Some states require this agreement in writing; some states just require certain provisions in writing; and some states handle it as a partnership and require no writing.

Recording Requirements

The Articles of Organization creates the limited liability company and is recorded (filed with the Secretary of State). In some states it is also an agreement between the members.

Types of Limited Liability Companies

There are two types of limited liability companies: member-managed and manager-managed. In member-managed, each member is an agent with authority to make decisions. In manager-managed, the members are not agents, and generally have authority to make only major decisions. Managers, who may not be members, have statutory control and the authority to make most decisions. Many states have "flexible statutes" that allow the members to enter into an agreement as to how the internal affairs of the company will be governed, limited only by provisions that may change its tax status from partnership to corporation. Other "bullet proof statutes" limit the areas that can be varied by members to guarantee that a partnership classification for tax purposes remains. The ability to contract arrangements that afford limited liability like a corporation, yet allow management relationships on the contract, and have it treated as a partnership for tax purposes, is possibly the ideal business vehicle. It has the best of both corporation and partnership status.

A Legal Entity

The limited liability company is a legal entity (it can do everything in its own name). It operates through its statutorily authorized agents (members or manager).

History

Basically, limited liability companies are **hybrids** (parts of different things) of general partnerships, limited partnerships, and corporations.

Until 1995 there was no uniform limited liability company (LLC) statute for states to base their legislation on. Therefore, there are **variables** (differences) in state statutes although they share certain **characteristics** (things).

Non-Corporate Business

An LLC is a non-corporate business organization, created by statute, and generally provides limited liability for all of its owners (members). The members can all participate in management and, if properly structured, can be taxed as a general partnership. Therefore, it provides the limited liability similar to that of a corporation and the tax advantages of a general partnership. It has more benefits than a limited partnership as all of its members can participate in management. Ownership interest in some LLCs may be considered a security and therefore subject to state and federal regulation. The formation is formal and must comply strictly with the statute creating it. Many of the states require at least two members. Once formed, the LLC is a legal entity and operates on its own. In many states it can own and dispose of property in its own name. The Articles of Organization must be filed in a designated state office. The information required for filing varies from state to state. You must check the statute of your state. Some states limit the life of an LLC to thirty years or less. Some states require the date of dissolution of the LLC in the filing. "LLC" or "Limited Liability Company" is generally required in the name. This allows all who deal with it to know the liability situation.

Investment in Limited Liability Companies

The investment by members can be work, labor, knowledge, money, real property, or personal property. Most states require an Operating Agreement in writing between the members. The agreement states how profits and losses will be handled and the method of management.

Taxation of an LLC

Most people want an LLC to be taxed as a partnership rather than as a corporation. Remember, there can be dual taxation with a corporation if you are not careful. The corporation pays a tax on earnings and then the stockholder (shareholder) receives a dividend that is again taxed as income to the shareholder. In a general partnership, earnings of the partnership are divided between the partners either according to a written agreement, statute, pursuant to the percentage of ownership of each partner, or equally by common law. Each partner then has this profit added to his or her ordinary income.

Dissolution of an LLC

Death, dissolution or bankruptcy that causes a member to cease being a member will cause dissolution unless the remaining members agree to continue. Most statutes allow a member to withdraw at any time and demand payment for his or her interest.

Rule of IRS for Taxation as a Partnership

The U.S. Internal Revenue Service has a regulation that must be complied with for an LLC to be taxed as a partnership. If it fails to meet the criteria, it will be taxed as a corporation. A partnership can only have two of the following four characteristics. If it has more than two, it will be deemed a corporation for tax purposes. The criteria are:

(1) Continuity of life
(2) Centralized management
(3) Limited liability
(4) Free transferability of interests

Items 2 and 3 above are usually satisfied. Continuity of life is prohibited by not making it perpetual (setting a time or method when it will end). Free transferability is prohibited by placing a restriction on the interest so that it must first be offered to other members, then to the company, before it can be sold to anyone else.

Note: Caution. Since the LLC is formal and requires a writing to be filed, there is no need to file a fictitious name. However, if the LLC sets up as a division that is not incorporated, in many states the rules apply as to fictitious filing (check your state statutes). Whenever you have a fictitious name, you must register that name with the county, city, town, or village; check local statutes (laws). The certificate to file is usually just a notice with the name of the fictitious business, its address, and the name and address of the owner. Some states require you to place a small ad in the legal notices section of a local newspaper that your client is carrying on a business under an assumed name at a named address. Some states require the newspaper notice and a filing. The way to tell if a name is fictitious is simple. Just check the client's birth certificate. If the name of the business is not exactly the same as on the birth certificate, it is fictitious and requires either a filing, notice, or both, depending on the area.

Note: If your client is going to hire employees, it must have an Employer ID number from the U.S. Internal Revenue Service (IRS). The accountant or CPA for the client will usually obtain it. You can obtain one by calling the local IRS office, obtaining their form, completing it, and filing it with the IRS.

Note: If your state has a sales tax and your client is selling an item that requires sales tax, this number is usually obtained by the accountant or CPA. If you desire to obtain it, just call the sales tax department in your state, obtain its form for a tax number, complete it, file it, and you will be sent a number.

Note: If your client has employees, check your state requirements. Usually, your client will have to obtain workers compensation insurance and unemployment insurance. Again, usually the accountant or CPA takes care of this. If you are going to do it, simply call an insurance agent, and he or she will take care of both insurance needs.

LIMITED LIABILITY PARTNERSHIP (LLP)

[handwritten margin note: no general partners only liable up to the extent of their investment]

There is no uniform LLP statute. It is a general partnership that limits the liability of its partners for some or all of the partnership's obligations. It is formal and must be recorded with the Secretary of State. Some states require annual renewals, some periodic reports, and a few require no renewal or reports. Some statutes have limited liability only for negligent acts, some for all torts, and contracts from negligence, as in malpractice, misconduct, or wrongful acts by a partner. Some states have unlimited liability for ordinary contracts. A few states have limited liability for all debts and obligations, but this does not apply to a partner committing the wrongful acts. Check your local statute in the state where you are looking to form this vehicle and in the states in which the company will be doing business.

SUMMARY

There are various vehicles available to enter into a business relationship and ownership: sole proprietorship, general partnership, limited partnership, corporation, close corporation, limited liability company, limited liability partnership, joint venture, business trust, professional corporation, non-profit corporation, and public corporation. Each entity has advantages and disadvantages. It is necessary to match the needs of the client with the form of business entity. Different states have different laws and these must be taken into consideration, especially if the client is going to operate in more than one state. An improper decision as to the vehicle to use can be a very costly error in terms of taxes, ability to manage, profits, and liability of the parties. Therefore, great care must be exercised and careful research of the business of the client and the needs of the client must be considered before making the decision.

WORDS TO KNOW

apparent authority	business entity
assets	close corporation
bind	corporation

deceased

division

general partnership

heirs

indemnify

infinite

joint and several liability

liability

limited partnership

personal property

real property

sole proprietorship

statutes

vehicle

REVIEW QUESTIONS

1. What is a fictitious name?
2. What do you have to do if you use a fictitious name for a business?
3. What are the advantages and disadvantages of a sole proprietorship?
4. What is a general partnership?
5. What are the advantages and disadvantages of a general partnership?
6. What is the purpose of a partnership agreement?
7. Who owns the assets in a partnership?
8. Define a limited partnership.
9. What are the advantages and disadvantages of a limited partnership?
10. Which vehicles are formal (require a filing)? Where are the filings filed?

SHORT ESSAY

1. Your client has great knowledge and little cash to invest, in fact, only $500. The business is consulting. The industry is hydro-electric. The client will advise how best to build and construct a plant, the equipment needed, and where and how to place it to produce maximum results for the plant. The client can receive fees upward of $250,000 per consultation client. The client will operate in all fifty states. Analyze the facts and state what you feel is the best vehicle and why. If the client may expect problems, point out problems that the client may face and possible solutions.
2. The client wants to start a business but is afraid that the business may terminate on his death. The client is also concerned about the ability to raise capital. There is also concern that he may not like his partners. What suggestions can you make?

C H A P T E R

WHAT IS A CORPORATION?

OBJECTIVES

After completing this chapter, you will be able to:

1. Perform the duties of a legal secretary and/or paralegal with reference to corporations.
2. Define a corporation and what it can do.
3. Identify a domestic, foreign, and alien corporation.
4. Know the different types of corporations.
5. Know how different corporations are taxed.
6. Discuss the principle of sovereignty.

DUTIES OF A LEGAL SECRETARY AND/OR PARALEGAL WITH REFERENCE TO A CORPORATION

The duties are set by the law firm where you are employed and may vary from firm to firm. Some duties are as follows:

(A) Interview the client to determine the best vehicle for the client to use to enter into the business venture. Discuss all the advantages and disadvantages of all types of business vehicles with the attorney.

(B) Monitor the choice of corporate name to assure that it does not violate any of the prohibitions. Check the availability of the name desired. A corporation can use any name except one that requires a license unless the corporation has the necessary license. If the corporation wants to act as a bank and call itself The First

17

Federal Bank of Oz, it must have the necessary state and federal licenses required to run a federal bank prior to incorporating. Corporations cannot use any name that denotes a government use and ownership unless it is a government corporation. A corporation cannot call itself The Florida Department of Motor Vehicles because they are in the business of selling cars unless it is a corporation owned by the State of Florida. Reserve the name if it is available. The availability of a corporate name is generally checked at the Department of State, Division of Corporations in the state where the corporation wants to be chartered. Some states permit the reservation of a corporate name for up to 90 days. There is a fee for this reservation, usually $25 to $100. The reservation is also generally obtained from the Department of State, Division of Corporations.

(C) Draft necessary documents, including but not limited to, promoter's agreement, stock subscriptions, certificate of incorporation, by-laws, organization meeting, first meeting of stockholders, first meeting of directors, etc.

(D) Obtain minutes book, stock book, stock ledger, and corporate seal.

(E) Draw and issue original issue stock certificates. Obtain and place revenue stamps on stock certificates and cancel same. Keep stock ledger accurate and up to date.

(F) Prepare minutes for all board of directors and shareholder meetings, including waiver of notice forms.

(G) Prepare all minutes of annual meetings.

(H) Draft proxy statements.

(I) Prepare and draft amendments to bylaws and/or certificate of incorporation.

(J) Aid in the preparation of and draft annual reports to stockholders.

(K) Aid in copyright, trade mark and patent searches.

NATURE OF A CORPORATION

A corporation is an artificial person. It can do anything a person can do. It can buy and sell property, both real and personal, in its own name. It can sue and be sued in its own name. It is formal. The existence of the corporation must be recorded in writing with the secretary of state. The corporation is the dominant form of business in the United States. Over 80 percent of the gross revenue from all business organizations in the United States is corporate.

REVISED MODEL BUSINESS CORPORATION ACT

There is a Revised Model Business Corporation Act (**RMBCA**) that has been adopted by the majority of states either in whole or in part. The RMBCA was adopted by the American Bar Association in 1984. At one time each state had their own business corporation act, stock corporation act, general corporation law or some other name or names of acts to cover the formation, governing and laws pertaining to corporations operating in their state. The revised model business corporation act known as RMBCA was formulated and adopted by the American Bar Association to homogenize (uniform) the laws of all states pertaining to corporations. Over the last 35 years the desire has been to uniform the laws of all states. This is not an easy task, as it interferes with the sovereignty of the states, and the states are not that fast in giving up parts of their sovereignty. Progress is slow but both the federal government and states are more inclined now to waive their sovereignty rights in many areas. Lawsuits against the federal government and states are an example of this new trend, where governments are permitting the commencement of more lawsuits against them. There are numerous uniform acts, the more popular being the Uniform Partnership Act, Uniform Model Professional Corporate Act, and the most well known, the Uniform Commercial Code (UCC), which has been adopted by the European Union (EU) as their commercial law. States adopt these acts either in toto (whole) or in parts that they prefer. Very often the differences are minor such as times to record documents and requirements for serving and answering documents. Certainly it is much simpler for a corporation to function knowing that every jurisdiction operates under the same laws.

Domestic, Foreign, and Alien Corporations

A corporation chartered by a state is called a **domestic corporation** in that state. If it does business in another state, it is called a **foreign corporation** in that state. An **alien corporation** is a corporation from another country. Therefore, a corporation can be domestic in the state chartered and foreign when operating in another state.

Sovereignty

Each state in the United States is a **sovereignty** (has the rights of a separate nation). As a sovereignty, each state has its own state constitution, state government, laws, army (state guard) and courts. No state can tell another state what to do, although each state grants **comity** (enforcement) to the **judgments** (court orders) of other states as long as they do not differ from the laws of the state granting comity. Therefore, each state has its own **statutes** (laws) concerning corporations. If a corporation is chartered in Nevada and does business in Georgia, it must obtain permission from Georgia to do business in the state, and must thereafter follow the laws of Georgia when doing business in Georgia.

ATTRIBUTES OF A CORPORATION

(1) Legal entities.
(2) Creatures of the state.
(3) Freely transferable stock certificates.
(4) Centralized management.
(5) Perpetual existence.
(6) Citizens of a state.
(7) Investors can only lose their investment.
(8) No other liability as a general rule.

Taxation

A corporation pays a United States income tax on its earnings. The tax rate is usually different from that of an ordinary person. The corporation can declare **dividends** (form of payment) to its shareholders, and the shareholders must then pay a tax on the dividends as ordinary income. Therefore, some claim there is double taxation. This double taxation can be avoided by small corporations; this will be discussed later in this book. A Subchapter S corporation pays no federal taxes; the shareholders are taxed as partners. A non-profit corporation pays no federal income taxes.

Legal Entity

A corporation is a legal entity. It can do anything a person can do. It can contract in its own name. It can sue in its own name. It can be sued in its own name. It is separate and apart from its shareholders. A sale of stock from one party to another has no effect on the legal existence of the corporation. Corporation property belongs to the corporation, not to the shareholders. Even if all shares are owned by one person, he or she is still distinct from the corporation.

Creature of the State

A corporation is a creature of the state. It is created by the state and regulated by the state. Every state has some kind of general incorporation statute which must be complied with for the secretary of state to issue a charter or certificate of incorporation. The U.S. Constitution prohibits anyone from **impairing** (changing or canceling a contract). Therefore, the corporation has a contract with the state. The state in its statute reserves the right to amend the statute from time to time. Without this reservation, the state could not change its statute as it would be impairing a contract.

Freely Transferable Stock

Generally the shares of stock of a corporation are freely and easily traded, i.e., bought or sold by shareholders. If there are no restrictions on the stock, the owner can sell it, **hypothecate** it (pledge it for a loan), give it as a gift, or **bequest** it as personal property in a last will and testament.

Centralized Management

A corporation has centralized management. The **stockholders** (owners) elect a board of directors; and the board of directors elect or appoint officers. Neither the officers nor the directors have to be stockholders. Therefore, ownership and management can be totally different. Generally this is true in large corporations to a degree, and often in small and closely held corporations.

Perpetual Existence

The corporation can be set up to be **perpetual** (in existence forever), or it can be for a limited time or number of years. If there is no limit stated in the certificate of incorporation, it is deemed to be perpetual.

Citizenship

A corporation is a citizen of the state in which it was **chartered** (some states use "chartered," others "incorporated"). This is only for purposes of lawsuits, both federal and state. For instance, a New York corporation wants to sue a California corporation. It can sue in New York, California, or in federal court on the grounds of **diversity of citizenship** (when all parties to a lawsuits are not citizens of the same state). Remember, you obtain a **judgment** (court order) if you win in the state where you sue.

Liability of Stockholders

The general liability of a shareholder is his or her investment. As a general rule, that is all a shareholder can lose. The phrase that shareholders have limited liability is a **misnomer** (incorrect designation). Shareholders have no personal liability. Their risk is the amount of their investment. The corporation has the **sole** (only) liability for its debts. Of course, if the party was a major shareholder or one of a group intending to use the corporation to **defraud** (cheat) a business, individual, or group, there would be additional personal liability.

TYPES OF CORPORATIONS

There are:

(1) Public corporations
(2) Publicly held corporations
(3) Domestic corporations
(4) Foreign corporations
(5) Alien corporations
(6) For profit corporations
(7) Professional corporations
(8) Nonprofit corporations
(9) Closely held corporations
(10) Private corporations
(11) Subchapter S Corporations

These are not necessarily exclusive; nor is there a need to choose just one. They can be combined in almost any grouping. For example, you can have a professional, private corporation, or a closely held, for profit, domestic, and Subchapter S corporation.

Public Corporation

A public corporation is created by a government, for a government purpose, such as the United States, a state, county, city, town or village. A federal (U.S.) example would be the Federal Deposit Insurance Corporation (FDIC) or the Tennessee Valley Authority (TVA). Created by Congress to perform a specific duty, its power comes from Congress. A school district or park district would be an example of a municipal corporation (when local, sometimes called a municipal corporation). Its powers come from the local legislative body.

Publicly Held Corporation

A publicly held corporation is usually traded on a stock exchange and has many stockholders (**shareholders**). A publicly held corporation is required to be registered under the Federal Securities and Exchange Act of 1934. Almost any company wanting to sell a large quantity of shares to the public must be registered. Any corporation so registered is deemed a publicly held corporation. For example, General Motors and AT&T are publicly held corporations.

Domestic, Foreign, and Alien Corporations

A corporation chartered in a state, and doing business in that state, is called a **domestic** corporation. If a corporation does business in a state other than where it is chartered, it is called a **foreign** corporation in that state. Remember, each state is a sovereignty; therefore, you must obtain permission to do business in a state other than where you are **chartered** (incorporated). Each state has a procedure to obtain **a certificate of authority** (qualifying it) to do business in that state. Certificate of authority (name may be different in different states, intent is always the same) is an application to a state by a foreign corporation to obtain the privilege to carry on a business in that state. Once granted the privilege the corporation will thereafter have to file and pay a yearly franchise fee to the state, generally based on gross income earned by the corporation for the year in that state. If there is a state income tax the corporation will also have to file and pay the state income tax the same as any other corporation operating in the state. All corporations domestic, foreign and alien doing business in the state pay a yearly franchise fee to that state. In some states the penalty for failing to obtain permission to do business in the state is that the corporation is restricted from the use of the courts in that state. This means that if a customer owes the corporation $100,000 the corporation cannot sue to collect it. If the corporation is sued in the state, the corporation cannot defend the action, must default, and therefore the plaintiff (party suing) wins. In other states it is a felony to fail to obtain permission. The penalties vary from state to state and can be as stated above civil or criminal (fines and/or prison or both). You pay a fee to the secretary of state and list a **resident agent** (any person) in that state who can take **service of process** (summons and other legal or government notices) in the state. When you qualify, you are subject to the regulation of, taxation of, and **litigation** (lawsuits) in the state. States have statutes for the state to obtain revenue in return for the corporation's use of the state's roads, courts, police, etc. The corporation can remain in the state where chartered and do interstate business in every state, without registering in each state, as long as the corporation does not have an office in the state. As soon as the corporation has an office—a place where someone can contact a corporate representative to get information or place orders in the state—the corporation is doing business in the state and must register. Once registered, the corporation is subject to the laws of the state, and to taxation on business done in the state. An **alien corporation** is a corporation chartered in a foreign country. A foreign corporation and/or an alien corporation with offices in each state and doing business in each state (other than just doing free repairs or service based on warranties) can be registered in 50 states, paying 50 franchise fees and 50 state income taxes in addition to a federal income tax.

For Profit Corporation

A for profit corporation is any corporation that operates to make a profit. It pays its shareholders dividends from earnings and profits. If you wanted to go into business, you would probably use a corporation for profit. AT&T, GMC, Compaq, Toyota, etc., are all corporations for profit. Once you decide to incorporate the type of incorporation is pretty much fixed by law. For example; public corporations are restricted to the government. Publicly held are restricted to local and federal securities exchange commission regulations and only if you want to sell large amounts of stock to the public. Professional held are only if you qualify as professional. Non profit held are only if you are a charity or public service. Basically, your only real decision in most instances is for profit and whether or not you want to be a subchapter S for tax purposes or a close corporation to restrict the sale of the corporate ownership or both.

Professional Corporation

There is a Model Professional Corporation Supplement to the Model Business Corporation Act. People licensed to practice a profession may take advantage of these statutes. Some states allow all professionals in the state to incorporate; other states limit the professions that are so allowed (if limited it is usually limited to doctors, lawyers, dentists, and CPAs). The designation **PA** (Professional Association) after the name indicates a corporation. Other states use **PC** (Professional Corporation) as the designation. The statutes are for tax purposes. They do not limit the liability of the professional. In some circumstances the professional may not be liable for acts committed by other members of the PC or PA. However, the professional is personally liable for acts he or she commits.

Nonprofit Corporation

A nonprofit corporation is chartered not to make a profit for its members. It is used for charitable, educational, or scientific purposes. Although nonprofit, it may still make a profit. However, the profits cannot be distributed to members, directors, or officers; they must be used exclusively for the purposes chartered. It cannot pay dividends. There is a Model Nonprofit Corporation Act (MNPCA). Many states have special requirements and statutes covering nonprofit corporations. Usually the consent of the attorney general of the state is needed to become chartered. Examples of nonprofit corporations are fraternities, sororities, hospitals, library clubs, athletic and social clubs, some private schools, colleges and universities, and charities.

Close Corporation (Closely Held)

A close corporation, or closely held corporation, comes about by an agreement between all stockholders that they will not sell their shares of stock without first offering the shares to the corporation, then to the other stockholders, and then to strangers. Stockholders agree for all to vote their shares to keep the same officers and directors. Chapter 5 discusses the close corporation agreement in more detail.

Private Corporation

A private corporation is not owned or run by or for any government purpose. It has no government duties. It is run by private people for private purposes and may be for profit or nonprofit. It could be closely held if desired by its stockholders. It could be domestic or foreign. It is run by the board of directors for the benefit of the stockholders. One of the duties of the directors is to maximize the value of the business for the benefit of the stockholders. It is probably the corporation that one would start to go into business.

Subchapter S Corporation

Subchapter S is a section of the Internal Revenue Code that permits a corporation to be taxed as a partnership, instead of as a corporation, while keeping all the other advantages of a corporate structure. Congress divided corporations into two groups: S corporations, that have so elected to be; and all other corporations known as C corporations. To designate a business as an S corporation there are numerous requirements that must be satisfied. Following are the more important qualifications:

(1) The corporation cannot have more than thirty-five stockholders. It can have from one to thirty-five.

(2) It must be a domestic corporation.

(3) No stockholder can be a nonresident alien of the corporation.

(4) Only one class of stock is permitted, but all shareholders need not have the same voting rights.

(5) The corporation cannot be a subsidiary or division of another corporation and cannot be affiliated with a group of corporations.

(6) Corporations, partnerships, and nonqualifying trusts cannot be shareholders. The stockholders must be individuals, qualified trusts, or estates.

S Corporation Benefits   Sometimes it is advantageous to be an S Corporation for tax purposes. Some of the benefits are:

(1) If the corporation has losses, the shareholders take the losses, as pro rata to their ownership and may deduct the amount on their personal income tax return against other gains from businesses. For example, you own 50 percent of the corporation stock. T, the corporation, has a $10,000 loss. You may take $5,000 off your personal income tax as against other gains. The corporation pays no income tax.

(2) If the shareholders' tax brackets are less than the corporate tax bracket, the entire earnings of the corporation will be taxed at the lower rate even though the shareholders did not personally receive the money. This allows the corporation to accumulate profits at a much lower tax rate.

(3) A single tax on the corporation, paid for by shareholders at the shareholders' tax rate, whether or not distributed to the shareholder. This gives the corporation a tax benefit. This is also a benefit to the shareholders. The corporate tax rate in many instances can be larger than the tax rate of an average person. In that instance if the corporation was taxed at the rate of the person there would be a tax advantage to the corporation. An S Corporation (1–35 shareholders) means that the shareholder or shareholders will be taxed as a general partnership rather than as a corporation. General partners' earnings are taxed whether or not actually distributed to the partner (profits left in the business for expansion purposes). For example, a shareholder is in the 40 percent tax bracket. The corporation has a loss of $10,000 and only one shareholder. The shareholder has another business where he has earned $10,000. The shareholder takes the $10,000 loss against the $10,000 earnings (40 percent of $10,000) and pays no tax. This amounts to a savings of $4,000 for the shareholder.

SUMMARY

A corporation is an artificial person. It can do anything a person can do: buy and sell realty, give gifts, enter into contracts, pay income taxes, receive, and amongst other things, bequest and **devise.** A bequest is an inheritance of personal property. A devise is an inheritance of real property. If a corporation does business in the state where it was chartered, it is called a domestic corporation; when it leaves the state, it is called a foreign corporation in the other state. An alien corporation is a corporation from another country. Each state is sovereign, so each state has its own laws that must be followed. If you have a Florida corporation which does business in California, it must obey the laws of California while doing business in California. In California it is a foreign corporation. In Florida it is a domestic corporation. To do business outside the state the corporation must file for authority to do business in a foreign state. It is a revenue statute, i.e., a way for the state to be compensated for your using their courts, streets, police, etc.

A corporation pays a federal income tax and a state income tax, if necessary. A corporation is a legal entity. The stock of a corporation is freely transferable. It has perpetual existence, central management, and citizenship in the state in which it was chartered for special purposes. An Ohio corporation can sue a Maine corporation in federal court, the jurisdiction being diversity of citizenship.

A shareholder generally has no personal liability because if the shareholder commits a wrong on behalf of the corporation, there may be personal liability at that point.

A corporation needs resident agent or someone who can take service of process in the state where chartered.

There are C corporations, profit corporations, nonprofit corporations, Subchapter S corporations, professional corporations, public corporations, close corporations, publicly held corporations, alien corporations, foreign corporations, domestic corporations, private corporations, and charitable corporations.

WORDS TO KNOW

alien corporation	judgment
bequeath	legal entity
C corporation	litigation
certificate of authority	perpetual
chartered	public corporation
comity	RMBCA
defraud	resident agent
devise	Subchapter S corporation
diversity of citizenship	shareholder
dividend	sole liability
domestic corporation	sovereignty
foreign corporation	statute
hypothecate	stockholder
impairing	

REVIEW QUESTIONS

1. What are the duties of a paralegal in the corporate area?
2. Define a corporation and what it can do.
3. What are foreign corporations, domestic corporations and alien corporations?
4. Name five different types of corporations.
5. What does sovereignty mean?
6. Why do we say a corporation is a legal entity?
7. Can a corporation be formed orally?
8. Why do we say shares of stock are freely transferable?
9. Why would perpetual duration for a corporation be good?
10. Explain diversity of citizenship.

11. What kind of liability does a shareholder have?
12. What is the benefit, if any, of a Subchapter S corporation?
13. Is a corporation better than a general partnership? Why?

SHORT ESSAYS

1. You are the president of a Georgia corporation. The corporation is going to do business in New York. You advise your attorney and ask if you can go ahead and conduct business in New York. The attorney says the necessary documents will be filed. Eight months later you sue a customer for $40,000 owed for merchandise the customer received and has refused to pay for. The defense is that your corporation is not authorized to do business in New York. The attorney was busy and forgot to file the necessary documents. What result?

2. You are the vice-president of human resources of a taxicab company. The corporation has 250 cabs. You hired drivers for all 250 cabs. The cabs are on the street 24 hours a day. You check each driver for a valid driver's license, and you read their license carefully. Mr. Jones, a pedestrian, was struck by one of the cabs and hospitalized. Mr. Jones is suing the corporation that owns the cab, the driver of the cab that was in the accident, and you for negligence. Mr. Jones claims the license of the driver was a forgery and if you had caught it, the driver would not have been given the job, and he would not have been injured. Decide this case and give your reasoning.

CHAPTER

3

DECIDING WHETHER AND
HOW TO INCORPORATE

OBJECTIVES

After completing this chapter, you will be able to:

1. Select a state in which to incorporate.
2. Know how to organize a corporation.
3. Have knowledge of pre-incorporation transactions.
4. Be able to prepare the documents for incorporation.

INTRODUCTION

A client wants to go into business. The attorney explains to the client the different ways that one may enter into business. Then the attorney and the client decide that it is best to incorporate as a for profit C corporation. The next decision to make is in what state to incorporate.

SELECTING A STATE IN WHICH TO INCORPORATE

A corporation's internal affairs are governed by the laws of the state where it incorporates even if it has no other contact with the state of incorporation. This means that if you incorporate in state A and thereafter do all your business in state B, your internal affairs are still governed by state A. A small corporation, operating in only one state with few stockholders, will generally incorporate locally.

A **close corporation** will, most likely, incorporate **locally** (in the state where its principal office and business is). A close corporation is selected when there are a few stockholders and they want to limit the sale of existing stock to persons whom they all approve. An agreement is drawn, and the stock is subject to this agreement. Usually it will be unnecessary to incorporate out-of-state because various state statutes now offer fairly comparable laws for close corporations. This will be discussed in greater detail in Chapter 5.

Increase of Start-Up Costs

If a business incorporates in a state other than where its principal office and business are located, it will tend to increase start-up and other costs. To maintain its corporate status a corporation must pay taxes to the state in which it incorporates. Likewise, it must also pay taxes to the state where it does business for the privilege of doing business in the state. It uses the roads, courts, police, etc.; therefore, it must pay in the form of an incorporation franchise fee for the right to do business in the state. The taxes overlap so that it will usually be less expensive to incorporate in the state where it does the most business and has its **principal** (main) office. In addition, local attorneys are familiar with the laws of the state in which they practice and may be hesitant to offer formal opinions and advise it on the laws of another state, necessitating the hiring of additional out of state counsel for advice. This will cost additional money.

Publicly Traded Corporations

When dealing with publicly traded corporations, other factors apply. The corporation laws of various states can differ significantly. For example:

- what transactions require stockholder approval and what percentage of stockholders are required for that approval
- how appraisal rights are treated
- how are the **fiduciary duties** (highest degree of fairness must be shown) of directors and officers enforced
- annual reporting requirements
- taxes and fees for corporations.

These laws differ in various states. The extra costs on out-of-state incorporation for a publicly held corporation may be a small percentage of the corporation's total revenues, as compared to the advantages afforded by the particular laws of a state.

Delaware Corporations

Franchise tax revenues represent an enormous source of revenue for a state like Delaware with a small fiscal base. The state, therefore, has a significant economic and financial interest in having laws that will attract corporations to incorporate in Delaware. Delaware has many more publicly held firms incorporated in it than any other state. Delaware is reliable and consistent in being responsive to corporate needs. Its history and political climate help assure its reliability to favor corporations. Delaware has had **litigation** (lawsuits) on just about every question imaginable concerning corporate law, and their highest court has ruled on these questions, creating a very reliable case law base (**common law**). Most questions can be answered by researching its case law. The case law is well settled. There are good legal precedents for business decisions that may need to be made.

A Delaware **corporate address** is well accepted by the financial community and may even be prestigious. The financial community likes a corporation to take advantage of Delaware laws. Therefore, a corporation chartered in another state that reincorporates in Delaware would be looked upon favorably by the financial community. In contrast, if a corporation reincorporated in another small state for the same purposes, the decision might cause concern to the financial community.

Revised Model Business Corporation Act

The Revised Model Business Corporation Act (RMBCA) adopted by the American Bar Association Committee on Corporate Law has been a **template** (model) for the statutes of many states.

ORGANIZATION OF CORPORATION

A decision to incorporate has been made. The attorney has discussed with the client the various states in which the client could incorporate with the advantages and disadvantages of each state. The discussion would be based on where the corporation is expected to do most of its business, the tax laws of the various states, the costs involved, and benefits and disadvantages. The state in which the business is going to incorporate is then decided on. Now, the corporation must be organized.

From the legal side, the first step in organization is to file certain documents with the appropriate state official, usually the secretary of state. A **certificate of incorporation, articles of incorporation,** or a **charter** will customarily be filed. The names are different in the different states. The information required is more or less the same in every state.

Certificate of Incorporation, Articles of Incorporation, Charter

The certificate of incorporation, articles of incorporation, or charter (different names in different states, but the same function) is recorded with the secretary of state in the state in which it is desired to charter the corporation. The document provides the state with the following information:

(1) The name of the corporation.

(2) The **principal** address (main office) of the corporation.

(3) The purpose of the corporation and the powers of the corporation.

(4) The total number of shares the corporation will have authority to issue. If there will be various classes, all classes must be listed and the amount of each to be issued must be stated. You must state if the stock is to be par or no par. If par, you must state the par value.

(5) Some states require a resident agent.

(6) The name and mailing address of the incorporators.

(7) A statement that the board of directors is authorized to make, alter, or repeal bylaws of the corporation. A statement that the stockholders can also make, alter, or repeal bylaws of the corporation.

(8) A statement that election of directors need not be by written ballot, except and to the extent provided in the bylaws of the corporation.

(A form for certificate of incorporation can be found in Appendix A.)

Powers of a Corporation

Since a corporation is an artificial person, it derives its power to act from the powers listed in the certificate, articles, or charter. At one time the certificate, article, or charter had to list each and every power or the corporation could not perform anything not listed. Today, the certificate, article, or charter simply states that the corporation may engage in any lawful act or activity for which corporations may be organized in the state.

Resident Agent

Some states require a resident agent that resides in the state to be named. This resident agent will accept all **service of processes.** Service of process means complaints, summonses, and any other legal documents needed to be served on the corporation. In states that do not require a resident agent, service of process is on the secretary of state. In those states when a corporation files with the secretary of state, it automatically appoints the secretary of state as the agent to take service on behalf of the corporation.

Issuance of Stock

The board of directors has the power to **issue** (sell) **authorized stock** (stock listed in the certificate of incorporation) and set the price of the stock. The various kinds of stock the corporation wishes to issue and the maximum number of shares that may be issued for each kind of stock it intends to have is listed in the certificate of incorporation. Each kind of stock is called a **class,** to wit: common shares, common shares A, preferred, or some identification like common stock class Z1 or Common stock #7676. Each group is called a class. If the corporation intends to issue only one class of common stock, the certificate can say the number of shares to be issued without designating class. If there is more than one class of stock, the certificate must designate the terms of each class or permit the board of directors to issue portions from time to time and designate the terms of each series as it is issued. Issuance of stock will be more fully discussed in Chapter 7. Stockholders elect the board of directors, and the board appoints or elects the officers.

Subscription Rights

At common law a shareholder had a right to **subscribe** (offer to buy) a proportionate share of a new issue of stock of the class **held** (owned). This was known as a preemptive right. There were many **exceptions** (times when no preemptive right existed) to the right. Modern statutes provide for no preemptive rights unless the certificate of incorporation expressly says they exist. Not very many certificates of incorporation provide for preemptive rights. The board of directors may also not issue stock for the purpose of **perpetuating** (keeping) themselves in office.

Common law is case law. The decision of a judge in a case becomes common law. If the legislature of a state or congress on the federal side passes a statute that is opposite the common law then the statute prevails and the common law on that issue terminates. The courts then interpret that statute and once again their decisions become common law. Assume a shareholder bought 100 shares of preferred stock class A in the XYZ corporation, representing 10 percent ownership of the class. At common law that preferred shareholder had a preemptive right to buy additional shares issued in that class to maintain the original 10 percent ownership. If the corporation decided to issue another 1000 shares of preferred class A shares, the preemptive right allowed the purchase of another 100 shares to maintain the original 10 percent ownership of the class.

HOW TO INCORPORATE

At one point in time most states required three or more people to be **incorporators** (persons that sign the certificate of incorporation), two or more had to be citizens of the state, and at least one had to be a citizen of the United States. It was required to have a minimum of three officers, i.e., a president, a treasurer, and a secretary. The same person could not fill more than one office. Also required were three subscribers to subscribe to purchase shares once the corporation was formed. The price for the purchase of the shares had to be included in the subscription. This guaranteed the corporation a minimum amount of money to commence operation.

Delaware Corporation Benefits

Delaware was the first state to allow one person to incorporate, and the person did not have to be a citizen of Delaware. One person could be the subscriber, incorporator, president, secretary, treasurer, and chairman of the board. Most states require a corporation to have at least one annual stockholders' meeting a year in the state of incorporation. Delaware requires one meeting a year minimum but has no requirements as to where the meeting must be held. This, in addition to the other benefits mentioned, attracts companies to incorporate in Delaware.

Today, most states allow one person to incorporate, similar to the requirements of Delaware. However, the only state today that allows one stockholder meeting a year minimum and has no restriction as to where that meeting takes place is still Delaware.

Promoters

The party or parties wanting to form the corporation are called promoters. The promoter promotes the formation of the corporation by doing all of the initial work to get it **chartered** (giving birth to the corporation). The major duties of the promoter are:

(1) Seeking investors to loan money to the corporation or buy an **equity** (stock) interest in the corporation.

(2) Finding persons called **subscribers** to purchase stock at a given price if and when the corporation is chartered.

(3) Arranging for people to serve on the board of directors.

(4) Seeking officers for the corporation.

(5) Finding the necessary employees that the corporation will need to function.

(6) Retaining an attorney.

(7) Retaining an accountant or CPA.

(8) Locating appropriate space for the corporation to carry on its business. Signing a lease or reserving the space until the corporation is chartered and in a position to **execute** (sign) the lease itself.

(9) Drawing the business plan and the marketing plan.

(10) Getting all necessary documents drawn, executed, and recorded.

Incorporating

A certificate of incorporation is then drawn and **executed** (signed) by the **incorporators.** The incorporators are the people who sign the certificate of incorporation. The promoters can also be subscribers and incorporators. The certificate of incorporation is recorded with the secretary of state in the state in which the corporation is to be chartered. The promoter promotes; subscribers subscribe, and the incorporators **incorporate** (sign the certificate of incorporation). Once chartered a corporate kit is needed. This can be purchased at any major office supply store in or out of state. The kit has printed minutes already drawn on which the blanks need only to be filled in: Minutes of the organization, first meeting of stockholders, first meeting of directors, and forms for notices of waiver. Most law offices will already have these minutes on their computer and all that is needed is to fill in the blanks. The kit also has forms for special and annual meetings of stockholders and directors. There is also a stock ledger where are listed the names and addresses of all stockholders, the number of shares they own, the number of the stock certificate issued to them, and on the **original issue** (first sale of stock by the corporation) is also listed the amount paid to the corporation. Sales by owners to others after the original issue are not original issue sales and list the change of ownership, the address of the new owner, and the number of shares transferred. There is no need to list the price paid after the original issue. For example, you are one of the founders of the corporation. You subscribed for the purchase of two hundred shares at $10 per share, for a total of $2,000. The $2,000 was paid to the corporation. This is an original issue stock. The corporation received and used the money as working capital. Five years later you sell your stock to Mrs. X. She pays the money to you, not to the corporation. She then notifies the corporation that she is the new owner, **tenders** (delivers) the stock certificate in your name to the corporation, and asks them to draw a new certificate to her in her name. There is also a stock ledger book with stock certificates printed with the corporation name, ready to be issued. All this comes in a binder with a corporate seal which is a metal instrument to impress the corporation seal on documents.

The way to incorporate is by filing a certificate of incorporation, articles of incorporation, or a charter (depending on the state) with the secretary of state.

Once the corporation is chartered by the state it is under way. The board of directors manages the corporation. The board is elected by shareholders. There are no shareholders until stock is issued by the board of directors. Therefore, there must be a way to either name directors before stock is issued or to issue stock before the directors are elected by the shareholders.

There are two basic ways to solve this problem. In New York the incorporators (people named in the certificate of incorporation and who sign the certificate) have the power of shareholders until stock is issued and the power of directors until directors are elected (NY Bus Corp Law, sec. 404[a], 615[c]). Under this statute, the incorporators will adopt the bylaws, fix the number of directors, and elect directors to serve until the first meeting of the stockholders.

In other states like Delaware, the incorporators have the power of shareholders and directors unless initial directors are named in the certificate of incorporation (Del. Gen. Corp. Law Sec 107, 108[a]). If initial directors are named in the certificate, they have the power of the incorporators as soon as the corporation is **chartered** (filed).

Once the directors are named by the incorporators or certificate of incorporation, they hold an organization meeting. A sample form of a **certificate of incorporation** can be found in **Appendix A.** At the organization meeting, bylaws are adopted, and directors and officers are named to serve until the first meeting of shareholders and the first meeting of the board of directors. After the organization meeting there is a first meeting of shareholders that elects a board of directors (sample form in **Appendix B**). Next, there is a first meeting of the board of directors and they elect or appoint officers (sample form in **Appendix B**). A typical form for an **organization meeting** can be found in **Appendix B; bylaws** can be found in **Appendix C.**

Subscriber

The usual method of a corporation issuing stock is an exchange, cash for stock. In some instances one wants to buy stock in the future, so they enter into a "subscription agreement" with the corporation that they will purchase a specific quantity of stock at a named price and payment will be made when the stock is delivered at a date mentioned in the future. In the case of a corporation not yet formed and needing subscribers, it enters into this agreement to purchase the stock as soon as the corporation is chartered. They are called subscribers or **pre-incorporation subscribers.** Since the corporation is not yet formed and cannot contract, the agreement is between the subscribers and the promoter (one who promotes a corporation). At old common law, since the corporation was not yet formed and could not contract, the subscribers could cancel the subscriptions at any time without liability. Modern corporation statutes have changed the treatment of subscribers. Most statutes today provide that pre-incorporation subscriptions are irrevocable for a specified time unless all subscribers consent to a revocation or the agreement otherwise provides. RMBCA (Revised Model Business Corporation Act) states that subscription agreements are irrevocable for six months unless all subscribers agree to revocation.

Pre-Incorporation Transactions

The **promoter** (party that brings about the creation of the corporation) may very often purchase or lease property for the corporation in the name of the promoter with the intention of assigning or selling it to the corporation once it is formed. This is the liability of the promoter. Until the corporation is formed it cannot have liability. Anyone acting in the name of the corporation before it is chartered has personal liability for the item, lease, etc. Any contracts made by the promoter in the corporation's name do not bind the corporation. If the corporation adopts the contract, the promisor is also still liable unless released by all parties. Prior to charter, a corporation has no power or capacity to contract.

SUMMARY

Where to incorporate? Is this a corporation that is now going to trade on a national exchange? If it is, probably Delaware is where to begin to search to incorporate. If it is a small corporation which is just beginning and its business is all local, the state to incorporate in is where it is going to carry on the local business. If it is going to do business in a few states, it is probably best to pick the one where it will do most of its business. Remember, it is not difficult to incorporate at a later date in another state and dissolve in the first state. The certificate of incorporation, articles of incorporation, or charter are names given in different states to the first document filed with the secretary of state to charter the corporation. The certificate is filed by incorporators or the incorporator if only one is needed. Most states today allow a corporation to be filed with one person holding all the offices and being the only director. You always need a resident agent or someone who can accept service for the corporation. There is a first meeting of stockholders and the board of directors is elected. The bylaws of the corporation are sometimes prepared at the shareholders' meeting, other times at the directors' meeting. Next, a first meeting of the board of directors is held at which the officers are elected or appointed. Stock is issued and the corporation is ready to do business. Any contracts signed by the promoters before the corporation was chartered are the liabilities of the promoters. The corporation can ratify the contracts and provide a **novation** to release the promoters from liability; otherwise, the corporation and the promoters are liable on the contracts. A novation is an agreement between three people, a debtor, creditor and a third party. The creditor agrees to release the debtor from liability and accept the third party as being liable. This must be in writing to conform to the statute of frauds.

CASE

Promoter's Contracts

COOPERS AND LYBRAND v. FOX
Colorado Court of Appeals 1988
758 P2d 883

Plaintiff is a national accounting firm. In November 1981 Gary Fox met with representatives of the Plaintiff and requested a tax opinion and other accounting services. He said he was in the process of forming G. Fox and Partners, Inc. Plaintiff accepted the assignment knowing the corporation was not in existence. On December 4, 1981, the corporation was formed. In mid–December plaintiff billed Gary Fox, Fox and Partners, Inc. for $10,827. When neither paid, plaintiff sued Gary Fox individually for breach of an express and implied contract based on the theory of promoter liability. The trial court ruled, in the absence of an agreement, since the plaintiff failed to prove that Fox would be personally liable. The complaint was dismissed.

The Court of Appeals reversed the trial court. Fox said plaintiff knew the corporation was not in existence and either impliedly or expressly agreed to look to the corporation for payment. The general rule is that promoters are personally liable for contracts they make, though made on behalf of the corporation. The exception is if the contracting party knows the corporation is not in existence but nevertheless agrees to look solely to the corporation, then the promoter is not liable. The trial court found no agreement express or implied. In the absence of agreement releasing him from liability Fox is liable. The burden is on the promoter to prove the agreement releasing him from liability.

Accordingly judgment reversed. Judgment for $10,827 to plaintiff.

WORDS TO KNOW

authorized stock
chartered
class of stock
close corporation
common law
corporate address
directors
equity
exceptions
execute
executed
fiduciary

fiduciary duties
incorporation
issue
litigation
novation
original issue
perpetuating
principal office
resident agent
service of process
subscribe
tender

REVIEW QUESTIONS

1. How would you select a state in which to incorporate?
2. List the steps to incorporate.
3. Who is liable for pre-incorporating transactions?

4. What document needs to be filed to incorporate?
5. With whom do you file the above document?
6. If you do business in five states, in which one do you incorporate?
7. What are subscription rights?
8. What is a subscriber?
9. What is an incorporator?
10. What is a resident agent?

SHORT ESSAYS

1. The XYZ corporation was formed with five shareholders. The certificate of incorporation said the corporation was to be in the business of preparation and serving of food as a restaurant. The corporation was chartered in Florida in 1998. The board of directors consisted of the five original shareholders and a majority vote was necessary to act. The Board has just voted to buy the building that the restaurant occupies. One of the members of the board says the certificate of incorporation does not give them power to buy real estate. Can real estate be bought? Explain your reasoning.

2. John and Tim acted as promoters for the ABC Corporation, now chartered in New York. John and Tim signed a twenty year lease at very favorable terms for space for the corporation. The corporation was not chartered at the time the lease was signed. Both John and Tim forgot to place a clause in the contract releasing them from personal liability when the corporation was chartered. Shortly after the corporation was chartered John and Tim became angry at the officers of the corporation who were the only shareholders. Neither John nor Tim were shareholders. They were promised they would be appointed officers if they obtained the lease and other items. Now they want nothing to do with the corporation and do not want to be liable on the lease. The officers/shareholders refuse to remove John and Tim from the lease. Decide the issue and give your reasons.

3. Fred and Mary subscribed for stock in the Equity Corporation. They were buying common shares and bought only one percent of the issue. They had subscription rights in their agreement. The corporation is now issuing a new issue of preferred stock class B that will have dividend rights superior to the common shares. Fred and Mary want the right to buy up to one percent of the new issue. The corporation has refused. Decide the issue and give your reasons.

CHAPTER

4

CORPORATION STRUCTURE

OBJECTIVES

After completing this chapter, you will be able to:

1. Know the different ways in which one can become a shareholder.
2. Be aware of the duties of a stockholder.
3. Know how a corporation is managed.
4. Tell what a board of directors is, and what they do and why.
5. Be aware of actions required by a board, and corporate officers and their duties.
6. Be aware of the duties of a board and corporate officers.
7. Know what a quorum is and why it is needed.

HOW TO BECOME A SHAREHOLDER

Shareholder and **stockholder** are synonyms. They are owners of stock in a corporation. While you are an owner of the corporation by owning stock, you do not own any specific asset or any part of an asset. For example, you own 100 shares of common stock in a corporation that has **issued** 1,000 shares of common stock. You have a 10 percent **interest** (ownership) in the corporation; you do not own 10 percent of the corporate offices or any other asset. You own an undivided 10 percent of the total corporation. You own 10 per-

36

cent of the corporate stock issued and outstanding. Assets of a corporation are owned by the corporation. Issued stock refers to stock to which the corporation has transferred ownership and which is in the hands of stockholders. In the above example, the 100 shares would be issued stock and the remaining 900 shares would be issued stock. When you obtain stock in a corporation, the corporation generally issues you a stock certificate. The stock certificate is proof of ownership and proof of interest in the corporation. While a stockholder is an owner of the corporation stock, the stockholder only has an indirect control of the day-to-day management of the corporation. Stock ownership conveys certain rights to the stockholder. These rights are discussed in Chapter 8.

You can become a stockholder in any of the following manners:

(1) By purchasing stock.

(2) By exchanging work for stock.

(3) By providing the corporation with knowledge in exchange for stock.

(4) By exchanging personal property or real property with the corporation for stock.

(5) By receiving stock as a gift from someone.

(6) By obtaining stock through a **bequest.** A bequest is an inheritance from a last will and testament.

MANAGEMENT OF A CORPORATION

Shareholders are the owners of a corporation. However, the corporation is managed by the board of directors. Shareholders elect the board of directors, and in many corporations retain the power and right to remove directors with or without cause. This right must be in the bylaws or certificate of incorporation to be retained. The average shareholder does not have a direct voice in day-to-day management. Usually, the shareholders cannot compel the board to take any action. The directors are not agents of the shareholders. Their duty is primarily to the corporation. In a close corporation the above may not apply as the close corporation agreement will govern how the board operates.

Publicly Traded Corporations

The board of directors makes business policy and manages the corporation. Officers are elected or appointed by the board. The officers act as agents of the board and execute the decisions and directions of the board. Shareholders elect the board and usually decide fundamental and major corporate decisions.

In a large corporation with millions of shares outstanding, there is a separation of ownership and control. The stock may be widely distributed all over the world. This allows control to be held by the directors or managers who can employ proxies to maintain control and self-**perpetuate** their control even though they own as a group a small percentage of the outstanding stock. This means that control can be maintained by a group that is not even a minority interest, merely a small insignificant interest. An example would be AT&T. In this instance, the corporation is controlled in actuality by its directors and management rather than by its stockholders. AT&T is an extremely large corporation with millions of shares outstanding. Its stock is widely distributed all over the world. In smaller corporations where the stock is not so widely distributed the stockholders can meet at the annual stockholders' meeting and maintain control of the corporation. The stockholders can at these meetings form alliances, voting agreements and discuss corporate problems and solutions.

They can even agree to hold additional stockholders' meetings or to form committees to solve corporate problems. When the stockholders are all over the world and in the millions, not too many will travel a long distance, at their own expense, to attend a stockholders' meeting. Therefore the directors and managers can draw and distribute proxies to the shareholders to vote by mail on various issues as well as election of directors. Information and recommendations of the board are included with the proxy. The cost of printing, mailing and postage is paid by the corporation. Anyone opposing the recommendations of the board would have to pay for printing, mailing and postage themselves. Hence, the directors and managers can perpetuate themselves in office even though they may hold a small or insignificant stock interest.

When stockholders own small amounts of a stock or hold a fraction of ownership, it is not cost effective for a stockholder to devote time to the affairs of the corporation. It is usually too expensive to travel to corporate stockholder meetings to vote, and so the proxy is used. The expense of use of the proxy by management is paid by the corporation. On the other hand, if someone wants to enter into a proxy fight for control, he or she must pay his or her own expenses for printing, artwork, drawing and preparing copy, addressing, stuffing, mailing, and associated costs. This is another reason that management can self-perpetuate itself. In a situation when a stockholder is unhappy with management, the approach should be to sell the stock rather than incur expenses in a fight.

BOARD OF DIRECTORS

Directors are elected by the shareholders to manage the corporation. They are not agents of the corporation. They are not agents of the shareholders. They are not trustees of the corporation. They are not the trustees of the shareholders. They serve in a **fiduciary** capacity to the corporation. As fiduciaries they must perform their duties in the best interests of the corporation with due care and good faith. Each director is committed to increasing the wealth of the corporation, and, hence, the wealth of the shareholders.

In some corporations, the members of the board are all actively involved in the day-to-day management of the business. In these cases, the corporate powers are exercised by the board of directors. This usually refers to small or closely held corporations. In publicly held corporations, most board members are unlikely to be actively involved in day-to-day management. In this case the corporate powers are exercised under the authority of the board which formulates major management policy but does not involve itself with day-to-day management.

In the normal scenario, the board of directors makes business policy and manages the corporation. The board is elected by the shareholders. Officers are elected or appointed by the board of directors. Officers acting as agents of the corporation and board of directors carry out the policies set by the board of directors. Shareholders are not involved in the day-to-day business of the corporation but do vote on major corporate changes; to wit: merging the corporation with another corporation, selling off major corporate assets, issuing new stock or a new class of stock, and dissolution of the corporation. In a public corporation with millions of shares outstanding and ownership widely scattered, it is possible for a small minority of people, not necessarily stockholders, to obtain control of the corporation by use of the proxy machinery and self perpetuate themselves in office as directors, thereby becoming titular managers of the corporation. Where stock ownership is widely scattered, the corporation may be controlled by management rather than by the stockholders.

The Revised Model Business Corporation Act (Section 8.01 (b), RMBCA)

"All corporate powers shall be exercised by or under the authority of, and the business and affairs of the corporation managed under the direction of, its board of directors, subject to any limitation set forth in the articles of incorporation or in an agreement authorized under section 7.32 (close corporation agreement)."

Section 8.01 RMBCA requires that every corporation have a board of directors, except that a corporation with a shareholders' agreement (close corporation agreement) may dispense with or limit the authority of the board of directors. This limitation must be in the bylaws or certificate of incorporation, or the close corporation agreement must become part of the bylaws. It must be in writing and signed by all shareholders in existence at the time it is drawn. The agreement must be noted conspicuously on the front or back of each stock certificate issued. If at the time of the agreement there are outstanding shares, they must be recalled and new shares issued that comply with section 7.32. Any purchaser of stock that does not have notice of the existence of the agreement on the face or back of the certificate and who is not aware of the agreement shall be entitled to rescind the purchase. The validity of the agreement will not be affected.

Qualification of Directors (Section 8.02, RMBCA)

"The articles of incorporation or by-laws may prescribe qualifications for directors. A director need not be a resident of the state of incorporation of the corporation, nor a shareholder of the corporation. The bylaws can provide that directors be residents of a particular place, or own shares in the corporation, or have certain qualifications deemed necessary to serve as a director of the corporation."

Number and Election of Directors

Traditionally, a minimum of three directors was required by most states to incorporate. Modern statutes and many states today only require a minimum of one director.

Section 8.03 (a), RMBCA

"The board of directors must consist of one or more individuals, with the number specified in or fixed in accordance with the articles of incorporation or bylaws."

Section 8.03 (b), RMBCA

"If a board of directors has power to fix or change the number of directors, the board may increase or decrease by 30 percent or less the number of directors last approved by the shareholders, but only the shareholders may increase or decrease by more than 30 percent the number of directors last approved by the shareholders."

The power to fix or change the board is set forth in the certificate of incorporation or the bylaws. If there is no mention in the certificate of incorporation or the bylaws, only the shareholders can fix, increase, or decrease the number of directors. The shareholders would do this in either a special meeting of stockholders called for this purpose and vote, or at the annual stockholders' meeting.

Section 8.03 (c), RMBCA

"The articles of incorporation or bylaws may establish a variable range for the size of the board of directors by fixing a minimum and maximum number of directors. If a variable range is established, the number of directors may be fixed or changed from time to time, within the minimum and maximum, by the shareholders or by the board of directors. After shares are issued, only the shareholders may change the range for the size of the board or change from a fixed to a variable-range size board or vice versa."

Term of Office

The initial directors are usually named in the organization meeting or the certificate of incorporation. They serve until the first meeting of shareholders at which directors are elected. Thereafter, directors are elected at the annual meeting of shareholders and serve for a stated term or until their successor is elected. If a quorum of shareholders does not exist at the annual shareholders' meeting or if the shareholders are deadlocked on the election, then the director or directors continue in office as "holdovers" until their successors are elected.

If there are nine or more directors, the articles of incorporation may provide for staggering their terms by dividing the total number of directors into two or three groups with each group containing one-half or one-third of the total, as near as may be. In that event, the terms of directors in the first group expire at the first annual shareholders' meeting after their election; the terms of the second group expire at the second annual shareholders' meeting after their election; and the terms of the third group, if any, expire at the third annual shareholders' meeting after their election. At each annual shareholders' meeting held thereafter, directors shall be chosen for a term of two years or three years, as the case may be, to succeed those whose terms expire. (RMBC Section 8.06)

Terms of Directors Generally (Section 8.05, RMBCA)

(a) The terms of the initial directors of a corporation expire at the first shareholders' meeting at which directors are elected.

(b) The terms of all other directors expire at the next annual shareholders' meeting following their election unless their terms are staggered.

(c) A decrease in the number of directors does not shorten an incumbent director's term.

(d) The term of a director elected to fill a vacancy expires at the next shareholders' meeting at which directors are elected.

(e) Despite the expiration of a director's term, the director continues to serve until a successor is elected and qualifies or until there is a decrease in the number of directors.

Resignation of Directors

A director may resign at any time by delivering written notice to the board of directors, its chairperson, or to the secretary of the corporation. A resignation is effective when the notice is delivered, unless the notice specifies a later effective date. The director continues to serve until a new director is elected and qualifies.

Removal of Directors by Shareholders

The shareholders may remove one or more directors **with or without cause,** unless the articles of incorporation provide that directors be removed only for cause. With cause means that you have a justifiable reason for removal. An example would be missing the last four meetings after being warned that if one more meeting was missed the director would be removed for cause. Being in competition with the corporation would be reason for cause. Without cause means removal for any reason whatsoever. All that is needed is enough votes for removal. A majority of shareholders call a special meeting of stockholders for the purpose of removing Mary Smith as a director. All that is required for the removal is a majority of votes of stockholders attending the special stockholders' meeting. This is an example of removal without cause.

Voting Group of Shareholders

If a director is elected by a **voting group of shareholders,** only the shareholders of that voting group may participate in the vote to remove that director. A voting group of shareholders is a group of shareholders who by written agreement have all agreed to either appoint one person to vote for them as a group or that they will vote together as one.

   If cumulative voting is authorized, a director may not be removed if the number of votes sufficient to elect the director under cumulative voting is voted against the director's removal. If cumulative voting is not authorized, a director may be removed only if the number of votes cast to remove the director exceeds the number of votes cast not to remove the director.

   A director may be removed by the shareholders only at a meeting called for the purpose of removing the director and the meeting notice must state that the purpose, or one of the purposes, of the meeting is removal of the director.

Removal of Directors by Judicial Proceeding

   (a) The proper court of the county where a corporation's **principal office** is located may remove a director of the corporation from office in a proceeding commenced either by the corporation or by its shareholders holding at least 10 percent of the outstanding shares of any class if the court finds that:
   (1) the director engaged in fraudulent or dishonest conduct, or gross abuse of authority or discretion, with respect to the corporation and
   (2) removal is in the best interest of the corporation. The proper court would be either county court or state court depending on the jurisdiction. If there is no principal office in the state, it would be the county where the registered office is or the registered agent is.
   (b) The court that removes a director may bar the director from reelection for a period prescribed by the court.
   (c) If shareholders commence a proceeding under subsection (a), they must make the corporation a party defendant.

A judicial removal as opposed to removal by the shareholders may be necessary or appropriate in any of the following instances:

   (1) In a closely held corporation, the director charged with misconduct is elected by a voting group or cumulative voting, and the shareholders with power to prevent the director's removal exercise that power despite the existence of fraudulent or dishonest conduct. The classical example is where the director charged with misconduct possesses sufficient votes to prevent removal and exercises the voting power to that end.
   (2) In a publicly held corporation, the director charged with misconduct declines to resign, though urged to do so, and because of the large number of widely scattered

shareholders, a special shareholders' meeting can be held only after a period of delay and at considerable expense.

A shareholder who owns less than 10 percent of the outstanding shares of the corporation may bring a **derivative stockholder's suit** (discussed more fully in Chapter 10) in the name of the corporation. A derivative stockholder's suit is an action brought by a stockholder for the benefit of the corporation. If the stockholder wins money, the money is paid to the corporation. A shareholder who owns at least 10 percent of the outstanding shares of the corporation may maintain a suit in the shareholder's own name and right. The corporation, however, must be made a **party** to the action. Party to the action means being included in the lawsuit, i.e. being sued.

Vacancy on Board (Section 8.10, RMBCA)

"**(a)** Unless the articles of incorporation provide otherwise, if a vacancy occurs on a board of directors, including a vacancy resulting from an increase in the number of directors:

(1) The shareholders may fill the vacancy;

(2) The board of directors may fill the vacancy; or

(3) If the directors remaining in office constitute fewer than a **quorum** of the board, they may fill the vacancy by the affirmative vote of a majority of all the directors remaining in office. (A quorum is a minimum number of directors necessary to be present to proceed with a meeting.)

(b) If the vacant office was held by a director elected by a voting group of shareholders, only the holders of shares of that voting group are entitled to vote to fill the vacancy if it is filed by the shareholders.

(c) A vacancy that will occur at a specific later date (by resignation that will take effect at a later date) may be filled before the vacancy occurs, but the new director may not take office until the vacancy occurs."

The quorum above referred to is the amount of directors in office, not the amount of directors wanting to act on a question. For example, there are eight members on the board; the quorum is six. This means that the board cannot act unless there are at least six directors present at a meeting. If there were two vacancies on the board, the board could not fill those vacancies at a meeting where five directors were present. The quorum is still six to act. On the other hand if there were three vacancies, that would leave five directors in office, less than a quorum, and the majority of the five could elect the three replacements for the vacancies under section 8.10 (a)(3).

Compensation of Directors

Unless the articles of incorporation or bylaws provide otherwise, the board of directors may fix the compensation of directors.

Meetings of the Board of Directors

The board of directors may hold regular or special meetings in or out of the state of incorporation. Unless the bylaws or articles of incorporation say otherwise, the board of directors may permit any or all directors to participate in a regular or special meeting by, or conduct the meeting through the use of, any means of communication by which all directors participating may simultaneously hear each other during the meeting. A director participating in a meeting by this means is deemed to be present in person at the meeting.

Action Without Meeting

Unless the bylaws or articles of incorporation specify otherwise, any action required or permitted to be taken by the board of directors may be taken without a meeting if the action is taken by all members of the board. The action must be evidenced by one or more written consents describing the action taken, signed by each director and included in the minutes or filed with the corporate records reflecting the action taken. This action is effective only when the last director signs the consent unless the consent specifies a different effective date. Any consent thus signed has the effect of a meeting vote and may be described as such in any document. (RMBCA Section 8.21)

The board can, therefore, act unanimously without a formal meeting; to wit: in a closely held corporation where there is a small number of directors, only one, two, three, or so. Very often the directors informally meet with various company managers and persons employed by the company. If action is necessary by the board after they have made a decision, a written consent by all directors is a lot easier and quicker than calling for a meeting.

In publicly held corporations formal meetings are more appropriate; however, there will always be situations where prompt action is necessary and the decision noncontroversial so that approval without a formal meeting may be preferred. Written consents would be appropriate in this case.

The requirement of unanimous written consent precludes the possibility of stopping or ignoring opposing arguments. A director opposed to an action that is proposed to be taken by unanimous consent, or uncertain as to the desirability of that action, may compel the holding of a formal directors' meeting to discuss the matter simply by withholding consent.

Notice of Meeting

Unless the bylaws or articles of incorporation say otherwise, regular meetings of the board of directors may be held without notice of the date, time, place, or purpose of the meeting.

Unless the bylaws or articles of incorporation provide for a longer or shorter period, special meetings of the board of directors must be preceded by at least two days notice of the date, time, and place of the meeting. The notice need not describe the purpose of the special meeting unless required by the articles of incorporation or bylaws.

Waiver of Notice

A director may waive any notice required by the bylaws, articles of incorporation, or act before or after the date and time stated in the notice. The waiver must be in writing, signed by the director entitled to the notice, and filed with the minutes or corporate records.

A director's presence or participation in a meeting waives any required notice to the director of the meeting unless the director at the beginning of the meeting objects to holding the meeting, or transacting business at the meeting, and does not thereafter vote for or assent to action taken at the meeting.

Quorum and Voting

A majority of board members constitutes a **quorum** in most states. A quorum is the minimum number of directors that must be present at a meeting to transact business. Most states require a majority to be the minimum for a quorum. The Revised Model Business Corporation Act allows the bylaws or articles of incorporation to set a quorum for the board as low as one-third of the members of the board. The articles of incorporation or the bylaws may require more than a majority of the board to constitute a quorum. In any event, a majority of the board present and voting is necessary to carry a motion unless the bylaws or articles of incorporation require greater than a majority of the board in attendance to carry a motion.

Close corporations sometimes require a unanimous presence of all directors for a quorum, and a unanimous vote of directors to carry a motion. This can create a problem as one member refusing to join the vote of all others can prevent action by the board. It may be very difficult to try to rule by unanimous decree.

If a director is present at a meeting of the board of directors, he or she **assents** (agrees) to the action taken at the meeting unless the director objects at the beginning of the meeting to holding or transacting business at the meeting, or the dissent or **abstention** from the action is entered in the minutes book or written notice of the dissent is given to the presiding officer of the meeting before adjournment or to the corporation immediately after adjournment. Abstention is when one passes on voting and refuses to vote.

The Revised Model Business Corporation Act requires a quorum of directors to be present at the time of a vote. At a shareholder meeting a quorum is necessary to start the meeting, and thereafter if some shareholders leave and there is not a quorum at voting time it is not a problem. At shareholder meetings you only need a quorum to start the meeting. At directors' meetings you need a quorum to start the meeting and a quorum to vote.

Directors cannot vote by proxy; they must vote in person. Shareholders, on the other hand, can vote by proxy. This is discussed more fully in Chapter 8.

Section 8.24, RMBCA

"**(a)** Unless articles of incorporation or bylaws require a greater number or unless otherwise specifically provided in this Act, a quorum of the board of directors consists of:

(**1**) a majority of the fixed number of directors if the corporation has a fixed board size; or

(**2**) a majority of the number of directors prescribed; or, if no number is prescribed, the number in office immediately before the meeting begins if the corporation has a variable-range size board.

(**b**) The articles of incorporation or bylaws may authorize a quorum of a board of directors to consist of no fewer than one-third of the fixed or prescribed number of directors under subsection (a).

(**c**) If a quorum is present when a vote is taken, the affirmative vote of a majority of directors present is the act of the board of directors unless the articles of incorporation or bylaws require the vote of a greater number of directors.

(**d**) A director who is present at a meeting of the board of directors or a committee of the board of directors when corporate action is taken is deemed to have assented to the action taken unless:

(**1**) The director objects at the beginning of the meeting (or promptly upon arrival) to holding it or transacting business at the meeting.

(2) The director's dissent or abstention from the action taken is entered in the minutes of the meeting; or

(3) The director delivers written notice of dissent or abstention to the presiding officer of the meeting before its adjournment or to the corporation immediately after adjournment of the meeting. The right of dissent or abstention is not available to a director who votes in favor of the action taken."

Committees of the Board

If the articles of incorporation or bylaws do not have a prohibition against forming one or more committees, the board of directors may, by majority vote of the full board, or if the quorum requirement is greater than a majority of the full board by quorum, appoint committees. All committee persons must be members of the board of directors. Some states require the articles of incorporation or bylaws to permit forming committees, otherwise they cannot be formed. No board member is relieved of any liability to the corporation by delegating authority to a committee. Some committees are audit committees to oversee the independent CPA; executive committees to guide management between meetings of the full board; finance committees, compensation committees, investment committees, and nominating committees. Audit committees composed of all outside directors are required by The New York Stock Exchange for all companies listed on the exchange. Committees can exercise all the authority that the board would have, except for declaring dividends and making distributions, amending the bylaws, filling vacancies on committees or boards, mergers, acquisitions, charter amendments, sale of stock, sale of substantial assets of the corporation, as well as any matters prohibited for committees by the articles or bylaws. Several states do not allow committees the power to change the principal corporate office, appoint or remove officers, fix director compensation, or remove agents. These are not prohibited by the Revised Model Business Corporation Act since the whole board of directors may reverse or rescind any action taken by a committee.

RMBCA Section 8.25 gives the board of directors power to act through committees composed of all directors. It specifies the powers that are not delegatable to the committee and that can only be performed by the full board of directors. (The board of directors or management can always establish nonboard committees composed of directors, employees, or others to deal with the corporate powers not required to be exercised by the board of directors.)

Committees (Section 8.25, RMBCA)

"(a) Unless the articles of incorporation or bylaws provide otherwise, a board of directors may create one or more committees and appoint members of the board of directors to serve on them. Each committee must have two or more members who serve at the pleasure of the board of directors.

(b) The creation of a committee and appointment of members to it must be approved by the greater of

(1) a majority of all the directors in office when the action is taken; or

(2) the number of directors required by the articles of incorporation or bylaws to take action under a quorum.

(c) Sections 8.20 through 8.24, which govern meetings, action without meetings, notice and waiver of notice, and quorum and voting requirements of the board of directors, all apply to committees and their members as well.

(d) To the extent specified by the board of directors or in the articles of incorporation or bylaws, each committee may exercise the authority of the directors.

    (e) A committee may not, however:

      (1) Authorize distributions.

      (2) Approve or propose to shareholders action that this Act requires to be approved by shareholders.

      (3) Fill vacancies on the board of directors or any of the committees.

      (4) Amend articles of incorporation.

      (5) Adopt, amend, or repeal bylaws.

      (6) Approve a plan of merger not requiring shareholder approval.

      (7) Authorize or approve reacquisition of shares, except according to a formula or method prescribed by the board of directors, or

      (8) Authorize or approve the issuance or sale, or contract for the sale of shares, or determine the designation and relative rights, preferences, and limitations of a class or series of shares, except that the board of directors may authorize a committee (or a senior executive officer of the corporation) to do so within the limits specifically prescribed by the board of directors.

    (f) The creation of, delegation of authority to, or action by a committee does not alone constitute compliance by a director with the standards of conduct of a director to eliminate the liability of directors."

Officers

Most states require a minimum of three officers: a president, secretary, and treasurer. The bylaws of the corporation may require or permit more officers. There is an **inifinite** (unlimited) number of officers permissible. Assistant vice president, vice president, treasurer, assistant treasurer, secretary, assistant secretary, and other variations that can be created and inserted into the bylaws. A person can hold more than one office; however, usually the same person cannot hold the office of president and secretary at the same time. Some states and the RMBCA allow one person to hold the office of president, secretary, and treasurer at the same time. A bank will generally not allow a bank account to be opened in the corporate name if there is only one person acting as all officers and that person signs the corporate bank resolution and is the only one to sign corporate checks. The bank will require someone else to sign an affidavit attesting to the resolution to allow only one officer and the same person to be the only one to sign checks. Usually the affidavit would come from the corporate attorney. If the president is also the secretary the same situation exists and an affidavit will be required from someone else—usually the corporate attorney. The reason for this is that the secretary of the corporation attests to the corporate resolution being accurate, an act of the directors and the signatures on the bank signature cards being accurate. This leads to too much possibility for fraud if one person holds all positions or if the president is also the secretary.

    Officers are fiduciaries of the corporation as are directors. In addition, officers are agents of the corporation and individually can **bind** (make liable) the corporation. Directors, while fiduciaries, are not agents. This means that as a body acting together, directors can bind the corporation, but not individually. Directors make policy and the officers carry out the policy on a day-to-day basis. The directors manage and the officers carry out the management goals delegated to them by the directors. Officers are selected, elected, or appointed by the board of directors. The board also has the power to remove an officer with or without cause. If the officer has a contract of employment with the corporation that restricts the right to fire, removal without cause may lead the officer to sue the corporation for **breach of contract.** Breach of contract means failing to perform the contract. "With cause" means that the officer was not performing his or her duties properly, possibly coming in late or leaving early; failing to return telephone calls; not preparing reports in a timely fashion or as required by the board of directors, exercising poor judgment on numerous occasions; in some way bringing disgrace to the corporation; being discriminatory in hiring, firing, and/or work ethic; sexual harassment, etc.

Required Officers (Section 8.40, RMBCA)

(a) A corporation has the officers described in its bylaws.

(b) A duly appointed officer may appoint one or more officers or assistant officers if authorized by the bylaws or the board of directors.

(c) The bylaws or the board of directors shall delegate to one of the officers responsibility for preparing minutes of the directors' and shareholders' meetings and for authenticating records of the corporation.

(d) The same individual may simultaneously hold more than one office in a corporation.

Officers' Term of Office

Officers are elected or appointed by the board of directors and serve at the will of the board of directors. Very often officers are hired with a contract; terminating the officer before the contract expires can lead to a breach of contract suit against the corporation. A few states allow the shareholders to elect the officers. In rare instances the state, courts, or shareholders can remove officers. Usually these involve removal "with cause." Some states are employment at will jurisdictions. Technically this means that the employer can terminate an employee at any time with or without cause. The employee can quit at any time with or without notice. There are exceptions to this doctrine. If a contract exists, oral or written, the employer may not be able to terminate without having good cause. Every interview with the officer before and after hiring and all said at the interviews become an express or implied contract, as well as all hiring and company manuals and memos sent during the course of employment. In addition there is various civil rights legislation that prevents termination or lawsuits will be precipitated. Age discrimination, minority status and disability are just a few of the laws that may prevent discharge or cause legal proceedings to be commenced against the corporation.

SUMMARY

Different ways to become a shareholder have been enumerated. The corporation is managed by the board of directors. The board is elected by the shareholders. The board of directors appoints or elects officers unless the bylaws or certificate of incorporation allows the shareholders to elect officers. In most states today a minimum of one director is required for incorporation. Most states allow one person to hold all the offices. A bank may, however, not let a bank account be opened if only one person holds all of the offices. The bank will require someone to verify the officers, so some other stockholder, director, or other party will have to make the verification. Directors usually have a one-year term and serve until they are replaced by a new duly elected director. The shareholders can remove directors with or without cause unless the bylaws or certificate of incorporation say otherwise. Directors can hold meetings within or outside of the state. Meetings can be attended electronically if the bylaws so permit. A quorum is necessary for a stockholders' meeting as well as for a directors' meeting. There are an infinite number of officers permitted.

WORDS TO KNOW

abstention	party
assents	perpetuate
bequest	principal office
bind	quorum
breach of contract	RMBCA
derivative stockholders' action	shareholder
fiduciary	stockholder
infinite	voting group
interest	with cause
issued	without cause

REVIEW

1. What is a fiduciary?
2. What is breach of contract?
3. What is a shareholder?
4. How do you become a shareholder?
5. What is a stockholder?
6. Explain quorum.
7. What is a bequest?
8. Explain a voting shareholders' group.
9. What does "without cause" mean?
10. Explain a derivative stockholders' action.
11. What does RMBCA stand for?
12. What does "with cause" mean? Give an example.
13. What is a corporation's principal office?
14. What does "party to the action" mean?
15. How does one become a member of the board of directors?

SHORT ESSAY

1. John Wise Guy was the principal, sole stockholder, president, chairman of the board, only officer, and only member of the board of directors of Good Fabrics, Incorporated. The company was chartered in the State of Delaware and had its principal office in Atlanta, Georgia. Good Fabrics, Incorporated, was in the retail business and sold ladies blouses. The corporation owned twenty-three retail stores which were located in various malls in five different states. Mr. Wise Guy, as president and chief buyer for Good Fabrics, Incorporated, purchased ladies blouses in the name of the corporation from various manufacturers. Good Fabrics, Incorporated, sold them at its various locations. The business was quite successful and grossed $22,000,000 a year. Mr. Wise Guy decided he was paying too much for the blouses he bought and that the manufacturers were making too much money. He decided to go into the manufacture of ladies' blouses and sell them at his retail locations.

Mr. Wise Guy, personally, in his own name, owned a building in North Carolina. The building had been empty for two years as it was in a depressed area and not in the best of condition. Mr. Wise Guy reasoned he could kill two birds with one stone by using this building to manufacture ladies' blouses that would be sold by Good Fabrics, Incorporated. He would have the property occupied and obtain blouses at a lesser cost.

Mr. Wise Guy formed a Delaware corporation, Cheap Labor, Inc. He was the only stockholder, only officer, and only director. He rented the building in North Carolina with a one-year lease to Cheap Labor, Inc., for $3,000 a month. Mr. Wise Guy decided Cheap Labor, Inc., would have fifty sewing machines with operators for each machine and run two shifts a day. Each machine cost $1,000, a total of $50,000. Mr. Wise Guy spent $3,000 to incorporate Cheap Labor, Inc., for the legal work and lease. He did not want to put more money into the corporation. He decided that he personally would buy and pay for the fifty machines. He would then own them in his personal name and lease them to Cheap Labor, Inc., for $100 a month per machine. Cheap Labor, Inc., would pay for them to be installed and maintained. Mr. Wise Guy decided he would use illegal aliens (people who entered this country illegally from a foreign country without visas) as operators of the machines and to manage the plant. Since they were illegal aliens, he would pay them below minimum wage and work them over forty hours a week; actually twelve hours a day, six days a week, without paying overtime. Mr. Wise Guy figured the cost of the fabric, rental of the machines, labor, lease, maintenance, electric, and sundries, and divided that cost into the number of blouses the plant would manufacture each week and that was the price Good Fabrics, Incorporated paid Cheap Labor, Inc., for the blouses. After expenses there was no profit left for Cheap Labor, Inc. The savings for Good Fabric, Incorporated came to 30 percent. Good Fabrics, Incorporated was now buying the same blouses for 30 percent less than they used to pay for them. Mr. Wise Guy was becoming very, very wealthy. After one year of operation, Mr. Wise Guy opened more retail locations and leased another fifty machines to Cheap Labor, Inc. Cheap Labor, Inc., obtained its fabric and sundries on credit and always paid timely. Cheap Labor, Inc., was now buying $100,000 of fabric a month and paying on thirty days credit.

One and one-half years after beginning the operation, the building in North Carolina had a fire on a Sunday and was totally destroyed. The fire was on the first day of the month. Fabric payments for the previous month were paid on the last day of the month. Mr. Wise Guy had the week's production picked up before the fire and paid for the merchandise when it was picked up. All the employees were paid, fabric cost for the previous month was paid, but no money was left. On the last day of the month, fabric for the new month was always delivered. It was paid for at the end of the month. One month's fabric was on the premises and burned. There was no insurance. The fabric company wants to be paid.

Cheap Labor, Inc., has no funds, no building, no fabric, and is effectively out of business. The fabric company sues Mr. Wise Guy and Good Fabrics, Incorporated as they were the parties that benefited from the production of Cheap Labor, Inc. How would you decide? Explain your reasoning.

CHAPTER

5

DO YOU WANT A CLOSE CORPORATION?

O BJECTIVES

After completing this chapter, you will be able to:

1. Know what a close corporation is.
2. Know the value of the use of a close corporation.
3. Solve the problems facing a small corporation.
4. Know what clauses and items go into a close corporation agreement.
5. Protect the participants in a small corporation.
6. Know how to draw a close corporation agreement.

INTRODUCTION

A close corporation resembles a partnership in that it usually has a small number of owners, is owner managed, and has non-transferability of ownership. The Uniform Partnership Act and The Revised Uniformed Partnership Act are formidable in the absence of a written agreement on a given issue. If there is no written agreement the acts apply. A written agreement can supersede what the acts say. The Uniform Partnership Act and the Revised Uniform Partnership Act are basically **suppletory.** That is, they govern only those areas that the stockholders agreement fails to cover; if there is no agreement, the acts govern. Therefore, the acts apply unless a written agreement says otherwise as to specific issues. The acts actually validate, in an implied manner, the written agreements between partners. A short discussion on general partnerships and corporations is necessary at this point to understand close corporation agreements. Basic characteristics of a general partnership are:

(1) In the absence of a writing to the contrary, all partners have an equal voice in the business i.e., equal rights in the management and conduct of the business.

(2) In the absence of writings, differences among the partners as to ordinary matters are settled by a majority vote of the partners. Outside the ordinary course of business, for example, amendments to the partnership agreement would require unanimous consent of the partners unless the agreement says otherwise.

(3) Every partner is an agent of the partnership and can bind the partnership in the ordinary course of business unless the third party, with whom the partner is dealing, knows the partner does not have authority to bind the partnership.

(4) In the absence of a written agreement, partnership profits are shared equally among the partners.

(5) In the absence of a written agreement, partnership losses are shared equally among the partners.

(6) No partner is entitled to a salary.

(7) No new partner can be admitted without the unanimous consent of all partners, unless an agreement exists to the contrary.

(8) Partnerships are usually for a limited time; they are not **perpetual** (forever). If the partnership is for a specified time, dissolution occurs at that point. If not for a specified time, any partner can terminate the partnership and cause dissolution at any time.

(9) Death of a partner terminates the partnership unless an agreement to the contrary exists.

(10) A partnership pays no federal taxes. The partnership must file a tax return. However, the taxes are paid by each partner as ordinary income on the partner's individual income tax return.

(11) Partners are in a fiduciary relationship to each other.

Basic characteristics of a corporation are:

(1) Corporate statutes are **regulatory** (must be followed) and not suppletory.

(2) Shareholders have no right to participate in the management of the corporation. The corporation is managed by a board of directors.

(3) Shareholders are unable to bind the corporation since they do not participate in the management of the corporation.

(4) Shareholders are not agents of the corporation.

(5) Shareholders are not in a fiduciary capacity to each other or to the corporation.

(6) Corporation profits are not shared by the shareholders. Shareholders receive dividends as, when, and if, so declared by the board of directors. The dividends are shared and received in proportion to stock ownership. The dividends become ordinary income to the shareholder, and the shareholder pays income tax on dividend earnings.

(7) Shareholders' stock interests are freely transferable unless an agreement to the contrary exists.

(8) Corporations generally have a **perpetual** (infinite) life. Consent of stockholders is necessary for dissolution.

(9) The Internal Revenue Code taxes profits of corporations; the corporation pays the tax, the shareholders do not. Likewise, tax losses belong to the corporation, not to the shareholders.

(10) A "Close Corporation" by agreement among the stockholders can and usually does change many of the above items.

Definition of a Close Corporation

A close corporation can best be defined as a corporation that has a relatively small number of shareholders. Some statutes require the number of shareholders to be less than fifty in a close corporation. Usually, it is designed in writing to be an owner–managed corporation with restrictions as to transferability of corporate shares.

Model Statutory Close Corporation Supplement

In 1982, the American Bar Association (**ABA**) Committee on Corporate Laws approved a Model Close Corporation Supplement. This is a model statute covering close corporations. This statute is **not** part of the Revised Model Business Corporation Act. It has not yet been fully adopted in all states although it is followed in many states.

LEGISLATIVE INTENT—VARIOUS STATES—AS TO CLOSE CORPORATIONS

The principal statutes are those enacted by California, Delaware, New York, and the Model Statutory Close Corporation Supplement. Nearly all other states have adopted one and/or parts of these state statutes. There are three different intents in these statutes:

1. **Unified Intent:** The legislature makes no special provisions for close corporations but does modify their statutes to meet the needs of close corporations. These statutes will apply to all corporations—publicly held corporations as well as small privately held corporations. This is not the modern view.

2. **New York and The Model Statutory Close Corporation Supplement:** In this intent New York and The Model Statutory Close Corporation Supplement deviate from The Unified Intent by adding provisions that apply only to defined shareholder situations. For example, the New York Business Corporation Act, Section 620 (a), authorizes voting agreements in all corporations. This is a unified intent. However, the New York Business Corporation Act, Section 620 (c), takes a definition intent by authorizing Certificate of Incorporation provisions as to Close Corporations "so long as no shares of the corporation are listed on a national securities exchange or regularly quoted in an over-the-counter market by one or more members of a national or affiliated securities association." The Model Statutory Close Corporation Supplement, Section 7.32, authorizes shareholder agreements in corporations that are not listed on a national securities exchange or traded in a market maintained by one or more members of a national securities association.

3. **Statutory Intent**—California and Delaware:

a. **California** has a unified intent with provisions which are useful to close corporations although any corporation can use them—whether a close corporation or not. It also has statutory provisions only for close corporations. California's close corporation provisions are not in any one subchapter but are scattered throughout the statute. The statute also has definitional differences. The Articles of Incorporation does not have to restrict stock transfers or public offerings. The Articles of Incorporation must say that the corporate shares cannot be held by more than thirty-five persons. The articles must say that this is a close corporation. Therefore, California is statutory, unified, and definitional as to close corporation intent.

b. **Delaware,** like New York, follows the unified intent to a point. Its statute is for close corporations as well as publicly held corporations. Delaware also has a subchapter applicable only to corporations that qualify **and** elect statutory close corporation status. Therefore, they are statutory close corporations. The way to qualify for a statutory close corporation is under Delaware General Corporation Law Subchapter XIV, Section 342.

"A close corporation is a corporation organized under this chapter whose certificate of incorporation . . . provides that:

(1) All of the corporation's issued stock of all classes, exclusive of treasury shares, shall be represented by certificates and shall be held of record by not more than a specified number of persons, not exceeding 30; and
(2) All of the issued stock of all classes shall be subject to one or more of the restrictions on transfer permitted by Section 202 of this title; and
(3) The corporation shall make no offering of any of its stock of any class which would constitute a "public offering" within the meaning of the United States Securities Act of 1933."

Section 202 requires a **legend** (notice) to be conspicuously written on each security that transferability and/or **registration** is restricted either by agreement, the bylaws, or the certificate of incorporation. Registration is required of certain securities before they can be sold under the 1933 Securities Act. This refers to Private Placement Offers (**PPO**) and other public offerings used to raise **equity capital** for the corporation. Equity capital means the purchase of a **stock interest.**

Qualify and Elect Close Corporation Status—Delaware

A corporation can qualify for close corporation status under Section 342 above, and then elect to be a close corporation under Section 343. You elect under Section 343 by placing a heading on your certificate of incorporation that the corporation is a close corporation.

The Delaware statute is **enabling** rather than **regulatory.** Enabling means that shareholders are allowed if they choose and are free to enter into agreements that might otherwise be unenforceable or of doubtful validity. Therefore, the drafting of the certificate of incorporation, bylaws, and agreements are of paramount importance in Delaware. Regulatory means that you must have certain requirements and follow the statute.

EXISTING CORPORATION TO BECOME A CLOSE CORPORATION—DELAWARE

Section 344, Delaware General Corporation Law, permits an existing Delaware corporation to become a close corporation by amending its certificate of incorporation and complying with Sections 342 and 202, above. There must be at least two–thirds of the holders of record of each class of stock to approve the amendment.

WHY WOULD YOU WANT A CLOSE CORPORATION?

Let us assume that you and four friends are contemplating going into business together. You have all reviewed the various vehicles to begin a business and have agreed upon a corporation. The corporation name shall be Best Friends, Inc. One of the five owners is an accountant, one is in marketing, one is in sales, one is in insurance, and the last one has executive talents. This is a good combination of talents for just about any service or other business venture. You have all agreed that each wants to devote and work full time in the business. Each has agreed to invest $40,000, a total capitalization of $200,000. It has been agreed that each would receive the same stock interest and the same salary. The executive would be the president; the insurance party would be the secretary; and the accountant would be the treasurer. The marketing person would be the vice president in charge of marketing and development. The sales party would be the vice president in charge of sales and training. You have all been very close friends for over fifteen years. Each trusts the others. Each of the five will be a director of the corporation.

Possible Future Problems Without a Close Corporation

Using the above set of facts some potential future problems exist. How do you guarantee each one's salary? How do you guarantee each one's title and duties? What happens to the stock if someone dies? What happens to the job of the **deceased** (dead party)? What happens if one of the five wants to sell his or her stock to an unknown third party? What happens if, down the road, three of the five join forces against the other two? Remember, shareholders elect directors with a majority vote. Shareholders do not have to be personally present to vote; they can vote by **proxy.** Proxy is a piece of paper that authorizes a particular person or group of persons to vote on behalf of the shareholder. The proxy can limit the vote to certain areas and state how the proxy is to be voted, or it can be a general proxy and allow the party or group to vote in their best judgment. Once there is a quorum of shareholders the meeting is effective and business can be carried on. It does not matter if shareholders leave the meeting at any point. The quorum is only necessary to start the meeting. Once the meeting has been started with the quorum it does not matter thereafter how many are present and the meeting can continue even if only one person is left. There is a different rule for directors' meetings. At directors' meetings a quorum is necessary to begin the meeting **and** a quorum is necessary for each vote. If directors leave during the meeting and the number left is less than a quorum, the meeting cannot transact any more business. Directors then elect or appoint officers with a majority vote. A quorum of directors is usually a majority of the directors on the board. A majority vote of the directors on the board is necessary to transact business, not a majority of the quorum. Therefore, if at any time during the meeting the number of directors present is less than a majority of the full board, the meeting cannot transact any more business.

With the above information, it is apparent that three of the above friends can join together and elect their own board of directors and their own officers, effectively cutting out the remaining two stockholders from management.

Close Corporation—Advantages

The major reason that a corporation was chosen as the vehicle for this business venture was that there would be no personal liability. A general partnership was discussed and everyone liked owner management in the partnership but feared the personal liability. Now, there is a way to get owner management, perpetuity, restrictions on the transferability of ownership, no personal liability, and a few other benefits. The way is with a close corporation.

FREEZE-OUTS

A corporation, while having many advantages, also supplies an opportunity for majority shareholders to take advantage of minority shareholders. The majority shareholders can subject the minority shareholders to a variety of actions, generally referred to as "freeze-outs." Remember, the board of directors has the power to declare dividends or refuse to declare dividends. The majority vote of the board governs. The majority may refuse to declare dividends. The majority may elect themselves as officers. The majority may pay themselves exorbitant salaries to drain off corporate funds. They may declare themselves huge bonuses. They may lease premises and/or equipment to the corporation at inflated prices. They may purchase supplies from friends or relatives at higher than usual prices. They can prevent minority shareholders from becoming officers, directors, or even employees of the corporation. The minority may seek judicial relief in the form of a lawsuit against the directors' self-serving conduct and attempt to show violation of their fiduciary duties. However, dividend policies are within the discretion of the board. Likewise, employment practices are within the discretion of the board. The business judgment rule, which will be discussed later in detail, will prevail. Basically, the business judgment rule allows the directors a great deal of leeway in making decisions on a purely business basis.

When the majority attempts a freeze-out, the minority are cut off from all corporate related monies. If the minority shareholders are unwilling to wait for the corporate policy of freeze-outs to change, they must either suffer their losses or seek a buyer to purchase their shares. It would be difficult to find a buyer who would be willing to enter an investment with freeze-outs in place. Perhaps one would buy at a fraction of the worth of the stock in the hope that management would change its strategy at some point and stop the freeze-out.

HOW DO YOU SET UP A CLOSE CORPORATION?

The Model Statutory Close Corporation Supplement, the New York State Business Corporation Law, the Delaware General Corporation Act, and the California Corporations Code all authorize close corporations. They can be set up in the Articles of Incorporation and sometimes be called a statutory close corporation. They can be formed at a later date as long as all shareholders agree to enter into a close corporation agreement.

VOTING

Statutory close corporations authorize voting agreements. The agreements can either be in the Articles of Incorporation or the Bylaws of the corporation. If the state does not have statutory close corporations, then any corporation formed can become a close corporation by having all stockholders enter into a close corporation agreement, sometimes referred to as a **stockholders agreement.**

Agreement

The agreement must be designed to solve all problems that may arise in the close corporation. The agreement must be clear enough for all to understand. There should be no **ambiguities** (confusion). A close corporation agreement is a contract. As with all contracts, it should clearly state the obligations and duties of all parties. If all parties know what they can and cannot do, lawsuits will be avoided. If one enters into an agreement with ambiguities, he or she is buying a lawsuit. Ambiguities are questions that get resolved in a courtroom. A businessperson wants to carry on a business, not a lawsuit.

The Close Corporation Agreement Should Cover At Least the Following Areas

Remember the reason money was invested in the corporation—the special abilities of the people who joined in forming the corporation. They all trusted each other and felt each would be a large contributor to the success of the corporation. They all agreed on the best job for each, salary, and other benefits. The close corporation agreement is for the purpose of protecting all so that no one is ever part of a freeze-out. The purpose of the close corporation agreement was to invest money in a corporation that each would be a part of. Each would have a management position, and be a director and a moving party in corporate strategy. Stock interest would be secure and no additional stockholders could come aboard without the unanimous consent of all charter stockholders. Likewise, no one could sell their stock interest to an outsider, only to the corporation or the other stockholders. A sample close corporation agreement can be found in Appendix D. Some of the minimum clauses in the close corporation agreement should be:

(1) The names and addresses of all stockholders in the corporation.
(2) The number of shares each stockholder owns.
(3) The names of the members of the board of directors to be elected.
(4) The names of the officers of the corporation to be elected.
(5) The job and duties of each stockholder—salary and work hours.
(6) Benefits for stockholders and other employees including vacation time; medical insurance; life insurance; vehicles, if any; and bonuses.
(7) Sick benefits for stockholders. What happens if one is permanently unable to work after a period of time?
(8) What happens to his or her stock if a stockholder dies?
(9) How does a stockholder sell his or her present interest?
(10) What happens if the corporation needs more capital?
(11) What happens to corporation assets if the corporation dissolves?
(12) How do you resolve problems that are not **amicably** (in a friendly way) settled?
(13) Placing of a **legend** (notice) on each stock certificate.
(14) Other items needed to be spelled out.

Stockholders   A corporation is formed because each stockholders trusts and has faith in the others and knows they can all work together to make a successful business. Some stockholders may put more assets in the corporation than others. Some may work more hours than others. Some may have technical skills, some educational knowledge, some experience; but all will contribute. In this section, list the names of each stockholder, their home addresses, and the number of shares of stock and the kind of stock they will own in the corporation.

Board Members   It is imperative that all stockholders become members of the board of directors. The board manages the corporation. Therefore, list the names of all stockholders and have each agree to vote all the shares that they own at all times to be listed as directors. This guarantees all to be directors as long as they wish. The object is to be sure that all stockholders become members of the board of directors. The board manages the corporation. Therefore, in the close corporation agreement list the names of all stockholders, electing them as directors of the corporation. Then, in the next sentence of the agreement all stockholders will agree to vote all the shares they own at all times, for the election of all the stockholders listed in the agreement as directors. This guarantees all stockholders to be directors.

Quorum   The close corporation agreement should require a quorum of all elected directors to be present for the board of directors to carry on any business. The required vote to carry a **resolution** (order of the board) should be **unanimous** (all directors present). In this manner all of the stockholders are guaranteed to be protected from and the possibility of a freeze-out.

Officers   The officers of the corporation will be named in the close corporation agreement. If their duties are not spelled out in the bylaws, this is a good place to list job duties, benefits, and all other items. This assumes that all of the officers are stockholders and **signatories** (signers) of the agreement. The purpose is to guarantee stockholders the positions they agreed to in forming the corporation and investing. Likewise, this is the legal manner giving them a right to this position. If it is ever taken from them, they would have a **cause of action** (the ability to sue the corporation and those who participated in the freeze-out).

Positions Other Than Officers   If a stockholder is going to hold a position with the corporation in any capacity other than an officer, this is the place to list that person. An example of these are director of research, state director, regional director, and other titles. Job duties, benefits, etc. should be spelled out in this section. Again, each person invested in the corporation to get the job. It must be in writing to protect his or her rights.

Sick Benefits, Disability   The close corporation agreement gives positions and salaries. If an attempt to freeze one out is successful, that party has a breach of contract, possibly fraud, suit and other causes of action against the corporation and the perpetrators. This can be a double edged sword if the drafter of the agreement is not careful. Assume one of the stockholders and a signer of the agreement is in charge of a corporate area and is receiving a six–figure salary. That party may become sick and on doctors orders may not be able to return to corporate duties for thirteen or more months. If the agreement does not provide for this kind of problem, the corporation may end up paying the salary for the thirteen months plus pay another party a salary to do the job of the disabled stockholder. Therefore, when preparing the agreement, it must be decided how long you will carry a sick or disabled person on full salary. It is possible to buy insurance to solve this problem, but that can become costly. You may want to specify full salary for the first two months, then one-half salary for four months, then one-fourth salary for four months, and no salary after that until there is a full return to duties. You may want to set a time limit and after that date no salary, and after a further period if unable to return to full duties you may require that party to sell their stock interest to the corporation or to all of the other stockholders in equal shares. The idea is that you do not want to carry someone who is not contributing to the corporation and you do not want a stranger to buy the party's stock. You may provide a similar time table if a party is declared totally disabled and unable to resume duties as a result of an accident, or physical or mental disability.

Death of a Stockholder   If a stockholder dies, what happens to the stock interest of that stockholder? Normally it goes to the estate of the deceased. One of the purposes of a close corporation is to prevent any new stockholders that are not unanimously agreed upon by all stockholders. Therefore, you must provide in the agreement for the purchase of the shares of the **deceased** (dead party). You do that by simply forcing the **tender** (offer) of the shares for sale to the corporation first. If the corporation does not want to or cannot buy, then the stock is offered in equal shares to the stockholders. If the stockholders do not want to buy, then it is offered to any stockholder or stockholders willing to buy. If no one wants to purchase the interest, the shares may be sold to anyone else without restriction. In this manner you are again controlling who the stockholders of the corporation are and you have the opportunity of preventing outsiders from becoming shareholders. Next you have to set up a formula for deciding the value of the stock interest, and the method of payment. This will be discussed in the section on selling an interest in a close corporation agreement.

Incapacity or Incompetence of a Stockholder   In the event a stockholder becomes incapacitated or **judiciously** (by order of a court) declared or otherwise found to be **incompetent** (unable to legally make decisions), you must have a formula to purchase this stock, similar to the above on the death of a stockholder. You certainly do not want one who is incompetent on your board of directors. Similarly, if one becomes permanently incapacitated, by any manner whatsoever, you do not want a party who may not be able to fully perform his or her duties to continue as a stockholder. You must make a provision to purchase the stock interest.

Sale of a Close Corporation Interest   If one of the stockholders, for any reason, wishes to sell the stock interest that is owned, you must provide a means for sale because the close corporation agreement is restricting the sale of the stock except as pursuant to the close corporation agreement executed by the parties. Therefore, you must provide for a means of sale and payment. First, the seller must offer the full stock interest for sale to the corporation. If the corporation does not wish to purchase for any reason, the stock interest should be offered to all present stockholders other than the selling stockholder in equal shares. This way all stockholders will retain their same percentage of ownership. If the stockholders do not want to equally purchase, then the interest should be offered to stockholders who are interested in purchasing, and they will buy equal amounts. If no stockholder wishes to purchase them, the selling stockholder can offer the stock for sale to anyone with no restrictions as to the close corporation agreement.

To determine the selling price, the agreement can provide for the parties each year to issue a **certificate of agreed value** and record it with the secretary of the corporation. The certificate of agreed value is accomplished by all stockholders agreeing to the value of the corporation on the date the certificate is dated. This is not difficult because, if someone puts a higher value than he or she should, he or she may be forced to pay that value if the stock is **tendered** (offered) to him or her. Therefore, he or she will be overpaying because of his or her own foolishness. On the other hand if one places a lower value than he or she should, because he or she feels if someone tenders the stock he or she will be able to buy it below its true value, he or she can be hurt. For instance if one dies, the **heirs** (next of kin) will receive less than true value. If one wants to sell, he or she will receive less than true value. These facts make the process orderly and generally a very fair number is agreed upon. That number goes into the certificate and is the price paid for stock if one dies or wishes to sell. The certificate of agreed value is good for one year or until a new certificate is executed by all stockholders. As the corporation grows and its value increases, it is necessary that all be sure to meet once a year to set a new value and record a new certificate of agreed value with the secretary of the corporation.

If they do not issue a certificate of agreed value, then they have to state a long formula as to exactly how to determine value when stock is tendered. It can provide for a certified public accountant to do an inventory of all assets and use either the purchase price of the items or present value as a basis. This way there is no value for good will in the final price. The choice must be made in the certificate, there cannot be two ways to figure value. This is costly, time consuming, and can lead to disagreements possibly requiring court intervention. The certificate of agreed value is fast, fair, and inexpensive.

The next problem is how the corporation, all stockholders, or individual stockholders that buy the stock, pay for the purchase. The stockholders can agree to 10 percent down and the balance to be paid in equal monthly installments over a five year period with 5 percent interest. This gives the selling stockholder or heirs an income for five years. The amount down, the interest percent, and the time for payment are all negotiated by the stockholders. This information as to method of payment is then incorporated into the certificate of agreed value. In this manner the price, method of payment, and interest are already settled upon in the certificate and when one tenders stock, the transaction can be concluded in days without expense to any of the parties.

Additional Capital Required by Corporation   The close corporation agreement does not permit additional stock to be sold, unless there is unanimous agreement by all stockholders to offer additional stock for sale. Since one of the main reasons for the close corporation is to keep strangers out and only have the original people who know and trust each other in the corporation, it is unlikely that all will agree to selling stock to a stranger. This leaves two basic means to obtain additional working capital for the corporation. The first is through a loan from a lending institution or an individual. Possibly one of the stockholders, or a group of stockholders, may be willing to loan the corporation money and receive repayment over a period of time with interest. The next method is by a mandatory assessment of all stockholders. Each would have to either give the corporation additional money as a **capital contribution** or as a loan, whichever is agreed upon by all. A capital contribution is when the lender is not paid back the money contributed; instead, it becomes a part of the original purchase price and is added to the original purchase price as cost for the original stock purchase.

Dissolution   When a majority of shareholders of a close corporation award dividends to all shareholders except a class of minority shareholders, it can be deemed an "oppressive action" and serve as a basis for dissolution under Section 1104-a of the Business Corporation Law of the State of New York. Under this statute, illegal, fraudulent, and oppressive acts are a basis for dissolution. Oppressive acts would be misappropriation of corporate assets or mistreatment of shareholders. A deadlock in voting would also trigger dissolution. In general, the corporation can dissolve on vote of the board of directors. This is why it is important to carefully agree on what percentage of voting is necessary by the board to carry a resolution. This writer suggests a unanimous vote to be necessary in most small close corporation agreements, especially if all stockholders invested a like amount and hold the same number of shares. Trouble starts when different percentages of stock ownership exist in a close corporation agreement.

Normally, when a corporation dissolves, all of the assets are sold. Creditors of the corporation are paid. Loans to the corporation by stockholders are repaid and what is left is divided on a **pro rata** ownership basis to stockholders. Pro rata means if you own 3 percent of the corporate stock, you will receive 3 percent of the funds to be paid to stockholders. Whatever your ownership percentage is, that is the pro rata percent you will receive. In a close corporation agreement the parties can agree to take dissolution property **in kind** as well as in cash. In kind means that if you are entitled to $300, you can either take the $300 or property valued at that amount. There can also be different treatment of stockholder loans to the corporation; whatever is agreed upon in the agreement will control.

Arbitration **Arbitration** is the use of a third party or third parties to settle a dispute. It is a contractual arrangement where all parties agree to submit an issue to either one or more parties mutually agreed upon by the contestants for resolution. The award of the arbitrator or arbitrators is binding with the same force and effect as a court order. It generally cannot be appealed. The only basis for appeal would be if the decision was arbitrary and capricious which is an extremely difficult issue to prove.

The best reason to include an arbitration clause in the close corporation agreement is that it will provide a speedy resolution of any dispute between the stockholders. You can name the arbitrator or arbitrators in the close corporation agreement and how much they will be paid and who will pay them—the corporation, the contestants, or the loser of the award. You can even set up a procedure for the arbitration. The grievant notifies the corporation, arbitrator, or arbitrators named in the close corporation agreement, and other parties who desire arbitration and for the issue to be arbitrated. Within five days the arbitrators will arrange a date for the meeting; the place to be used for the arbitration is the corporate offices. Within five days of the hearing an award must be issued. Therefore, the complete process will take about ten days. If one had to use the courts, it would take months, or in some jurisdictions years, to obtain a court trial. It is a very important item to consider for the close corporation agreement.

Legend A **legend** is a statement that must appear in a prominent place on each stock certificate of a close corporation. Basically it says, "This stock certificate is subject to a close corporation agreement, dated this __ day of __ 20 __. A copy of this agreement is on file with the corporate secretary and is available for reading during normal business hours."

SUMMARY

In this chapter we discussed how a close corporation resembles a partnership. It has a small number of stockholders, is owner managed, and its shares are subject to restrictions as to transferability. In addition, it has the protection of a corporation as to no personal liability for shareholders. It also has the benefit of being perpetual. A close corporation is easy to form. In some jurisdictions it is statutory; i.e., it is mentioned to be a close corporation in the articles of incorporation and/or bylaws. In other jurisdictions all that is required is a close corporation agreement as long as all stockholders agree. An existing corporation can become a close corporation if all stockholders agree.

A close corporation can protect the stockholder as to income by guaranteeing a job, salary, and the duties actually originally intended in forming the corporation. It assures the owner–management concept. If drawn properly, the close corporation agreement will protect against "freeze-outs"; the majority stockholders can run the corporation without any say by the minority stockholders.

We discussed the various areas a close corporation agreement covers and went over an actual agreement in Appendix D; the advantages of continuation of the corporation even after incapacity and/or death of some stockholders; how they would be paid; and how the valuation of the corporation would be figured. We covered dissolution and arbitration of disputes.

CASES

Close Corporation

DONAHUE v. RODD ELECTROTYPE CO.
Supreme Court of Massachusetts, 1975
367 Mass. 578, 328 N.E. 2nd 505, 307 N.E. 2nd 8

TAURO, Chief Justice

Euphemia Donahue is a minority stockholder in defendant company, Rodd Electrotype Co., a Massachusetts corporation. The suit is against the directors of Rodd Electrotype, Charles Rodd, Frederick Rodd, and Harold Magnuson; and against Harry Rodd, former director, officer, and controlling stockholder of Rodd Electrotype; and against Rodd Electrotype. The plaintiff seeks to rescind a purchase by the corporation of the shares of Harry Rodd, and to compel Harry Rodd to repay the corporation the $36,000 paid by the corporation for his shares together with interest from the date of purchase. The lawsuit claims the defendants caused the corporation to purchase these shares in violation of their fiduciary duty to her, a minority stockholder.

The trial judge dismissed the suit, finding the sale was without prejudice to plaintiff, carried out in good faith and fairness. The appeals court affirmed. It is now before the Supreme Court.

Harry Rodd and Joseph Donahue became employees of Royal Electrotype (predecessor of Rodd Electrotype) in the mid-1930s. Donahue's duties were operational in the plants and he never participated in the management aspect of the business. Rodd's advancement in the company was rapid. In 1946 he became general manager and treasurer. Thereafter, Rodd acquired 200 of the corporation's 1000 shares. Donahue acquired 50 shares. In 1955 Rodd became president and general manager. The remaining 750 shares were purchased by Royal. At this point Donahue and Rodd were the sole stockholders of Royal, owning 80% and 20% respectfully. In early 1960 the corporation was renamed to Rodd Electrotype Co., and Harry's two sons, Charles and Frederick, took management positions with the company. In 1965 Charles became president and general manager; and his father, Harry, remained active in the business.

Around 1967, Harry Rodd gave 117 of his 200 shares equally to his two sons and daughter. He gave two shares to the corporate treasury. He retained 81 shares. At this point Donahue owned 50 shares, Harry Rodd 81 shares, and the two sons and daughters of Harry between them, owned 117 shares. In 1970 Harry was not in good health and his sons wanted him to retire. Harry wanted a financial arrangement to be made for his 81 shares before he would retire. Charles Rodd, his son and now president, negotiated a purchase by the corporation of 45 shares from Harry at $800 per share. Charles Rodd then called a special meeting of the board of directors which consisted of Charles Rodd, Frederick Rodd, and an attorney. They voted to authorize the corporation to purchase the 45 shares from Harry Rodd at $800 per share. Charles testified that this was the book value and liquidating value of the shares. Subsequently, Harry Rodd sold 2 shares to each of his three children for $800 per share and gave each child 10 shares as a gift, leaving Harry with no more shares.

During this period Donahue died and his 50 shares passed to his wife and son. When they learned the corporation had purchased Harry Rodd's shares, they tendered their shares to the corporation for purchase at the same price. The offer was refused by the corporation and this suit commenced.

The plaintiffs argue that the purchase of Harry's shares was an unlawful distribution of corporate assets to a controlling stockholder and a breach of a fiduciary duty owed by the controlling stockholders (Rodds) to a minority stockholder (Donahue), because the Rodds failed to offer Donahue an equal opportunity to sell shares to the corporation at the same price. The defendants say the sale was fair and there is no right to equal purchase by the corporate treasury.

This court agrees with plaintiff and reverses the decision of the lower court. However, we limit the application to "close corporations" as hereinafter defined. We deem a close corporation to be typified by: (1) a small number of stockholders; (2) no ready market for the corporate stock; and (3) substantial majority stockholder participation in management, direction, and operation of the corporation. As thus defined, the close corporation bears striking resemblance to a partnership. . . . Just as in a partnership, the relationship among the stockholders must be one of trust, confidence, and absolute loyalty if the enterprise is to succeed. When this type of "freeze-out" is attempted by the majority shareholders, the minority shareholders are cut off from all revenue and must either suffer their losses or seek a buyer for their shares. . . . At this point the minority stockholder cannot easily reclaim his capital. . . . Two forms of suitable relief are set out hereafter. The judge below is to enter an appropriate judgment. The judgment may require Harry Rodd to remit $36,000 with interest from the date of purchase to Rodd Electrotype in exchange for 40 shares of Rodd's treasury stock. . . . In the alternative the judgment may require Rodd Electrotype to purchase all of plaintiff's shares for $36,000 without interest. We view this as the equal opportunity the plaintiff should have received. *(Note to students—Be sure you protect this possible scenario from occurring in your close corporation agreement.)*

ADLER v. SVINGOS
436 N.Y.S.2d 719 (N.Y. App. Div. 1981)

Plaintiff, defendant, and Shaw, were equal shareholders in a restaurant corporation known as 891 First Avenue Corporation. They entered into a stockholders agreement that basically said that all corporate operations and decisions, including changes in corporate structure, required unanimous consent of the three of them. In effect, at this time, they had a "close corporation." Adler and Shaw tried to sell the business alleging that all that was needed was a majority of the stockholders. Svingos objected, relying on the stockholders agreement and his refusal to consent to the sale. Adler and Shaw commenced an action to declare the shareholders agreement void, claiming it violated a statutory provision that said only the certificate of incorporation can allow greater than normal voting requirements for shareholders' action. Therefore, they alleged the voting agreement was void. The court ruled that the plaintiffs executed the agreement and are now estopped from denying its validity. The act of amending the certificate of incorporation is purely ministerial and the parties can now amend the certificate of incorporation to accomplish the same purpose as in their shareholders agreement. The parties by executing the agreement and believing it effective and intending it to be effective at that time, cannot now deny its validity.

WORDS TO KNOW

ambiguities

certificate of agreed value

close corporation

deceased

enabling

equity capital

freeze-outs

heirs

incompetent	resolution
in kind	signatories
judiciously	statutory intent
legend	stockholders agreement
perpetual	stock interest
PPO	suppletory
pro rata	tender
proxy	unanimous
registration	unified intent
regulatory	

REVIEW

1. What is a close corporation?
2. What is a "freeze-out"?
3. How does a close corporation help stockholders?
4. What is a close corporation agreement?
5. Name five items of concern in a close corporation agreement.
6. Is it difficult to form a close corporation agreement? How is it formed?
7. How can you determine the value of a corporation? Give two ways.
8. Are there a minimum and maximum number of stockholders necessary for a close corporation agreement? If so, what are the maximum and minimum?
9. What does an enabling statute mean?
10. What does a regulatory statute mean?
11. What is meant by "freeze-out"? Explain in full.

SHORT ESSAY

1. You and eight friends formed a closed corporation and entered into a close corporation agreement. All were signatories. The agreement gave each stockholder a management position in the corporation and spelled out the duties of each position, salary, and benefits. Each of the eight stockholders invested $150,000 in the corporation. Each had the same number of votes. Each was a member of the board of directors. A majority of stockholders was needed for a quorum and for any business to transpire at stockholders' meetings. A majority of the board was a quorum and necessary before the board could proceed to vote on any issue. A majority of the board was necessary to carry a motion.

   Recently, five of the stockholders have been voting together, and apparently the remaining three have been together. Voting has now become predictable. All agree to be voting their conscience and in the best interest of the corporation. All state they have made no previous arrangements as to voting with anyone. Yet, the votes have been consistent; five and three, same parties on the five and same on the three. It is becoming very apparent that the five group members are receiving more benefits than the three group members. The five group members each have a personal assistant. The three group members do not. The five group members each have a corporate charge account with American Express in their own names. The three group members do not. The five group members have each had their offices enlarged, repainted, and redecorated. The three group members have not. The five group members all have offices next to each other. The three group members have offices scattered around the facility; none is near any other stockholder. The five group members now want to move the corporation headquarters to another state. The three group members do not want to move.

The close corporation agreement is lacking as to what can be done concerning these problems. What suggestions can you make?

2. You would like any dispute that may arise concerning the close corporation agreement to be resolved through arbitration. List the points you would like to cover in the arbitration clause, and draw an arbitration clause for the agreement.

3. It is your intention to set up a means to determine the corporation value in the close corporation agreement. Draw up a clause on how you would like the corporate value determined.

CHAPTER

DUTIES OF OFFICERS AND DIRECTORS

OBJECTIVES

After completing this chapter, you will be able to:

1. Define fiduciary.
2. Be aware of the duty of loyalty in a corporate setting.
3. Know the duty of obedience and how it is applied.
4. Be aware of the duty of due care in a corporate setting.
5. Know what a controlling stockholder is and their duties and obligations.
6. Be aware of and know how to apply the business judgment rule.
7. Be aware of the liability of directors and some ways to protect directors.

INTRODUCTION

Officers and directors of a corporation are in a position of special trust and confidence. They make decisions that will affect the corporation and stockholders, ethically and financially. Therefore, we say that they are in a fiduciary capacity when dealing with the business of the corporation. A **fiduciary** is one in a special position of trust and/or confidence who is expected to act with the utmost good faith and loyalty. Sometimes, controlling stockholders will also be held to a fiduciary standard when dealing to the detriment of minority stockholders. The duties of a corporate fiduciary, generally, are loyalty, obedience, and due care. These duties are sometimes statutory, sometimes common law, and sometimes both.

LOYALTY

The loyalty required is that officers and directors must always place the interests of the corporation first. They cannot put their personal interests ahead of the corporation. They may not represent conflicting interests. Loyalty is one of strict allegiance to the corporation. Whenever a director or officer breaches a fiduciary duty, they forfeit any right to compensation that they might normally be entitled to during the period of the breach. These problems arise in conflict of interest situations and in corporate opportunities.

A business transaction that belongs to the corporation cannot be taken by an officer or director for his or her own personal gain. If you have a personal gain at the expense of the corporation, you have breached your fiduciary duty of loyalty. **Breached** means violated or failed to perform your duty.

For example, you are a president and/or a director of a corporation that owns restaurants that makes and serves pizza to customers to eat in or take out. Knowing that you are president of this corporation, a group comes to you and says they would like to sell their pizza restaurant to your corporation. You make an appointment with them to see the restaurant, their books, and their records. They tell you what they want as a selling price. After inspecting the restaurant, books, and records, you decide it is a good opportunity and the price is reasonable. You offer to buy the restaurant for yourself. You have just breached the duty of loyalty.

If it is reasonable to foresee that the corporation would be interested in the opportunity and it is something you discovered in your official capacity, it would be deemed a **corporate opportunity.** The transaction belongs to the corporation, not to you. If you purchased the business, the corporation could impose a constructive trust upon you and be entitled to all profits made from the transaction and insist that you convey ownership to the corporation for the same amount that you paid. A **constructive trust** is established by the court; it means that you would be holding property for the benefit of the corporation, not for your own benefit.

Remedies for Violation of Duty of Loyalty

At common law in the 1880s the general rule was simple. No director could benefit from a transaction with the corporation, regardless if there was full disclosure before the vote or not, and regardless if the director voted or not. Fairness or unfairness of the transaction to the corporation was not an issue. Any stockholder, or the corporation itself, could void the transaction. It was considered a voidable transaction from the start.

By the early 1900s the general rule changed. A contract between a director and the corporation was valid if it was approved by a disinterested majority of the board of directors and was found to be fair and not fraudulent. However, a contract in which the majority of the board was interested was voidable either by a shareholder or by the corporation without regard to fairness.

By 1960 the general rule changed, and today it is that no transaction of a corporation with any director or directors, officer or officers, is automatically voidable by a shareholder or the corporation. The courts will review each transaction and contract and invalidate it only if it is found to be unfair to the corporation. It does not matter if disclosure was made or not, or if a disinterested majority of the board approved the transaction.

The remedy for violation of the duty of loyalty is usually rescission. If rescission is not feasible, then the difference between the contract price and a fair price would be the measure of damages. If a director or officer improperly takes a corporate opportunity, the remedy would be a constructive trust for the benefit of the corporation. Any stockholder, group of stockholders, or the corporation itself can bring the action. This is an action in **equity.** Equity is used when there is no adequate remedy at law.

Punitive Damages

Trial courts have awarded **punitive damages** against directors or officers who breached the duty of loyalty when fraud was involved. Punitive damages are damages that are not proven. They are a sum of money set by a judge or jury without relation to the actual damages. It is used as a punishment when one has intentionally and maliciously intended to injure and cause damage to another. Fraud is a good example, as one element of fraud is the intent to injure.

Fairness requires that entering into a transaction on fair terms is not enough, it must also be in the corporation's best interest.

Duty of Obedience

Directors, officers, controlling stockholders, and corporate managers cannot exceed their authority or the authority of the corporation. Violation of a law, statute, rule, or ordinance is an act that exceeds authority and is illegal. It also breaches the duty of obedience. Any loss suffered by the corporation because of unauthorized acts in some jurisdictions causes the breaching party **strict liability.** Strict liability means that even innocent unknowing breaches are violations. In other jurisdictions the breaching party is personally liable only if the acts exceeding authority were negligently or intentionally performed.

Duty of Diligence

The **duty of diligence** means performing duties with the degree of **due care** that a reasonably prudent person would exercise in the conduct of his or her own personal affairs in the same situation. The use of due care means to perform your duties as a reasonably prudent person would, without negligence. Officers and directors are not liable for honest errors of judgment. Obviously, if they were, no one would want to be an officer or director.

Honest errors of judgment, made in good faith without being obviously negligent, are excused from liability and are not considered a breach of due diligence. This is called the **Business Judgment Rule** which will be discussed in more detail later in this chapter.

Failure of a director to attend meetings of the board of directors and/or coming to meetings unprepared could lead to liability for breach of due care and/or due diligence. A few other areas that could lead to liability for breach of due care and/or due diligence would be:

- Failure of a director to investigate signs of embezzlement by an employee.
- Reliance on totally unreasonable statements by accountants or others may lead to liability.
- Failure to take action against an employee who is obviously injuring the company on an ongoing basis could lead to liability.
- Directors have a duty to inform themselves prior to making a business decision. Failure to do so could lead to liability for breach of due care or due diligence.

- Directors may not shut their eyes to corporate misconduct and then claim that because they did not see the misconduct, they did not have a duty to look.
- Directors should maintain familiarity with the financial status of the corporation by a regular review of financial statements. They are not required to audit corporate books, just to be familiar with them.
- Directors should acquire at least a rudimentary understanding of the business of the corporation.
- If one feels unqualified, or lacks enough business experience or knowledge to be a director, the party should either acquire the necessary knowledge or refuse to act as a director.
- Directors are under a continuing duty and obligation to keep informed about the activities of the corporation.
- In general, failing to act as a reasonably prudent person may lead to liability.

STATUTORY DUE CARE

Twenty-two states have enacted statutory due care provisions similar to RMBCA, California, New York, and New Jersey. A few of these use a phrase as ". . . with that care which ordinarily prudent persons would exercise under similar circumstances in their personal affairs." *Selheimer v. Manganese Corporation of America*, 423 PA. 563 said the phrase "in their personal affairs" imposed a higher standard of care than the usual phrase, "in a like position."

Approximately half the statutes refer to officers as well as directors. The law of agency, however, imposes a duty on a paid agent to act with the standard of care and skill, which is normal in the locality for the kind of work the officers and directors are employed to perform and to exercise any special skill the agent has. This would imply that officers have the same standards as directors.

General Standards for Directors (Section 8.30, RMBCA)

(a) A director shall discharge his duties as a director, including his or her duties as a member of a committee:
  (1) In good faith.
  (2) With the care an ordinarily prudent person in a like position would exercise under similar circumstances; and
  (3) In a manner he or she reasonably believes to be in the best interests of the corporation.
(b) In discharging his or her duties, a director is entitled to rely on information, opinions, reports, or statements, including financial statements and other financial data, if prepared or presented by:
  (1) One or more officers or employees of the corporation whom the director reasonably believes to be reliable and competent in the matters presented;
  (2) Legal counsel, public accountants, or other persons as to matters the director reasonably believes are within the person's professional or expert competence; or
  (3) A committee of the board of directors of which he is not a member if the director reasonably believes the committee merits confidence.

    (**c**) A director is not acting in good faith if he or she has knowledge concerning the matter in question that makes reliance otherwise permitted by subsection (b) unwarranted.

    (**d**) A director is not liable for any action taken as a director or any failure to take any action if he or she performed the duties of the office in compliance with this section.

Standards of Conduct of Officers (Section 8.42, RMBCA)

    (**a**) An officer with discretionary authority shall discharge his duties under that authority:

       (**1**) In good faith;

       (**2**) With the care an ordinarily prudent person in a like position would exercise under similar circumstances; and

       (**3**) In a manner he or she reasonably believes to be in the best interests of the corporation.

    (**b**) In discharging his or her duties, an officer is entitled to rely on information, opinions, reports, or statements, including financial statements and other financial data, if prepared or presented by:

       (**1**) One or more officers or employees of the corporation whom the officer reasonably believes to be reliable and competent in the matters presented; or

       (**2**) Legal counsel, public accountants, or other persons as to matters the officer reasonably believes are within the person's professional or expert competence.

    (**c**) An officer is not acting in good faith if he has knowledge concerning the matter in question that makes reliance otherwise permitted by subsection (b) unwarranted.

    (**d**) An officer is not liable for any action taken as an officer, or any failure to take any action, if he or she performed the duties of his or her office in compliance with this section.

SELF INTEREST (CONFLICT OF INTEREST)

A director can have a conflicting interest in only three ways:

    1. Obviously, if the transaction is between the director and the corporation. If the director is not a party to the transaction but has a beneficial financial interest in the transaction, other than from being a director of the corporation, it would be a conflicting interest. Any time the director is going to benefit so that it is reasonably expected to influence his or her judgment if called on to vote, would constitute a conflict of interest. The other two ways can be found later in this chapter in the discussion of Subchapter F.

    The following two sections, 8.31 and 8.32 of The Revised Model Business Corporation Act address this issue. Although these two sections were amended in 1988 and superseded by Subchapter F, sections 8.60–8.63 of the RMBCA, they are nevertheless very important as many states that adopted 8.31 and 8.32 have not adopted the later sections 8.60–8.63.

    Section 8.31 deals only with conflict of interest transactions involving directors. It does not address transactions by officers, employees, or substantial stockholders unless they are also directors. The elimination of the automatic rule of voidability does not mean that all transactions under 8.31 are automatically valid. Remember, these transactions may be subject to attack because they constituted waste, were not authorized by the appropriate corporate body, violated other sections of the Act, or were unenforceable under other common law principals. The sole purpose of section 8.31 is to limit the common law principle of automatic voidability. The vote required for approval, authorization, or ratification is from a quorum present, and only the votes of directors or shares present or represented at the meeting can be considered. The prohibition of 8.31(d) may result in conflict of interest issues being resolved by a majority of the minority shares. Example, a majority shareholder who is a director of the corporation with a conflict of interest issue. His shares will not be counted; therefore, the decision will be by a majority of the minority shares.

Director Conflict of Interest (Section 8.31, RMBCA)

(a) A conflict of interest transaction is a transaction of the corporation in which a director of the corporation has a direct or indirect interest. A conflict of interest transaction is not voidable by the corporation solely because of the director's interest in the transaction if any of the following are true:

(1) The material facts of the transaction and the director's interest were known or disclosed to the board of directors or a committee of the board of directors, and the board of directors or committee authorized, approved, or ratified the transaction.

(2) The material facts of the transaction and the director's interest were disclosed or known to the shareholders entitled to vote; and they authorized, approved, or ratified the transaction; or

(3) The transaction was fair to the corporation.

(b) For purposes of this section, a director of the corporation has an indirect interest in a transaction if (1) another entity in which he has a material financial interest or in which he is a general partner is a party to the transaction, or (2) another entity of which he is a director, officer, or trustee is a party to the transaction, and the transaction is or should be considered by the board of directors of the corporation.

(c) For purposes of subsection (a)(1), a conflict of interest transaction is authorized, approved, or ratified if it receives the affirmative vote of a majority of the directors on the board of directors (or on the committee) who have no direct or indirect interest in the transaction; but a transaction may not be authorized, approved, or ratified under this section by a single director. If a majority of the directors who have no direct or indirect interest in the transaction vote to authorize, approve, or ratify the transaction, a quorum is present for the purpose of taking action under this section. The presence of, or a vote cast by, a director with a direct or indirect interest in the transaction does not affect the validity of any action taken under subsection (a)(1) if the transaction is otherwise authorized, approved, or ratified as provided in that subsection.

(d) For purposes of subsection (a)(2), a conflict of interest transaction is authorized, approved, or ratified if it receives the vote of a majority of the shares entitled to be counted under this subsection. Shares owned by or voted under the control of a director who has a direct or indirect interest in the transaction, and the shares owned by or voted under the control of an entity described in subsection (b)(1), may not be counted in a vote of shareholders to determine whether to authorize, approve, or ratify a conflict of interest transaction under subsection (a)(2). The vote of those shares, however, is counted in determining whether the transaction is approved under other sections of this Act. A majority of the shares, whether or not present, that are entitled to be counted in a vote on the transaction under this subsection constitutes a quorum for the purpose of taking action under this section.

Subchapter Definitions (Section 8.60, RMBCA)

In this subchapter:

(1) "Conflicting interest," with respect to a corporation means the interest a director of the corporation has respecting a transaction effected or proposed to be effected by the corporation (or by a subsidiary of the corporation or any other entity in which the corporation has a controlling interest) if
  (i) Whether or not the transaction is brought before the board of directors of the corporation for action, the director knows at the time of commitment that he or a related person is a party to the transaction or has a beneficial financial interest in or is so closely linked to the transaction and of such financial significance to the director or a related person that the interest would reasonably be expected to exert an influence on the director's judgment if he were called upon to vote on the transaction; or
  (ii) the transaction is brought (or is of such character and significance to the corporation that it would in the normal course be brought) before the board of directors of the corporation for action, and the director knows at the time of commitment that any of the following persons is either a party to the transaction or has a beneficial financial interest in or is so closely linked to the transaction and of such financial significance to the person that the interest would reasonably be expected to exert an influence on the director's judgment if he were called upon to vote on the transaction; (A) an entity (other than the corporation) of which the director is a director, general partner, agent, employee; (B) a person who controls one or more of the entities specified in subclause (A), or an entity that is controlled by, or is under common control with, one or more of the entities specified in subclause (A); or (C) an individual who is a general partner, principal, or employer of the director.

(2) "Director's conflicting interest transaction" with respect to a corporation means a transaction effected or proposed to be effected by the corporation (or by a subsidiary of the corporation or any entity in which the corporation has a controlling interest) respecting which a director of the corporation has a conflicting interest.

(3) "Related person" of a director means (i) the spouse (or a parent or sibling thereof) of the director, or a child, grandchild, or sibling of any thereof) of the director, or an individual having the same home as the director, or a trust or estate of which an individual specified in this clause (i) is a substantial beneficiary, or (ii) a trust, estate, incompetent, conservatee, or minor of which the director is a fiduciary.

(4) "Required disclosure" means disclosure by the director who has a conflicting interest of (i) the existence and nature of his conflicting interest, and (ii) all facts known to him respecting the subject matter of the transaction that an ordinary prudent person would reasonably believe to be material to a judgment about whether or not to proceed with the transaction.

(5) "Time of commitment" respecting a transaction means the time when the transaction is consummated or, if made pursuant to a contract, the time when the corporation (or its subsidiary or the entity in which it has a controlling interest) becomes contractually obligated so that its unilateral withdrawal from the transaction would entail significant loss, liability, or other damage.

Judicial Action (Section 8.61, RMBCA)

(a) A transaction effected or proposed to be effected by a corporation (or subsidiary or other entity that the corporation has a controlling interest in) that is not a director's conflicting interest transaction may not be enjoined, set aside, or give rise to an award of damages or other sanctions in a proceeding by a shareholder or by or in the right of the corporation, because a director of the corporation, or any person with whom or with which he has a personal, economic, or other association, has an interest in the transaction.

(b) A director's conflicting interest transaction may not be enjoined, set aside, or give rise to an award of damages or other sanction, in a proceeding by a shareholder or by or in the right of the corporation, because the director or any person with whom or with which he has a personal, economic, or other association, has an interest in the transaction, if:

  (1) director's action respecting the transaction was at any time taken in compliance with section 8.62;

  (2) shareholders action respecting the transaction was at any time taken in compliance with section 8.63;

  (3) the transaction, judged according to the circumstances at the time of commitment, is established to have been fair to the corporation.

Directors' Action (Section 8.62, RMBCA)

(a) Directors' action respecting a transaction is effective for purposes of section 8.61(b)(1) if the transaction received the affirmative vote of a majority (but no fewer than two) of those qualified directors on the board of directors or on a duly empowered committee of the board who voted on the transaction after either required disclosure to them (to extent information was not known to them) or compliance with subsection (b); provided that action by a committee is so effective only if (1) all its members are qualified directors, and (2) its members are either all the qualified directors on the board or are appointed by the affirmative vote of a majority of the qualified directors on the board.

(b) If a director has a conflicting interest respecting a transaction, but neither he, nor a related person of the director, specified in section 8.60(3)(i) is a party to the transaction, and if the director has a duty under law or professional canon, or a duty of confidentiality to another person, respecting information relating to the transaction, such that the director may not make the disclosure described in section 8.60(4)(ii), then disclosure is sufficient for purposes of subsection (a) if the director (1) discloses to the directors voting on the transaction the existence and nature of his conflicting interest and informs them on the character and limitations imposed by that duty before their vote on the transaction, and (2) plays no part, directly or indirectly, in their deliberations or vote.

(c) A majority (but no fewer than two) of all the qualified directors on the board of directors, or on the committee, constitutes a quorum for purposes of action that complies with this section. Directors' action that otherwise complies with this section is not affected by the presence or vote of a director who is not a qualified director.

(d) For purposes of this section, "qualified director" means, with respect to a director's conflicting interest transaction, any director who does not have either (1) a conflicting interest respecting the transaction, or (2) a family, financial, professional, or employment relationship with a second director who does have a conflicting interest respecting the transaction, which relationship would, in the circumstances, reasonably be expected to exert an influence on the first director's judgment when voting on the transaction.

Shareholders' Action (Section 8.63, RMBCA)

(a) Shareholders' action respecting a transaction is effective for purposes of section 8.61(b)(2) if a majority of the votes entitled to be cast by the holders of all qualified shares were cast in favor of the transaction after (1) notice to shareholders describing the director's conflicting interest transaction, (2) provision of the information referred to in subsection (d), and (3) required disclosure to the shareholders who voted on the transaction (to the extent the information was known by them).

(b) For purposes of this section, "qualified shares" means any shares entitled to vote with respect to the director's conflicting interest transaction except shares that, to the knowledge, before the vote, of the secretary (or other officer or agent of the corporation authorized to tabulate votes), are beneficially owned (or the voting of which is controlled) by a director who has conflicting interest respecting the transaction or by a related person to the director, or both.

(c) A majority of the votes entitled to be cast by the holders of all qualified shares constitutes a quorum for purposes of action that complies with this section. Subject to the provisions of subsections (d) and (e), shareholders' action that otherwise complies with this section is not affected by the presence of holders, or the voting, of shares that are not qualified shares.

(d) For purposes of compliance with subsection (a), a director who has a conflicting interest respecting the transaction shall, before the shareholders' vote, inform the secretary (or other office or agent of the corporation authorized to tabulate votes) of the number and the identity of persons holding or controlling the vote, of all shares that the director knows are beneficially owned (or the voting of which is controlled) by the director or by a related person of the director, or both.

(e) If a shareholders' vote does not comply with subsection (a) solely because of a failure of a director to comply with subsection (d), and if the director establishes that his failure did not determine and was not intended by him to influence the outcome of the vote, the court may, with or without further proceedings respecting section 8.61(b)(3), take such action respecting the transaction and the director, and give such effect, if any, to the shareholders' vote, as it considers appropriate in the circumstances.

Discussion of Sections 8.60–8.63 RMBCA (Known as Subchapter F)

(1) Subchapter F is limited, and targets only conflict of interest challenges concerning directors. It does not have any provision for controlling stockholders or minority stockholders having a conflict of interest in a corporate dealing. Conflicting interest requires that the director knew of his conflicting interest at the time of committing to the corporation.

(2) The sections are only applicable when there is a transaction by or with the corporation.

(3) Subchapter F contemplates deletion of section 8.32 which deals with loans to directors. A loan to a director is simply treated as a conflicting interest transaction under subchapter F.

There are three ways for a director to have a conflicting interest:

(1) If the transaction is between the director and the corporation. If the director is not a party to the transaction but has a beneficial interest in the transaction, separate from his interest as a director or stockholder, and it reasonably would be expected to exert an influence on his or her judgment if he or she had to vote on the matter. The gain of the director must lie in the transaction itself. A contingent, remote, or future gain will not give rise to a conflict under 8.60. If B company is in a transaction with C corporation and the director of C corporation is somehow linked to B company and will gain, or can reasonably be expected to exert an influence, it is a conflict. If B company is a party to or interested in the transaction with A company, and B company is somehow linked to the director of A company, it would be governed by subdivision (1)(ii). But if the director's economic interest in B company is so substantial and the impact of the transaction so important to B company, it becomes a conflicting interest under subsection (1)(i).

(2) A conflict of interest can arise by a related person to the director having a transaction with the corporation; related as a spouse, child, grandchild, sibling, parent, or spouse of any mentioned. A trust where the director is trustee would be a related person.

(3) Any entity other than the corporation of which the director is a director, general partner, employee, agent, CEO, or employee of the director, doing business with the corporation. If the director's interest is present, conflict is assumed.

The definition of directors "conflicting interest transaction," 8.60 (2) not only designates the area within which the rules of subchapter F are to be applied but also denies the power of the court to act with respect to conflict of interest claims against directors in circumstances that lie outside the statutory definition of "directors conflicting interest transaction" (see section 8.61[a]). To constitute a director's conflicting interest transaction, there must first be a transaction by the corporation, its subsidiary, or controlled entity in which the director has a financial interest. Subchapter F does not apply if there is no transaction by the corporation of which the director acts as director. Other areas of law prohibit a director from seizing corporate opportunities for himself and from competing against the corporation of which he is a director; subchapter F has no application to such situations.

COMPENSATION AND WASTE

The general rule is that: If a bonus payment has no relation to the value of services for which it is given, it is in reality a gift in part, and the majority stockholders have no power to give away corporate property against the protest of the minority. *United States v. American Tobacco Co.,* 60 F (2d) 113. Therefore, if the majority stockholders elect to and do place a clause in the bylaws that will compensate an officer or group of officers and/or director or group of directors on a percentage basis of the gross business or net profit, and the business expands ten or twenty fold over a period of years, it would be possible for minority stockholders to seek relief in a court of **equity,** based on misuse and waste of the monies of the corporation by the directors and/or majority stockholders, to the detriment of minority stockholders. There are two kinds of courts, law courts where you sue to recover dollar damages, and courts of equity where you do not have an adequate remedy at law. In equity you can obtain reformation or rescission of a contract or clause (e.g. clause in bylaws); injunctions to force someone to do something or stop them from doing something; and specific performance as when the subject matter is either unique or antique, the court can order specific performance and order the seller to complete the contract. Majority stockholders and/or directors cannot misuse the funds of the corporation to the detriment of minority stockholders. If they do it is called waste. There must be a reasonable relationship to monies paid and value received.

Normally, the board of directors sets the salaries of officers and directors. However, the original stockholders may have placed a clause in the bylaws concerning salaries of certain parties. These must have a reasonable relationship to value. Stockholders can always amend the bylaws and insert a new clause in the bylaws concerning salaries. Again, these must have a reasonable relationship to value. Minority stockholders can always bring an action in equity for misuse of funds by the corporation and/or waste.

COMPENSATION PLANS FOR EXECUTIVES

Some of the various methods to compensate executives and valuable employees, in addition to salary, titles, vehicles, credit cards, boats, vacations, use of vacation homes, company airplanes, company condos, and other perks, are incentive stock options, non-qualifying options, stock appreciation rights, phantom stock, and restricted stock. These are used either to aid in the hiring and attracting of new executives or retain valuable employees.

Incentive Stock Options

There is a large tax advantage with incentive stock options if the plan qualifies. Once the requirements are met, there is no federal income tax paid at the time the option is granted and no federal income tax paid at the time of its exercise. The income tax will be based on long-term capital gains rates, as long as the holding periods for long term gains are met. However, stock obtained by incentive stock options (ISO) cannot be sold or otherwise transferred for at least two years from the date the option was granted and at least one year from the date the stock was acquired by the employee from the option.

To qualify for incentive stock option treatment, the following conditions must be met:

(1) There must be a written plan by which the option is to be issued which specifies the employees eligible to receive the option, and the total number of employees or class of employees to receive the option.

(2) Options can be exercised by an employee for no more than $100,000 of stock during any calendar year. This must be in writing in the plan and be the fair market value of the stock.

(3) The plan must be approved by the shareholders within twelve months before or after it is adopted by the board of directors.

(4) The option must be granted within ten years after the plan has been adopted by the board of directors or approved by the stockholders, whichever is earlier.

(5) The option must be exercisable only during employment of the employee, or within three months after termination of employment, and may not be exercisable for more than ten years from the date of the grant.

(6) The option price must equal or exceed the fair market value of the stock on the date the option is granted.

Non-Qualified Stock Options (Sometimes Called Nonstatutory)

As executive compensation, a non-qualified stock option is a right granted to one or more employees by a corporation to acquire shares of the corporation's stock. Neither the options nor the shares, when the option is exercised, is qualified for the special favorable income tax treatment, provided under the Code, for incentive stock options, sometimes called statutory or qualified options. Thus, these are sometimes called nonstatutory options.

Stock options are used to offer a premium to an executive and to attract new, or retain the services of, valued existing executives. In this manner the employee will be able to share in the appreciation of the stock and value of the corporation.

The granting of a non-qualify stock option to an executive does not result in taxable income as the option is not a transfer of title to stock and is not considered property for federal income tax purposes unless the option has a fair market value. The option would have a fair market value if:

(1) The option is readily traded on an established market, or

(2) If not traded on an established market, the option is transferable, exercisable in full, and subject to no restrictions to affect fair market value of the option, and the option has a recognizable and readily ascertainable fair market value.

When a non-qualified option is exercised, and if the stock has no restrictions, the executive would have income immediately for federal income tax purposes (difference between the option price and the value of the stock after the option is exercised).

Stock Appreciation Rights

The difference between the value of the stock on the date the stock appreciation right (SAR) is granted and the value of the stock on the date that the SAR is exercised, is called a stock appreciation right. Stock appreciation rights are usually granted together with an option right to buy stock. Generally the stock appreciation right is granted together with the right to receive dividends that have been declared, as well as the value of the stock appreciation during the SAR period, prior to it being **exercised.** Exercised is the date when you transfer the option into a purchase of the stock, or the date that you cash in the SAR.

If the SAR has a stock option with it, the employee has a choice of which to exercise. If you exercise one, the other right is **extinguished.** Extinguished means terminated. The big advantage of an SAR is that the employee invests no money and does not have to buy anything. The employee just cashes in and receives the increase in value of the stock from the date of the SAR to the date of exercise and in some cases the dividends that were paid during the SAR period, if that option was also granted. For example, the SAR is granted to the employee on January 1, 1997. The stock is valued at $20 per share on January 1, 1998. On June 1, 2000, the stock has had $100 in dividends declared since January 1, 1997. The employee exercises the SAR. The stock is $30 per share. The employee will receive $10 for every share granted in the SAR plus $100 dividends on each share granted in the SAR. Payment can be either in cash or company stock, at the option of the employee. The employee invested no money for these rights. The money made from the SAR must be included in gross earnings and federal income taxes must be paid thereon.

Phantom Stock

Phantom stock plans are the least form of stock incentive plans used by *Fortune* 500 companies.

Whenever some form of unit, other than actual shares are used, it is called phantom stock. Thus, a phantom stock plan can grant outright shares and/or options for phantom stock. A naked SAR, described in the previous section, is substantially similar to phantom stock.

Restricted Stock

Restricted stock is generally common stock, although it can be any other class of stock, of the employer, issued to an employee, to attract or retain the employee, in the service of the employer. The stock is issued pursuant to a written agreement, either without cost to the employee, or at a nominal cost to the employee. The retention and ownership of the stock by the employee is subject to conditions or restrictions. **Vesting** is usually contingent upon the employee continuing in the service of the employer for a stated period of time. Voting means ownership. The vesting can be in stages. For example, 10 percent can vest after two years employment; 40 percent after five years employment; 100 percent after ten years employment; or any other schedule the employer may have. The plan will usually require continuous employment with the employer. Termination or resignation will cause the loss of all, or some stated portion of the stock, during a stated period prior to full vesting. Sometimes, shares may be subject to repurchase by the corporation at a stated formula or price. Nonvested stock may be repurchased at the cost paid by the employee, while vested stock may be repurchased at the fair market price of the stock or book value of the stock, as determined by the board of directors or some other written formula.

Under the Internal Revenue Code and Regulations of the IRS, stock transferred to an employee for services must be included in gross taxable federal income, the first taxable year the beneficial interest in the stock is transferred to the employee, or the first taxable year the stock is not subject to substantial risk of forfeiture. The taxable portion is the excess over the payment of the stock and the fair market value of the stock when transferred. (Employee paid $10 for the stock, fair market value is $100, the taxable portion is $90.)

DUTIES OF CONTROLLING STOCKHOLDERS

Controlling stockholders are stockholders who, because of their large holdings of stock and/or agreements or associations with others who have joined with them to give them enough stock, control the corporation through their votes. These controlling stockholders owe a fiduciary duty to the corporation and to minority stockholders. Any relationship or transactions they have with the corporation must meet the test of **intrinsic fairness.** Intrinsic fairness comprises two elements: (1) a high degree of fairness, and (2) a shift in the burden of proof so that the controlling stockholders must show and have the burden of proof that the transaction by controlling stockholders and the corporation were subjectively fair. The business judgment rule will not apply when controlling stockholders are trying to prove intrinsic fairness.

When a transaction involves a **parent** and a **subsidiary,** with the parent controlling the transaction and fixing the terms, the test of intrinsic fairness with its resulting shifting of the burden of proof will be applied. The test for application of this rule is where the parent received a benefit to the exclusion and at the expense of the subsidiary. When a corporation owns a controlling interest in another corporation, it is called a parent and the other corporation is called a subsidiary.

When controlling stockholders cause a corporation to pay excessive dividends to stockholders so that the industrial development of the corporation is effectively prevented, and it became in reality a corporation in dissolution, the minority stockholders have the basis for an action against the controlling stockholders. The intrinsic fairness standard would be applied, and the controlling stockholders would have the burden of proof that these dividends were intrinsically fair to the minority stockholders.

A controlling or dominated shareholder standing on both sides of a transaction, as in a parent-subsidiary context, bears the burden of proving its entire fairness. (*Weinberger v. UOP, Inc.,* Del. Supr., 457 A2d 701). A minority shareholder with 43.3 percent of the stock can still be declared a dominating shareholder and be held to a fiduciary standard and fairness test.

Majority shareholders, either singly or acting in concert to accomplish a joint purpose, have a fiduciary responsibility to the minority and to the corporation to use their ability to control the corporation in a fair, just, and equitable manner. Majority shareholders may not use their power to control corporate activities to benefit themselves alone or in a manner detrimental to the minority. Any use to control or use their power to control the corporation must benefit all shareholders proportionately and must not conflict with the proper conduct of the corporation's business (*Brown v. Halbert,* 271 Cal. App. 2d 252).

Use of an Independent Committee of Directors to Shift Burden of Proof

However, an approval of the transaction by an independent committee of directors or an informed majority of minority shareholders shifts the burden of proof on the issue of fairness from the controlling or dominating shareholder to the challenging shareholder-plaintiff. The power to say no is a significant power. "It is the duty of directors serving on an independent committee to approve only a transaction that is in the best interest of the public shareholders, to say no to any transaction that is not fair to those shareholders and is not the best transaction available. It is not sufficient for such directors to achieve the best price that a fiduciary will pay if that price is not a fair price." (In re *First Boston, Inc. v Shareholders Litig.,* Del. Ch., C.A. 10338–1990)

SALE OF A CONTROLLING INTEREST

One who invests capital to obtain a dominant position in the ownership of a corporation is entitled to the right of controlling that corporation. Absent fraud, bad faith, looting of corporate assets, or conversion of a corporate opportunity, a controlling stockholder is free to sell, and a purchaser is free to purchase, the controlling interest at any price agreed, including a premium price. (*Barnes v. Brown,* 80 NY 527)

Minority shareholders are entitled to protection against abuse by majority or controlling stockholders. But, they are not entitled to prevent legitimate dealings of the controlling stockholders. The purchase of a controlling interest, therefore, usually commands a **premium price.** The premium is the additional amount over the actual value that the purchaser is willing to pay to obtain control of the corporation.

PURCHASE OF A CONTROLLING INTEREST

The purchaser that desires to purchase an interest in a corporation, so that the purchaser has complete control over the business and assets of the corporation, has several choices to accomplish this intent.

(1) The purchaser can purchase all of the outstanding shares, and own 100 percent of the corporation. All selling stockholders receive the proceeds of their sale. All may receive the same amount per share or there may be different amounts paid for larger blocks of shares, and smaller amounts per share paid for smaller blocks of shares. All shareholders are free to make their own deal. The purchaser may not want to purchase any shares unless the purchaser can purchase all of the shares outstanding.

(2) The purchaser can just purchase enough of the outstanding shares to obtain voting control (sometimes a majority would be necessary, sometimes less). There probably would be a premium paid to large shareholders. Selling shareholders receive the proceeds of their own transaction. All outstanding shares are not purchased. This would be preferred by large shareholders as they can obtain the highest price for their shares in this manner.

(3) Induce a sufficient number of shareholders to vote for a merger with a corporation owned by the purchaser. The merger plan will generally treat all shareholders equally in receiving shares of the surviving corporation.

(4) Induce the necessary amount of shareholders to vote for a sale of the corporate assets to a corporation owned by the purchaser. The proceeds will go into the selling corporation's treasury. The corporation will then usually be liquidated and the proceeds divided pro rata to the shareholders.

Sale of Corporate Office (Directorships) or Management Control Without Voting Control

It is illegal to sell corporate directorships or management control of a corporation without selling voting control under New York State law. Persons holding office in a corporation or acting as a director of a corporation hold it on behalf of the corporation's shareholders. It is not their property to dispose of as they wish. Management must represent and be chosen by the shareholders of the corporation. Under New York State law, a controlling shareholder can sell its interest at a premium price.

BUSINESS JUDGMENT RULE

The Business Judgment Rule removes liability from a director and officer for honest mistakes of judgment. To avail oneself of this rule and protection, it is necessary that the decision was made in a prudent and reasonable manner, that proper inquiries were made to aid in the decision, that proper monitoring took place, and that the director or officer employed a reasonable process to make the decision. There can be no conflict of interest.

If a director or officer fails to employ this basic standard and the decision of the director or officer is the **proximate** cause of damage or loss to the corporation, then the director or officer would have personal liability to the corporation. Proximate cause would be the placing in motion of something that results in injury or damage. An example would be; Tom throws a book at Fred, Fred deflects the book with his hand, and it hits Mary. The proximate cause of injury to Mary was the throwing of the book by Tom. You apply the "but for" principle. But for Tom throwing the book at Fred, Fred would not have deflected it, and it would not have hit Mary. Therefore, the proximate cause of injury to Mary was Tom throwing the book at Fred. Consequently, Tom is liable for the injury to Mary.

Standards of Review and Standards of Conduct in Corporation Law

In corporation law the **standards of review** and **standards of conduct** are the same. Standards of review are the tests a court would apply to determine if liability exists and/or whether to grant injunctive relief. Standards of conduct are how one should perform and conduct oneself in a given activity. An agent in a transaction must deal fairly with his principal. That is the standard of conduct. If the principal were suing the agent for not dealing fairly, the standard of review would be "did the agent deal fairly with the principal." A director and/or officer has a duty to the corporation to perform his or her functions in good faith, in a manner reasonably believed to be in the best interests of the corporation, and with the care an ordinary prudent person would reasonably be expected to use in a like position under similar circumstances. This standard of care results in the duty to inquire, monitor, make reasonable and prudent decisions, and employ a reasonable process to make decisions.

For a decision to be in good faith it must be rational. To be rational it must have a minimal requirement of same basis of reason. An irrational decision shows bad faith. Reckless conduct would not be rational.

Under the business judgment rule there is no protection for directors who have made an "unintelligent or unadvised judgment" (*Mitchell v. Highland-Western Glass,* Del. Ch., 167 A. 831). A director's duty to inform himself or herself prior to the making of a decision, comes from his or her fiduciary duties in serving the corporation and stockholders. A director must proceed with a critical eye in assessing information. The director must proceed in an informed, deliberate manner, in determining approval of an agreement.

LIABILITY OF DIRECTORS

Over forty states authorize corporations with shareholder approval to limit or eliminate the liability of directors for some breaches. A few states allow shareholders to eliminate or limit the liability of officers. A small number of states have eliminated personal liability for money damages against directors, subject to certain exceptions. Other states have limited the amount of money damages that can be recovered against directors and/or officers. The State of Delaware permits a provision to be inserted in the articles of incorporation eliminating or limiting personal liability of shareholders and directors for money damages for breach of duties as a director except for:

(a) a breach of duty of loyalty to the corporation,

(b) acts of bad faith, intentional wrongs, or violation of law,

(c) unlawful dividend payments or redemptions, and

(d) any transaction where the director derived an improper personal benefit.

These statutes only operate as to money damages. Equitable relief is still available. None of these statutes affect the right of shareholders to remove directors with or without cause.

Limiting Liability of Directors (Section 2.202(b)(4), RMBCA)

Section 2.02(b)(4) is a provision eliminating or limiting the liability of a director to the corporation or its shareholders for money damages for any action taken, or any failure to take action, as a director, except liability for

(1) the amount of a financial benefit received by a director to which he is not entitled;

(2) an intentional infliction of harm on the corporation or the shareholders;

(3) a violation of section 8.33; or

(4) an intentional violation of criminal law.

Shareholders Liability—Optional

Shareholders of a corporation do not generally have personal liability. If a shareholder performs an intentional act that causes harm, that could lead to personal liability. However, the RMBCA Section 2.02(b)(2)(v) permits a corporation to impose liability on shareholders. This is an optional provision and can be incorporated into the articles of incorporation. Section 2.02(b)(2)(v) "The articles of incorporation may set forth . . . the imposition of personal liability on shareholders for the debts of the corporation to a specified extent and upon specified conditions." This is only an option, it is not mandatory.

PROTECTION OF DIRECTORS

As a general rule you will want to do everything possible to reduce the potential liability of directors in your corporation. You want to attract the best possible candidates to act as directors on your board. Therefore, you should do everything possible to prevent them from incurring personal liability. There are three methods to reduce the liability of directors as follows:

(1) Use of states to incorporate in that have statutes and/or allow provisions in the articles of incorporation that permit the elimination or limiting of personal liability of your directors.

(2) The purchase of insurance.

(3) Indemnification. Under Delaware law and New York State law a corporation may indemnify any person who was or is a party to any lawsuit by reason of being a director.

Just about every state has an indemnification statute. Some apply only to officers and directors, while others also apply to employees and agents. Some are **exclusive** and prohibit indemnification for items not mentioned in the statute. Others are **nonexclusive** and allow indemnification to be governed by the provisions in the articles of incorporation and can go beyond the items mentioned in the statute. Many indemnification statutes provide for indemnification when an officer or director has been successful in a lawsuit. Delaware and New York require the director or officer to win the lawsuit; the success must be on the merits or otherwise. Some statutes allow the director and officer indemnification for fines and judgments levied as a result of violation of some civil or penal law. Here the indemnification would be because the director and/or officer incurred the liability in good faith in furtherance of the business of the corporation.

SUMMARY

A fiduciary is one in a special position of trust, and/or confidence, and is expected to act with the utmost good faith and loyalty. Officers and directors are fiduciaries. Sometimes a controlling stockholder will be held to a fiduciary standard when dealing with minority stockholders. The duties of a fiduciary are loyalty, obedience, and due care. If a director takes advantage of a deal with the corporation, the remedy is usually rescission. If rescission were not practical, then damages would be the difference between the contract price and the fair price. Sometimes it is necessary to use a constructive trust as the remedy. Officers and directors cannot exceed the authority of the corporation. A breach of this is called a breach of obedience. Personal liability will attach to the breaching party.

The business judgment rule can protect directors from honest mistakes and honest errors of judgment, as long as the transaction was investigated and studied carefully by the director with good faith present and is carried out as a reasonably prudent person would.

A director cannot have a conflict of interest in dealing with the corporation unless the transaction is fair to the corporation, the material facts were disclosed to the board, and full disclosure was made prior to the transaction. A conflict of interest would arise if the deal was with the director and the corporation, the corporation and any entity the director had a financial or beneficial interest in, or the corporation and any person related to the director.

Executives and key employees sometimes need more than just salary. They require other **perks.** Perks are benefits. Some benefits are credit cards; use of boats, airplanes, automobiles, and vacation homes; incentive stock options, non-qualified stock options, stock appreciation rights, phantom stock, and restricted stock.

Controlling stockholders either own or control a large block of shares. Any dealings with the corporation that they enter into must be intrinsically fair to the corporation and the burden of proving that fairness is on the controlling stockholder. A controlling stockholder can sell his, her, or its holdings at a premium price, that is for more than its actual value. Controlling stockholders cannot sell seats on the board of directors or sell jobs as officers of the corporation. They are in a fiduciary capacity when dealing with the corporation and/or other minority stockholders.

Directors and stockholders can limit their liability or eliminate it by incorporating in states that permit this. Other methods of limiting liability are insurance and/or indemnification by the corporation.

CASES

A Corporate Opportunity

CHEMICAL DYNAMICS, INC., v. NEWFELD
728 S.W.2d 590 (1987)

Chemical Dynamics, Inc., was a close corporation. The Schultz family consisted of Abe Schulz, Sol Schulz, and Harry Schulz. The family owned twenty-three shares of Chemical Dynamics. Lawrence Newfeld owned seventeen shares. Total capitalization was forty outstanding and issued shares. Abe Schulz, Sol Schulz, and Lawrence Newfeld, were managing officers and directors of the corporation. The corporation was in the manufacturing business and leased a building for its offices and manufacturing in 1967. The lease had an option to purchase the building for $300,000. In 1970 the corporation was in financial difficulty and unable to

pay its rent on the building. The corporation needed $21,492 to avoid being evicted from the premises. Sol Schulz assigned the lease and option to Lawrence Newfeld in exchange for the $21,492 needed to prevent eviction. In 1973 the owners of the building notified Lawrence Newfeld that they would like to sell the building for $300,000 even though the option had already expired. In October, 1973, Newfeld, with the help of Harry and Sol Schultz, purchased the property. Two years later, after all creditors had been paid, Abe Schulz demanded the return of the building to the corporation. Newfeld refused, and Abe Schulz brought this action on behalf of the corporation claiming Newfeld took a corporate opportunity when purchasing the property.

The issue here is whether the option to purchase the building was a corporate opportunity and whether Newfeld usurped that opportunity. In 1970 the corporation was in serious financial difficulty. It was unable to pay its rent and facing eviction from the business premises which would have left the corporation without office space and without manufacturing space. The corporation did not have the money, the means, or the credit, to raise the funds needed to pay the back rent and prevent eviction. Newfeld was willing to invest his own funds to save the corporation that was operating at a loss and unable to pay its creditors. Because Newfeld had risked his own money, when other experienced businessmen had refused to do so, the assignment of the lease constituted consideration for the business risk Newfeld was willing to take. Moreover, by admission of Abe

Schulz, the corporation had not been in the financial position to buy the building in 1973. It was not until 1975 that the corporation could afford to buy the building which was two years after Newfeld paid for it and owned it. Therefore Newfeld had not appropriated a corporate opportunity. He exercised a right the corporation assigned to him. The fact that Harry and Sol helped Newfeld finance the purchase was also immaterial. Had Newfeld not funded the corporation in 1970, the corporation would probably not have continued and the investment of all shareholders would have been lost. All of the shareholders, directors, and officers knew of the transaction of Newfeld paying the corporation $21,492 for the lease assignment. The option to purchase in the assignment expired. The owners offered to sell the property to Newfeld, not as part of the option, as it had expired, but as a new offer. No offer was made to the corporation by the owner of the building. Hence, no corporate opportunity existed.

Indemnification

HEFFERNAN v. PACIFIC DUNLOP GNB CORP.
United States Court of Appeals
Seventh Circuit (1992)
965 F. 2d. 369

In this diversity case, the court considered whether Delaware law precludes a former director from obtaining indemnification from the corporations he served. The district court prematurely dismissed this case, concluding it was one in which the director could prove no set of facts entitling him to indemnification. The Circuit Court of Appeals reversed this decision and remanded the case for futher proceedings.

Daniel Heffernan owned 6.7% of the stock of GNB Holdings, Inc. (Holdings), and was a director. Holdings owned GNB, Inc. (GNB), a wholly owned subsidiary. In 1987 Pacific Dunlop Holdings, Inc. (Pacific) acquired control of Holdings and its subsidiary GNB, by a stock purchase of approximately 60% of Holdings stock. This gave Pacific 92% of Holdings (previously owned 32%). Prior

to the purchase, Holdings filed a registration statement with the Securities and Exchange Commission, pursuant to an intended initial public offering. Holdings then abandoned the public offering and instead entered into the transaction with Pacific. The transaction was a stock purchase agreement with Pacific, Holdings, certain shareholders, and an investment company (the investment company owned 29% of Holdings stock and Heffernan was a vice president of the company). The stock agreement incorporated Holdings material previously prepared for the Securities and Exchange Commission. Pursuant to this agreement Heffernan sold his 6.7% interest in Holdings to Pacific and resigned as a director.

Litigation started from the stock purchase agreement. In 1990 Pacific sued

Heffernan and the investment company. Pacific sought to rescind its purchase of Heffernan's and the investment company's shares in Holdings, alleging the material in the agreement previously filed with the SEC was materially misleading as to disclosure of certain liabilities of Holdings and GNB. Heffernan requested indemnification and an advance on his litigation expenses from Holdings and GNB pursuant to Delaware General Corporation law and the bylaws of the corporations. Holdings refused Heffernan's request, whereupon Heffernan commenced this action to establish his rights to indemnification and advances.

Delaware General Corporation Law, section 145, "a corporation may indemnify any person who was or is a party to any lawsuit by reason of the fact that he or she was a director . . ." Holdings and GNB's bylaws make the provision in section 145 mandatory. Holdings' bylaws state, "the corporation shall, to the fullest extent permitted by the Delaware General Corporation Law . . . indemnify and hold harmless any person who is or was a party to any lawsuit by reason of his status, or the fact that he is or was or has agreed to become, a director of the corporation or of an affiliate,

and as to acts performed in the course of the director's duty to the corporation . . ." GNB's bylaws state "the corporation shall indemnify its officers, directors, employees, and agents to the extent permitted by the laws of Delaware."

The district court dismissed the complaint saying he had been sued for wrongs he committed as a individual, not as a director. Standing alone, neither the fact that Heffernan sold his own shares in Holdings nor the statutory provision on which Pacific is based thwarts Heffernan's right to indemnification as a matter of law. The nature of the transaction indicates that Heffernan may have been sued, at least in part because he was a director of the corporations. We find no support in Delaware's indemnification statute for the defendant's argument that it limits indemnification to suits against a director for breach of a duty of his or her directorship for acting wrongfully on behalf of the corporation he or she serves. Hence the complaint was improperly dismissed. The indemnification statute permits Heffernan to proceed to establish his right to advances and indemnification from Holdings and GNB. Reversed and remanded.

Duty of Loyalty

KLINICKI v. LUNDGREN
Supreme Court of Oregon
298 Or. 662 (1985)

Klinicki and Lundgren were both former Pan American pilots stationed in West Berlin. They agreed to go into the air transport business in West Berlin, starting with an air taxi and later expanding into scheduled service or chartered flights. They formed an Oregon Corporation, named Berlinair, Inc. It was a close corporation. Klinicki was president and director, responsible for developing and promoting the business. Lundgren was vice president and director, responsible for operations and maintenance. Each owned 33% of the corporate stock. Lelco, Inc., a corporation owned by Lundgren and his family, owned

33% of the corporate stock. The corporation's attorney owned the remaining one percent of stock.

In November 1977, Klinicki and Lundgren representing Berlinair, met with representatives of BFR, a consortium of Berlin travel agents that contracted for charter flights to take German tourists to sunnier climates. The BFR contract was considered a lucrative business opportunity, and Klinicki and Lundgren had contemplated pursuing the contract when they formed Berlinair. After the first meeting, all subsequent contacts with BFR were made by Lundgren and/or other employees under his direction.

Lundgren believed that Berlinair could not obtain the contract as BFR was satisfied with its present carrier. In June 1978, Lundgren learned there was a good chance the BFR contract might be available. He informed BFR that he would make a proposal on behalf of a new company. In July 1978, he incorporated Air Berlin Charter Company (ABC) and was its sole owner. In August 1978, ABC presented a proposal to BFR, and after discussions was awarded the contract on September 1, 1978. Lundgren concealed all negotiations with BRF from Klinicki and his diversion of the BFR contract to ABC, even though he used Berlinair working time, staff, money, and facilities.

Klinicki, a minority shareholder in Berlinair, commenced a derivative stockholders action against ABC for usurping a corporate opportunity of Berlinair. He also sued Lundgren for compensatory and punitive damages based on breach of fiduciary duty.

The trial court held for plaintiff and found Lundgren breached his fiduciary duties of good faith, fair dealing, and full disclosure, and owed plaintiff and Berlinair. Also, as an officer and director of Berlinair, Lundgren breached his fiduciary duties of good faith, fair dealing, and full disclosure. Also, that ABC through Lundgren wrongfully diverted the BFR contract which was a corporate opportunity. The court imposed a constructive trust on ABC in favor of Berlinair, ordered an accounting by ABC, and enjoined ABC from transferring its assets.

When a director, officer, or senior executive of a close corporation wishes to take personal advantage of a corporate opportunity, the following procedures must be strictly followed: (1) The opportunity must be promptly offered the corporation with all the material facts disclosed to disinterested directors and/or shareholders. (2) The corporate opportunity may only be taken advantage of after full disclosure and after being rejected by a majority of disinterested directors. If there are no disinterested directors, then a majority of disinterested stockholders. (3) An appropriation of corporate opportunity may be ratified by rejection of the opportunity by a majority of disinterested directors or a majority of disinterested stockholders after full disclosure.

The court finds that: Lundgren as director, and principal executive officer of Berlinair owed a fiduciary duty to Berlinair. The BFR contract was a corporate opportunity. Lundgren formed ABC for the purpose of usurping the opportunity presented to Berlinair by the BFR contract. Lundgren did not offer Berlinair the BFR contract. Lundgren did not attempt to obtain the consent of Berlinair to his taking the BFR corporate opportunity. Lundgren did not disclose to Berlinair his intent to appropriate the opportunity for himself and ABC. Berlinair never rejected the opportunity presented by the BFR contract. Berlinair never ratified the appropriation of the BFR contract. Lundgren, acting for ABC, misappropriated the BFR contract. If the challenging party satisfies the burden of proving that a corporate opportunity was taken without being offered to the corporation, the challenging party will prevail. Judgment for plaintiff affirmed.

WORDS TO KNOW

breached

business judgment rule

constructive trust

corporate opportunity

due care

duty of diligence

equity

exclusive

extinguished

fiduciary

intrinsic fairness

parent

proximate

punitive damages

standards of conduct

standards of review

strict liability

subsidiary

vesting

REVIEW

1. What is a fiduciary and who are fiduciaries?
2. Explain the duty of loyalty.
3. How do you breach a duty?
4. What are the remedies for violation of the duty of loyalty?
5. Explain the duty of obedience.
6. What is the duty of due diligence?
7. Give five examples of the duty of care.
8. What are the standards of conduct for directors and officers?
9. Explain conflict of interest.
10. What are the remedies for conflict of interest?
11. How many executive compensation plans can you list?
12. What is a controlling stockholder?
13. What, if any, duties does a controlling stockholder have?
14. Explain the business judgment rule.
15. What is the liability of directors and officers?
16. Do shareholders have any liability? Can they ever be liable?
17. Is there any way to protect directors from personal liability? Explain.

SHORT ESSAYS

1. John Commission was a vice president of purchasing for ABC Pizza, Inc. Unbeknownst to the corporation, he charged vendors 5 percent of the selling price of the items he purchased. He has now retired to an island in the Pacific. ABC just learned that John Commission charged 5 percent to vendors for all items he purchased during the last three years of his employment. ABC is suing John Commission for the amount of 5 percent of all the items he purchased for them during the last three years. In addition, the corporation is suing to recover the salary he was paid during those three years. Explain your decision.

2. State and explain three different ways that a director can have a conflict of interest with the corporation that he is a director of.

3. John Employee owns 5 percent of the shares of XYZ Corporation. He received the 5 percent stock interest as a bonus from his employer about five years ago. John Employee is a vice president and second in charge. He acts as president when the owner who is president is unavailable. Sam Boss owns 95 percent of the stock. Sam Boss is seventy-five years old. The corporation employs 250 people. Sam Boss has two sons, aged 45 and 52. Neither has ever worked for the corporation. In fact, neither has ever worked anywhere. Both sons like auto racing and spend all their time racing at various tracks around the

world. Sam Boss has decided he wants his sons in the business and wants them to take over slowly. He hired both sons three months ago, with titles of vice president. Each receives $275,000 a year salary. John Employee receives $125,000 per year salary. The sons come in about two days a month. They each have corporate credit cards, and for the last three months have run up bills of about $60,000 per month. Mostly air fares, hotel bills, entrance fees for racing, and food bills. John Employee fears that in a short period of time the corporation will be in financial trouble if the boys continue to spend the way they are. Sam Boss told John they are his sons and he will not restrict their spending. John Employee fears his 5 percent stock interest will be worthless if this continues. This was his pension-retirement fund. What, if anything, can John Employee do?

4. John Employee (see above) has just thought of an alternative. There is a new corporation coming into existence in about two months, The Big Corp. They will be in direct competition with ABC Corporation. John Employee has talked with the major executives of The Big Corp., and they have offered him an increase in salary and many new benefits if he joins them. Of course he will have to bring with him some customers from ABC corporation, but John does not believe that will be a problem. What advice, if any, can you give John?

RAISING CAPITAL

OBJECTIVES

After completing this chapter, you will be able to:

1. Know the difference between equity securities and debt securities.
2. List the various kinds of debt securities.
3. List the various kinds of equity securities.
4. Know the difference between the various equity securities.
5. Know the difference between the various debt securities.
6. Be aware of par value stock and what its benefits are.
7. Be aware of no par value stock and what its benefits are.
8. Know what stock options, warrants, and rights are and their uses.

INTRODUCTION

A corporation is a business. To run a business you must have capital. A corporation can obtain capital by either selling **debt securities** or **equity securities**. Debt securities do not represent ownership but create a debtor-creditor relationship. Equity securities create an ownership interest. There are two kinds of equity security, common and preferred. There are many variations of debt as well as equity securities that a corporation can issue.

The certificate of incorporation lists the type of shares, various classes of shares, and the number of shares of each type and/or class that the corporation is authorized to issue. If the board desires to issue additional shares, types or classes other than those listed in the certificate of incorporation, an amendment must be filed to the certificate to amend the number and types of shares the corporation is authorized to issue.

At common law shareholders had **preemptive rights**. Preemptive rights gave the shareholder the right to subscribe to the same percentage of stock now held if a new issue of stock was authorized. For example, Mr. Smith purchased 2 percent of the **original issue** of the common stock issued and outstanding. Now the corporation is going to issue preferred stock. Mr. Smith would have the right to subscribe to 2 percent of the preferred stock to be issued. Original issue means the first sale of stock of a particular class or kind of security by the corporation. The funds paid for the stock go to the corporation treasury. Today, by modern statutes, shareholders have no preemptive rights unless the certificate of incorporation provides such a right which very few do.

The board of directors cannot re-allocate or issue new stock for the sole purpose of perpetuating themselves in office, whether or not there are preemptive rights. Directors are fiduciaries, and, therefore, cannot issue stock or options to themselves at an unfairly low price.

Another way the corporation can help finance itself is through retained earnings. This, of course, only works after the corporation is in business and generating profits. Equity and debt securities raise capital even if there have been no retained earnings and/or profits.

BLUE SKY LAWS

All states have regulations concerning the issuance and sale of securities. These are called **Blue Sky Laws**. There are provisions in these regulations to prohibit fraud and require full disclosure of all facts prior to the sale of any security to the public. Many states regulate brokers, dealers, and all others in the security business. Some states require registration of securities prior to sale to the public. The federal government regulates securities through the Securities and Exchange Commission which will be discussed in Chapter 12.

DEBT SECURITIES

Some of the major forms of **debt security** are:

- bonds
- debentures
- indentures
- notes

A debt is a fixed amount that the corporation owes, and consists of **principal** and **interest**. When paying back a debt, the monthly, yearly, or other method of payment usually consists of principal and interest. Principal is return of the money borrowed, and interest is the interest that needs to be paid on the borrowed amount. For example, you borrow $100 to be paid back in one year, with 6 percent interest. The payment would be $100 principal, plus $6 interest, for a total payment of $106.

Bonds, debentures, and indentures are all basically promissory notes. They can be issued as they are, or as indentures, if the borrower desires.

The board of directors can issue one debt security, all kinds of debt securities, or none at all. Assume a corporation has ten plants, numbered one to ten. It can issue a secured bond using a piece of equipment in plant number Another secured bond can be issued using a piece of equipment in plant number. Another secured bond can be issued using a piece of equipment in plant number. This can go on as long as there are assets to secure the bond being issued. The point is, there is no limit to the amount of debt securities a corporation can issue. As long as people are buying them, the corporation can sell them.

Debt securities can be offered after a vote is carried by the board of directors to issue them. The stockholders do not have to participate or be advised of the intention of the board to consider or issue them. It is solely a decision of the board of directors to issue debt securities, take bank loans, obtain private loans or mortgages, or seek other financing when needed.

Bonds

Bonds are generally secured obligations. They are promissory notes. As a general rule bonds are long term, ten years or more. The interest can be paid monthly, three times a year, four times a year, once a year, or in accordance with any other terms stated in the bond. The principal of the bond is paid at maturity. The bond is a negotiable instrument. A **negotiable instrument** is generally an instrument that is easily transferred either in blank or by endorsement. **In blank** means to transfer ownership by handing it to another, assuming the instrument was originally in blank or payable to bearer. **Bearer** is the party in possession of the instrument. **Instrument** refers to any writing or agreement. **Endorsement** means to sign it on the reverse side similar to a check.

Bonds are debt securities that are issued by a corporation in large amounts, to raise many millions of dollars of capital. They have long maturity dates, 5, 10, 15, 20 or more years. **Maturity date** is the date the bond comes due and must be paid by the corporation to the holder of the instrument. Very often the corporation can not obtain a loan from a lending institution in the sum of money that they seek because the lending institution feels the corporation is too great a risk and may default in payment. Other times the lending institution wants an extremely high interest rate and a short maturity date hence, the issuance of bonds. Bonds are purchased by the public, mutual funds, and various investors as an investment, since they generally pay higher interest rates than available elsewhere in the financial market.

Debentures

Debentures are generally unsecured obligations. They are promissory notes. As a general rule they are long term, ten years or more. The interest can be paid monthly, quarterly, yearly, or in accordance with any other terms stated in the bond. Some bonds and/or debentures have coupons at the bottom; each interest period you clip a coupon and deposit it into your bank account or cash it at your bank. This is sometimes referred to as clipping coupons for a living. The principal is paid at the maturity of the bond. The promise to pay runs directly to the bondholder. The debenture is a negotiable instrument.

Indentures

An **indenture** is an agreement between the debtor (borrowing corporation) and a trustee. The trustee acts as an administrator and pays the interest and eventually the principal on the indenture to the holder of the indenture. The trustee monitors and enforces compliance on behalf of the bondholders as a group. The indenture states the obligations of the borrower, the rights and remedies of the bondholder, and the duties of the trustee. The indenture is a negotiable instrument. It is also a bond. The trustee allows for many investors, scattered in various areas, to buy the indentures in small denominations. The trustee enforces compliance on behalf of all holders; therefore, it is cost effective for the small investor. The indenture is a promise that runs to the trustee. The holders of the bonds are third party beneficiaries. The bondholders do not individually have to litigate a default by the borrower because the trustee will do it. An advantage for the borrower is only one lawsuit instead of a multitude of suits. An advantage for the investor is that on default, the trustee brings the action; costs, if any, will be distributed pro rata amongst all holders of the indenture. Therefore, it becomes cost effective. A trustee of an indenture is appointed by the corporation (debtor party raising capital) and is a fiduciary for all parties with the legal obligations of a fiduciary. The difference between a bond and an indenture is that the bond does not have a trustee. The greatest advantage of the indenture is that the trustee enforces the obligation and brings all lawsuits on default by the debtor (corporation). An example would be as follows; June 7, 2000, millions of investors purchased bonds from a corporation, with an 8 percent interest rate, principal and interest payable at maturity date June 6, 2005. If on June 6, 2005 the corporation defaults (fails to pay the interest and principal to bondholders) each bondholder must hire an attorney at their own expense, which could be considerable and commence a lawsuit action against the corporation. In an indenture the trustee would commence the lawsuit and the costs would be shared by all creditors (holders of the indenture). This lowers the cost to holders for enforcement. The advantage to the corporation is that it only has to defend one lawsuit rather than defending many.

Promissory Notes

Corporate debt securities are usually long term **promissory notes**. A promissory note is a piece of paper promising to pay someone—a company, corporation, or entity—a sum of money with interest over a period of time or in one future payment. Notes are usually short term, unsecured, and **mature** in ten years or less. The date on which the note matures is the date when it has to be paid.

Notes are similar to promissory notes except as to maturity date. Generally, notes are short term obligations, sometimes as short as 90 days or less.

To quickly obtain capital, very often as a bridge for other financing, notes will be considered as the vehicle of choice. A **bridge** is a fast infusion of capital to keep the business functioning while seeking other sources of long term financing, possibly issuance of stocks, indentures, debentures or bonds. Technically, promissory note is a generic term, encompassing all debt securities. As an example, the popular certificate of deposit (CD) that is offered by banks to investors, is a promissory note.

CORPORATE POWER TO ISSUE DEBT SECURITIES

The revised Model Business Corporation Act, Section 3.02, grants the power necessary for corporations to issue debt securities. There are callable bonds, convertible bonds, income bonds, secured bonds, and unsecured bonds. These can also be issued as indentures. If issued as indentures, they would be administered by a trustee.

Any bond, regardless of name, can be issued as an indenture instead of a bond by the addition of a separate agreement annexed to the bond, called the indenture agreement which appoints a trustee. For further clarification of an indenture see the indenture explanation previously discussed.

General Powers (Section 3.02, RMBCA)

Unless its articles of incorporation provide otherwise, every corporation has perpetual duration and succession in its corporate name and has the same powers as an individual to do all things necessary or convenient to carry out its business and affairs, including without limitation power

(5) to sell, convey, mortgage, pledge, lease, exchange, and otherwise dispose of all or any part of its property;

(6) to purchase, receive, subscribe for, or otherwise acquire, own, hold, vote, use, sell, mortgage, lend, pledge, or otherwise dispose of and deal in and with shares or other interests in, or obligations of, any other entity;

(7) to make contracts and guarantees, incur liabilities, borrow money, issue notes, bonds, and other obligations (which may be convertible into or include the option to purchase other securities of the corporation), and secure any of its obligations by mortgage or pledge any of its property, franchises, or income.

Callable Bonds

Callable bonds are bonds that are issued with a long maturity date. The borrower retains the right to **redeem (or call)** all or part of the issue at a specified price, at the option of the borrower, by accelerating the maturity date. Redeem means to pay off. Call means to call in the bonds prior to maturity and pay them off. The advantage to the corporation is that the corporation has the option at any time prior to maturity to call all or part of the issue. The corporation may want to do any one or a group of the following after redemption: reduce its fixed costs, reduce its proportion of debt, refinance at a lower cost, free mortgaged property, or improve its credit rating. This gives the borrower the ability to restructure its financing.

The corporation can issue as many series of callable bonds as the board desires and is able to sell. For example, Series A is a thirty year callable bond bearing interest at 7 percent per annum and callable at a price of face value. Series B is a thirty year callable bond bearing interest at 9 percent per annum and callable during the years ten through fifteen at a price of 2 percent less than face value. This can go on to issue Series C, D, E, etc., as far as the imagination of the board will take it. There is no limit as to the number of debt securities the corporation can issue.

Convertible Bonds

Convertible bonds can be converted to stock, usually common stock of the corporation, at a pre-determined rate at the option of the holder of the bond. For example, the holder may be able to convert the bond to seventy–five shares of common stock of the company within five years, twenty shares within ten years, and five shares within twenty years. Sometimes there is only one option to convert during the lifetime of the bond. Sometimes there is one option to convert up to a period of time. Sometimes there is a group of options at various prices during a particular period. There are as many options and formulas to convert as one can draft. The bond has all the details stated in the bond.

Again, the corporation can issue as many series of callable bonds as it desires, with the terms it desires. There is no limit to how many callable bonds it can issue as long as the market will **absorb** them. Absorb means to take up.

Income Bonds

Income bonds can be tied to a percentage of earnings of the corporation. They can be tied to a percentage of earnings from a particular division or area of the corporation, for example, a percentage of profits earned from the midwestern division. This insulates the corporation from having to pay a fixed interest during a fiscal crisis when there are no earnings or very small earnings. Normally debt securities pay a fixed interest without regard to earnings. The fixed interest becomes a fixed expense. Income bonds remove the fixed expense and remove the burden if there are no earnings or small earnings.

Again, the corporation can issue as many income bonds as the market can take. One bond can be based on a percentage of income from the Chicago plant; another income bond can be based on a percentage of income from the St. Louis plant, etc. There is no limit to how many the corporation can issue.

Participating Bonds

Participating bonds have an interest rate that is fixed regardless of earnings, plus an additional interest rate based on earnings. This would be a combination of a traditional bond (secured or unsecured) and an income bond.

Once again, the corporation can issue as many series of participating bonds as it desires. There is no limit.

Secured Bonds

Secured bonds place a specific named asset as security for the bond. Sometimes all the assets of the corporation can be the security. In addition to the holder of the secured bond being a secured creditor as to the secured items, the bondholder is also a general creditor, against all of the assets of the corporation. Suppose that a bond is secured by a specific piece of machinery. The bond places a **lien** on the piece of machinery in the bond. A lien means that the piece of machinery is subject to a first claim by the bondholder. The only way a purchaser or new lender can remove the lien is by payment, or upon the consent of the bondholder to remove the lien. On default, the bondholder can bring an action to **foreclose** the lien. **Foreclose** is a term used when property, real or personal, is placed as security for a loan and there is a default by the borrower (in this instance the corporation). Foreclosure is the action (lawsuit) brought to foreclose (sell) the security. After obtaining an order of foreclosure from the court, the marshal or sheriff will sell the piece of machinery at public auction. If there is not enough money received from the sale to cover the obligation and all costs and disbursements of the sale, the bondholder then becomes a general creditor of the corporation against all the remaining assets of the corporation for the balance due.

Again, the board can authorize the issuance of as many series of secured bonds as it desires, and use whatever security it desires.

Unsecured Bonds (Debentures)

Unsecured bonds are generally referred to as **debentures**. Certainly debentures sound a lot more important, and safer, than unsecured bonds. Being unsecured, it is only as good as the corporation. It is a general obligation of the corporation. There is a debtor-creditor relationship with the bondholder, but the bondholder is only a general creditor and stands in no better position than any other creditor. Frequently, these are sold as indentures to add a little more security for the bondholder. The indenture may impose limitations on the corporation's right to declare and/or pay dividends until the bonds mature and are paid in full. There may also be limitations on the corporation's right to redeem stock, call other bonds, or in any way acquire, reacquire, or purchase back its shares. There can also be a prohibition on future borrowing or a limitation placed on future borrowing until the bonds are paid in full. The indenture gives the bondholder a little security. It also makes the debenture more marketable and saleable.

The board of directors can issue as many series of debentures as it desires, always changing some of the terms from the prior issue.

EQUITY SECURITIES

Equity securities are stocks sold by a corporation to raise capital. The proceeds from the original issue belong to the corporation as capital. **Original issue** is the first sale of the security by the corporation to a purchaser.

Equity securities create an ownership interest in the corporation and are a means of raising capital for the corporation. Evidence of ownership interest is by a certificate of stock which is recorded by the corporation and lists the number of shares owned and the class of security. While the stock certificate creates title to an interest in the corporation, it does not create title to the corporate property. The assets of a corporation are owned by the corporation, not by the shareholders. The certificate of stock does give the holder the following rights: (1) to participate in the right to control the corporation by voting, (2) to participate in the earnings of the corporation, and (3) to participate in the residual assets of the corporation upon dissolution.

Right to Issue Shares

Before a corporation can issue stock, it must be authorized in the articles of incorporation. A corporation is limited to the sale of the shares authorized in its certificate of incorporation. This initial number is pursuant to the desires of the promoters and/or incorporators. To raise or lower this number requires an amendment to the certificate of incorporation. The filing fee of the secretary of state is determined by the number of shares the corporation intends to issue. For example, in Delaware it costs $.01 a share for the first 20,000 shares ($200 minimum fee). The corporation does not have to issue all 20,000 shares. It can issue one or more shares at $.005 per share for up to two million shares, $.004 per share for all shares over two million. The number the corporation can issue is infinite as long as the filing fees are paid. Various states have various costs and minimums: New York State 200 shares, Florida 2,000 shares.

If a corporation issues shares that are unauthorized, the shares are void pursuant to Section 6.03, RMBCA. Article 8, Section 8-104, of The Uniform Commercial Code requires the corporation to obtain an identical security that is valid or pay the person (the last **bona fide purchaser**) the amount paid for it with interest. A bona fide purchaser is one who takes for value without notice of a defect.

Stock that has been authorized and not yet sold by the corporation is called **authorized and unissued**. Stock that has been authorized and sold by the corporation is called **authorized and issued or outstanding stock**. Stock that has been authorized and sold by the corporation and then bought back by the corporation is called **treasury stock**. Treasury stock is issued and not outstanding.

Par Value

Par value can be arbitrarily set by the board of directors or shareholders if the certificate of incorporation allows shareholders this right. This is the minimum price that the corporation can sell the shares for; there is no maximum price. This is only for the first sale by the corporation. The price does not have to have any relationship to the value. The par value, if there is to be one, must be stated in the articles of incorporation. Par value can be amended by the board or shareholders. After the first sale by the corporation, the price of the stock freely floats and is set by the bid and asking prices of buyers and sellers. There is no minimum price. After the initial **original issue**, per value has no significance to either add or detract from the value of the shares. Original issue means the first sale by the corporation. The sale proceeds go to the corporation. After the original issue, the selling price goes to the seller. The corporation no longer has a financial benefit from the sale.

The original purpose for par value was to protect stockholders from a corporation issuing watered stock. The par value was the actual market value; when set as par value, the corporation could not issue stock to friends for less than the actual market value. A sweetheart deal is when a corporation sells stock at less than market value to friends, thereby reducing the value of other stockholders' holdings.

When a corporation sells par value original issue stock, the par value amount received by the corporation is called stated capital. Any amount received over the par value on the original issue is called capital surplus. This is for accounting purposes. The corporation can never sell par value initial issue stock for less than par value.

Over twenty states plus Section 6.21 of the RMBCA eliminate par value, stated capital, and capital surplus. All shares can be issued at a price set by the board of directors. If the certificate of incorporation allows the shareholders to set the price, the shareholders can set the price of all shares. Section 2.02 (b)(iv), RMBCA, allows a corporation to elect to issue shares with par value if desired by the articles of incorporation.

Articles of Incorporation (Section 2.02 (b)(iv), RMBCA)

(**b**) The articles of incorporation may set forth:
　　(**iv**) a par value for authorized shares or classes of shares

No Par Value

No par value stock means that the board of directors, or shareholders if authorized, may set the selling price for the original issue. There need not be any relation to market value in setting the price. No par value shares can help directors in some jurisdictions to provide distributions to shareholders by establishing capital surplus. As long as the stock does not have a **liquidation preference,** the directors can allocate the funds to capital surplus. **Liquidation preference** on no par stock means that the stock certificate states a fixed value for each share in the event the corporation dissolves and the assets have to be liquidated. The stockholders receive a minimum amount as stated in the stock certificate plus a pro rata portion of any remaining monies pursuant to the amount of their stock ownership. As an example; Mr. A owns 10 shares of no par stock with a liquidation preference of $50 per share. On liquidation, after all debts have been paid, Mr. A would receive $500 for his 10 shares plus a pro rata amount of any other monies left. If it has a liquidation preference, only the amount in excess of the preference can be allocated to capital surplus. Dividends are paid from capital surplus in many jurisdictions. States that recognize par value, stated value, and capital surplus must apply all proceeds from the sale of the original issue stock to stated capital.

Issuance of Shares (Section 6.21, RMBCA)

(**a**) The powers granted in this section to the board of directors may be reserved to the shareholders by the articles of incorporation.

(b) The board of directors may authorize shares to be issued for consideration consisting of any tangible or intangible property or benefit to the corporation, including cash, promissory notes, services performed, contracts for services to be performed, or other securities of the corporation.

(c) Before the corporation issues shares, the board of directors must determine that the consideration received or to be received for shares to be issued is adequate. That determination by the board of directors is conclusive insofar as the adequacy of consideration for the issuance of shares relates to whether the shares are validly issued, fully paid, and nonassessable.

(d) When the corporation receives the consideration for which the board of directors authorized the issuance of shares, the shares issued are fully paid and nonassessable.

(e) The corporation may place in escrow shares issued for a contract for future services or benefits, or a promissory note, or make other arrangements to restrict the transfer of the shares, and may credit distributions in respect of the shares against their purchase price, until the services are performed, the note paid, or the benefits received. If the services are not performed, the note is not paid, or the benefits are not received, the shares escrowed or restricted and the distributions credited may be canceled in whole or part.

Treasury Stock

Treasury Stock is shares that the corporation has issued and later repurchased. They are issued, but not outstanding. The board of directors can set any price for the sale of treasury stock, even if it is par value stock (the original issue, first sale). No dividends are paid on treasury stock; no voting rights attach to treasury stock; and there are no preemptive rights with treasury stock. Of course, when the corporation sells treasury stock, all these restrictions are terminated and the buyer has voting, dividend, and preemptive rights if they existed before. Section 6.31, RMBCA, allows corporations to repurchase their own shares; they are then authorized but unissued. If the articles of incorporation prohibit the reissue of acquired shares, the number of authorized shares is reduced by the number of shares acquired.

Reports to Shareholders (Section 16.21, RMBCA)

(a) If a corporation indemnifies or advances expenses to a director under Sections 8.51, 8.52, 8.53, or 8.54 in connection with a proceeding by or in the right of the corporation, the corporation shall report the indemnification or advance in writing to the shareholders with or before the notice of the next shareholders' meeting.

(b) If a corporation issues or authorizes the issuance of shares for promissory notes or for promises to render services in the future, the corporation shall report in writing to the shareholders the number of shares authorized or issued, and the consideration received by the corporation, with or before the notice of the next shareholders' meeting.

Consideration Needed to Purchase Shares

The RMBCA allows anything of value to be valid consideration for the purchase of shares: cash, promises of cash (promissory notes), personal property, promises to contribute personal property, real property, promises to contribute real property, services rendered, and services to be performed.

A majority of states do not consider promissory notes and promises for future services to be adequate consideration for the purchase of shares. Cash, property, and services already rendered are considered good consideration in these states.

Section 6.21(c), RMBCA, provides for the board of directors before issuing shares to determine if the consideration is adequate. The determination by the board is conclusive.

Section 6.21(e), RMBCA, allows the corporation to hold shares in escrow when issued for a promissory note, or future services or benefits to the corporation. If not held in escrow, other restrictions can be imposed on the stock by the board of directors. If the services are not performed, the note not paid, or the benefits received, the shares escrowed or restricted may be canceled in whole or in part.

The majority of states hold the valuation of consideration to be a matter of opinion for the board of directors, and in the absence of fraud the judgment of the board of directors is conclusive. The RMBCA only requires the consideration to be adequate, and the decision of the board of directors is conclusive as to the decision of adequate consideration.

STOCKS CORPORATIONS CAN ISSUE

Generally corporations issue common stock, preferred stock, stock options, and stock warrants. Each has a specific purpose; each can be used to raise capital for the corporation; and each can be issued in a series. Examples of these are common stock class A, common stock class B, and to infinity common stock class ZZZ. Preferred stock class A and preferred stock class B for as long as the board wishes to go on issuing. It can issue preferred stock issue number 2300. The different series can vary as to voting rights. Examples of these are one series can have the exclusive right to vote on liquidation of the corporation; one series can have a 30 percent vote on liquidation of the corporation, with another or group or series equaling the remaining 70 percent. Different shares can have different dividend rights and different treatment in the assets of the corporation in the event of liquidation. The board of directors can become as creative as it wants to. But, it can only issue what the certificate of incorporation authorizes. Therefore, it may need to amend the certificate to issue additional shares or series of shares. The RMBCA Section 6.01, eliminated the terms common and preferred. However, it does allow the issuance of shares with different preferences, dividend rights, preferences and rights.

Authorized Shares (Section 6.01, RMBCA)

(a) The articles of incorporation must prescribe the classes of shares and the number of shares of each class that the corporation is authorized to issue. If more than one class of shares is authorized, the articles of incorporation must prescribe a distinguishing designation for each class; and, prior to the issuance of shares of a class, the preferences, limitations, and relative rights of that class must be described in the articles of incorporation. All shares of a class must have preferences, limitations, and relative rights identical with those of other shares of the same class except to the extent otherwise permitted by Section 6.02.

(b) The articles of incorporation may authorize (1) one or more classes of shares that together have unlimited voting rights, and (2) one or more classes of shares (which may be the same class or classes as those with voting rights) that together are entitled to receive the net assets of the corporation upon dissolution.

(c) The articles of incorporation may authorize one or more classes of shares that:

(1) have special, conditional, or limited voting rights, or no right to vote, except to the extent prohibited by this Act;

(2) are redeemable or convertible as specified in the articles of incorporation (i) at the option of the corporation, the shareholder, or another person, or upon

the occurrence of a designated event; (ii) for cash, indebtedness, securities, or other property; (iii) in a designated amount or in an amount determined in accordance with a designated formula or by reference to extrinsic data or events;

(3) entitle the holders to distribution calculated in any manner, including dividends that may be cumulative, noncumulative, or partially cumulative; and

(4) have preference over any other class of shares with respect to distributions, including dividends and distributions upon the dissolution of the corporation.

(d) The description of the designations, preferences, limitations, and relative rights of share classes in subsection (c) is not exhaustive.

Notwithstanding the RMBCA, many states allow nonvoting shares to vote on certain mergers, exchange of shares, and fundamental changes that affect the shares of the class as a class.

Common Stock

Common stock is generally the main stock used for raising capital. It is often the only stock issued. The RMBCA Section 6.01 allows common stock to be issued in classes with various limitations as to voting, dividends, and/or relative rights. The RMBCA allows the stock to be redeemable and/or convertible. Any limitations or relative rights restrictions as well as redeemable or convertible ability must be stated in the articles of incorporation.

For example, Class A common may have two votes per share in electing directors, while Class D common may have no votes for electing directors. Class C common may be able to elect two directors, while class E common can elect four directors. Class A common may receive two times the dividends received by class B common. The point is, almost anything can be done as long as it is stated in the certificate of incorporation.

Classes and Series of Stock

A corporation can issue different **classes of stock**. Class is a type of stock, sometimes referred to as a category which can be further divided into **series**. All stock in a series have the same rights. There are sometimes minor differences in some series of a class. All shareholders in a series may be entitled to a dividend. Shareholders in another series may be entitled to a larger or smaller dividend. A class or series may have any one or a combination of the following:

(1) Voting rights. Usually used to elect directors and vote on amendments. Different series and different classes can have different rights to vote. For example, one series may have the right to elect five directors while another series may have the right to elect only one director.

(2) Liquidation rights. The order in which stockholders will be paid upon dissolution can be different in different series and/or classes.

(3) Dividend rights. Different classes and series can have various rights to dividends. Dividends can only be paid when the corporation is solvent. In many states dividends can only be paid out of earned surplus.

(4) Conversion rights. The right to convert into a different class. For example, if the company does not meet financial goals, non-voting stock can be converted into voting stock.

(5) Preemptive rights. Each shareholder has the right to buy additional shares whenever offered by the company to maintain their original percentage of ownership. For example, the corporation issues ten shares to each of ten people. Each share-

holder has a 10 percent ownership. Later, the board of directors decides to issue an additional one hundred shares to new stockholders. This would dilute the ownership of the original ten people and leave them each with only a 5 percent ownership. Preemptive rights mean they can each buy enough of the new issue to maintain their 10 percent ownership position.

(6) Redemption rights. Shareholders with this right can force the corporation to re-purchase their shares at a stated price, in the event financial goals or other stated goals of the company are not met.

Preferred Stock

Preferred stock is a hybrid of stock ownership and senior debt. Preferred stock is referred to as a senior debt because generally a corporation must first issue a dividend to preferred stock-holders prior to declaring a dividend for common shareholders. Preferred and common stock are both in the net worth section of the balance sheet. Dividends of both common and preferred stock are a distribution of profits to stockholders. Bond interest is a cost of doing business. When both common and preferred stock are issued, the common shareholders agree that the pre-ferred stockholders will have first claim in the event the board of directors issues a dividend.

Straight Preferred Stock

Straight preferred stock is nonparticipating and is the most frequent type issued. It has a fixed dollar dividend per share stated in the certificate. If par value, it has a fixed percent-age of par value as the dividend stated in the certificate. Usually preferred stock also has a preferred status as to disposition of assets in the event of dissolution. The dividend is usu-ally payable quarterly, but the period of payment can be at any stated time. Debt holders have a fixed claim for interest and principal. Preferred stockholders usually do not. If the board declares a dividend on common stock, it must first pay the designated preferred stock dividend. In liquidation, the preferred stock is satisfied (its preference as stated in the cer-tificate) before common stock shareholders receive anything. Often the preferred stock is given the right to vote for directors if the preferred stock dividend is in default for a stated period mentioned in the certificate. The dividend most often is cumulative. This means that no common stock dividend can be paid until all defaulted preferred stock dividends have been paid. If the dividend on the preferred stock is not cumulative, then the common stock can be paid a dividend as long as the preferred stock gets its current stated dividend first.

Stock Options, Stock Rights, and Stock Warrants

To reward and/or attract executives, the corporation can offer warrants and/or options. These can also be used by the corporation to raise capital. The corporation can make a particular se-ries of stock more attractive by including a **stock right** which allows the purchaser to purchase a stated amount of stock in another series or class an inducement to purchase the offered se-ries. **Stock options** are usually used in incentive stock options to attract or reward executives. **Stock warrants** are a kind of stock option that generally runs for a longer period of time, is freely transferable, and is usually actively traded on a stock exchange. The board of directors decides the terms of the stock options, rights, and warrants, as well as the price and the use thereof.

Retained Earnings

The third method of financing a company is the sale of equity securities, debt securities, and retained earnings. Generally, the corporation will not retain earnings unless it has a foreseeable use for the funds. The only method of return for stockholders is through the receipt of dividends and appreciation. Without dividends the stock can only appreciate based on future potential.

SUMMARY

There are three major ways to raise capital for a corporation: through the sale of equity securities, debt securities, and retained earnings. Debt securities are bonds. Bonds are a debt and have to be repaid with principal and interest. Equity securities represent ownership and do not have to be repaid. A corporation must be authorized in its certificate of incorporation to issue shares of stock. If necessary, the certificate of incorporation can be amended to include the authorization to issue additional shares, classes, and series. Debt securities include callable bonds, convertible bonds, income bonds, participating bonds, secured bonds, and unsecured bonds.

Stock can be authorized and issued, authorized and unissued, authorized issued and outstanding, or authorized issued and not outstanding (treasury stock).

A corporation can sell par value stock and/or non par value stock. There can be various classes and series of stock sold, each with its own benefits and attractions.

Common stock and preferred stock can be sold in classes and series, each with its own benefits to attract purchasers. It is almost limitless as to the combinations of benefits to be included in various classes and series. Common stock is generally voting stock that elects the board of directors; preferred stock is generally nonvoting. Preferred stock must be paid dividends before common stock can be paid dividends. If the corporation is in default of dividends to preferred stockholders, the preferred stockholders can very often have the right to vote for directors during the default period.

Stock rights, options, and warrants can be used to raise capital or to attract and/or reward executives.

Retained earnings, the sale of debt securities and equity securities are the methods used to finance a corporation. As a rule, the corporation will only retain earnings if there is an immediate need for working capital or the corporation is planning some form of near term expansion. The reason is that stockholders only have two ways to earn a return on their investment in stocks; one is dividends and the other is capital appreciation. If dividends are not declared by the corporation then, the stock can only appreciate through future potential. This can take a fairly long period of time and waiting for the investor.

CASES

Disputed Common Shares from Preferred Stock

STAAR SURGICAL COMPANY v. WAGGONER
588 A.2d 1130 (1991)

Waggoner was president and CEO of Starr. Starr had a line of credit with the Bank of New York and used its accounts receivable as collateral for the line of credit. In late 1987, Bank of New York lowered the value (wrote down) of the accounts receivable of Starr that it had for collateral. This caused the bank to be $2,000,000 short in collat-eral. The bank asked the president and CEO of Waggoner to personally guarantee the debts of Starr to the bank. Waggoner, in 1987, advised the board of directors that he would guarantee the debts only if he received voting control of the company during the time of the guarantee. The board agreed that Waggoner would be issued some kind of convertible security in exchange for his guarantee. Four days later the board passed a resolution giving Waggoner and his wife newly created preferred shares that would be converted into two million shares of common stock if the guarantee remained in force more than thirty days. Waggoner signed the minutes but the rest of the board never formally signed the minutes. On January 11, 1988, some dissatisfied board members called a meeting and tried to delay the conversion feature which was now in effect. On January 19, 1988, Waggoner exercised his option and received two million shares of common stock. In August 1989, Waggoner exercised his voting rights on the rest of the preferred stock and removed the Starr board. The removed directors and two shareholders contested under Delaware law. The court found that the preferred stock shares were void. The certificate of incorporation authorized the board by resolution to issue blank check preferred stock. However, Delaware law requires a board resolution specifically authorizing the issue of such preferred stock. The board must issue a certificate of designation in conjunction with the resolution. The board never formally adopted the resolution or issued a certificate of designation. Failure to comply with Delaware law rendered the shares void. The conversion from the void shares rendered the new common stock void as well. Stock issued in violation of Delaware law is void.

Attempt to Restrict Stock

DEAN WITTER REYNOLDS, INC. v. SELECTRONICS, INC., ET AL.
594 N.Y.S.2d 174, 188 A.D. 2d 117 (1993)

The subject stock was original issue and issued to Stephen Nagel, a director and officer of Selectronics, under the private placement exemption section 4 (2) of the Securities Act of 1933. The issuer failed to place a legend on the certificates that they were unregistered and distributed as a private placement. Nagel later exchanged those certificates for five shares of common stock (stock in question here). Selectronics again failed to place a legend on the certificates and did not register the stock. The stock was pledged by Nagel as security for a loan from the defendant F.I.G. Corporation, and finally came into the possession of defendant Bil Banque Internationale, a Luxembourg (Suisse) S.A.

Plaintiff, Dean Witter Reynolds, Inc., is attempting to recover losses sustained when Depository Trust Company rejected the certificates for clearance. Defendant Bil deposited five certificates with Plaintiff Dean for Dean to sell for its account. The certificates seemed negotiable and Dean sold the shares and remitted the proceeds to Bil. The securities clearance house where the shares went for re–registration rejected the shares and for the first time had a restrictive legend on their face. Plaintiff Dean is now suing Bil, Selectronics, Mellon Bank (Selectronic Transfer Agent), et al.

The Supreme Court and this court granted plaintiff's motion for summary judgment and remanded for assessment of damages. Under UCC 8-204 defendants were liable for failing and neglecting to indicate the restrictions on the face of the certificates.

Section 8-204 of the Uniform Commercial Code says "a restriction on transfer of a security imposed by the issuer even though otherwise lawful is ineffective against any person without actual knowledge of it unless (a) the certificate has a restriction noted conspicuously thereon."

Plaintiff as a pledgee was among the persons protected by Section 8-204 against a restriction not conspicuously noted on the security except as to persons with actual knowledge. The wrongful refusal to transfer gave rise to the right to sue for conversion.

The U.C.C. Section 8-204 does create liability for damages against issuer and/or transfer agent who omitted to include restrictions on the face of the certificate in a conspicuous manner.

The Appellate Division of the State of New York affirmed the decision of the Supreme Court and remanded the case back to the Supreme Court for an assessment of damages.

WORDS TO KNOW

absorb

authorized stock

Blue Sky Laws

bona fide purchaser

bonds

call

callable bonds

classes of stock

common stock

debentures

debt securities

equity securities

income bonds

indentures

interest

issued stock

matures

no par value

original issue

outstanding stock

participating bonds

par value

preemptive rights

preferred stock

principal

promissory notes

redeem

secured bonds

series of stock

stock options

stock rights

straight preferred stock

treasury stock

unsecured bonds

warrants

REVIEW QUESTIONS

1. What is the difference between equity securities and debt securities?
2. List the various equity securities and explain the differences.
3. List the various debt securities and explain the differences.
4. What is the difference between par value stock and non par value stock?
5. What are the uses for stock options, warrants, and rights?
6. Explain preemptive rights.
7. Explain the difference between principal and interest.
8. What does issued and outstanding mean?
9. What does authorized mean?
10. What is treasury stock?
11. Where and how does a corporation obtain the right to issue shares of stock?
12. What is a bona fide purchaser?
13. What is the maximum number of shares a corporation can issue?

14. What is a minimum number of shares a corporation can issue?

15. Who decides the price of the shares the corporation will sell?

SHORT ESSAYS

1. Delft Corporation is authorized to issue 10,000 shares of no par nonparticipating common stock. Fred, Tom, and John, the incorporators, each own two thousand shares for which they each paid $20,000. The original capitalization was $60,000. The corporation has a three–person board of directors. Fred, Tom, and John are each a director. The corporation is being sued for $30,000 on a contractual obligation. The board of directors does not believe the corporation is liable. Allan, an attorney, has been consulted by the board. Allan wants a $2,000 retainer and has said the total fees could go as high as $5,000. The board has decided by a two-thirds vote that instead of offering Allan money they will offer him 500 shares of stock in exchange for his services to be performed. John was the dissenting vote. Allan has agreed to the stock being placed in escrow pending his completion of the work to be performed. Five weeks later Allan attends a board meeting to report progress to the board. At this time he advises that he made a motion for summary judgment and the complaint was dismissed. He now wants his stock released from escrow. John feels that since it only took one court appearance, Allan should not be entitled to the 500 shares. He says it is not adequate consideration to the corporation. The other two board members do not feel that strongly and are willing to keep their agreement. Discuss your decision and explain.

2. D corporation is authorized to issue 2,000 shares of $50 par value common stock. Ten shareholders each own 150 shares and Mr. Smith owns 500 shares. All the shareholders except Mr. Smith have agreed to file an amendment to the articles of incorporation to increase the capitalization and authorize an additional 2,000 shares of $50 par value common stock. What are the rights of Mr. Smith? Explain fully.

3. The corporation has 25 stockholders. Ten of the 25 stockholders represent 51 percent of the issued and outstanding stock. Only two of the ten are members of the seven member board. The board of directors has passed a resolution to issue and sell $50,000 of corporate debentures. The ten shareholders representing 51 percent of the outstanding stock disagree and want to block the issuance and sale of these debentures. Explain in detail the rights of all parties.

4. You have been retained as a consultant for the Need Money Corporation. The corporation is in need of $200,000 to build a pilot machine of a new invention that the corporation owns a patent on. This machine will be able to prepare optical lenses and cut them to the size specified and to fit a prescription that is set in the controls. It will also coat the lenses so that they will get darker as sunlight hits them. It will also fit the lenses into a frame so that the complete product will be ready for delivery without anyone touching the frame or lenses. The complete operation will take two minutes. Presently it takes two days to send this work out and receive the frames and lenses. Need Money Corporation wants to set these machines in malls to fit prescription lenses for customers as they wait. All of the common stock is presently owned by five people. None of them wants to issue new stock. Lending institutions have not been receptive because this is a new corporation. Can you help this corporation raise the $200,000 it needs? How do you propose accomplishing it? Explain totally and fully all possible scenarios for raising this capital and present your recommendation to the board.

CHAPTER

8

SHAREHOLDER RIGHTS

OBJECTIVES

After completing this chapter, you will be able to:

1. Know what an ultra vires act is.
2. Know the duty of the board of directors to maximize the wealth of shareholders.
3. Set up voting rights for stock that you issue.
4. Tell when a shareholder is personally liable for corporate debts.
5. Know that shares of stock can be issued without issuing a stock certificate.
6. Know the different kinds of shares that can be issued with different voting rights.
7. Know who gets notice of shareholders meetings in a public corporation.
8. Know when a majority vote is necessary and when a plurality vote is necessary, and the difference.
9. Know how to be assured of representation on the board of directors by minority shareholders.
10. Know how to stagger election of the board of directors.
11. Define cumulative and noncumulative voting.
12. Know the difference between a de jure and a de facto corporation.

13. Know the liability for acting as a corporation without having a charter from the state.
14. Know what piercing the corporate veil means.
15. Be aware of the consequences of commingling corporate funds.
16. Know what a proxy is and how to draft one.
17. Know when you can inspect the corporate books and records.

INTRODUCTION

Can a corporation act in a manner that is not intended to maximize profits? If it did, it probably would be an **ultra vires act.** An ultra vires act is an act that the corporation is not authorized to make or perform. The corporation receives its powers from the articles of incorporation and charter. A corporation is supposed to act for the monetary benefit of its shareholders. The traditional concept of a corporation was: What is good for the corporation is good for the shareholder.

This concept was based on two assumptions: (1) The welfare of the shareholder is incident to the welfare of the corporation, and (2) Earnings or earnings per share are appropriate indications of the corporation's performance.

Today, both these assumptions are incorrect: (1) Corporations concerned about the shareholders will generally take more risks than corporations concerned with their own well being, and (2) Maximizing corporate earnings or per share value does not always maximize shareholders' wealth.

From a shareholder's perspective, the best thing to do with a corporation that is steadily losing money is to liquidate it. The shareholders then receive their money and can put it to better use. From the employees', managers', and corporate point of view, it is better to continue keeping the company alive and working to rejuvenate it.

The duty of the board of directors, and officers today, is to maximize shareholders' wealth.

RIGHT TO VOTE

Common stock usually gives the shareholder the right to at least vote for directors and any amendments that change the original charter. These rights, however, can vary between different classes and series of common stock. In 1956 Ford Motor Company went public. Class B common stock was issued to the family. Class B common stock has a 40 percent voting power in the corporation, and, therefore, can elect 40 percent of the directors. This stock, in effect, gives the Ford family control of the corporation.

LIABILITY OF SHAREHOLDERS

Unless the articles of incorporation say otherwise, a stockholder is not personally liable for the acts or debts of the corporation. The only liability is to the corporation to pay the consideration agreed to for the shares. Once paid, the shares are fully paid and **nonassessable** thereafter (Section 6.21(d) RMBCA). Nonassessable means no further money need be paid for the shares once they are issued. A purchaser buying these shares without notice or knowledge that the full consideration had not been paid to the corporation is *not* personally liable to the corporation or its creditors for the unpaid consideration owing the corporation.

Liability of Shareholders (Section 6.22, RMBCA)

(a) A purchaser from a corporation of its own shares is not liable to the corporation or its creditors with respect to the shares except to pay the consideration for which the shares were authorized to be issued or specified in the subscription agreement.

(b) Unless otherwise provided in the articles of incorporation, a shareholder of a corporation is not personally liable for the acts or debts of the corporation except that he may become liable personally by reason of his own act or conduct.

SHARES REPRESENTED BY CERTIFICATES AND SHARES WITHOUT CERTIFICATES

Shares of stock are generally represented by certificates of stock. However, shares can be issued without certificates as long as there is no statute prohibiting same (Section 6.26, RMBCA). If issued without certificates, the corporation, within a reasonable time after issue, must send the shareholder a written statement containing the information required in a certificate (Section 6.26, RMBCA). The minimum information required in a certificate of stock is:

(1) The name of the corporation and state of charter.

(2) The name of the person to whom issued; the number of shares and class or series.

(3) If different shares are issued by the corporation, a summary of all classes or series with the rights, preferences, and limitations for each class and series. This must be on the front or back of the certificate or in a conspicuous place the statement that this information will be furnished in writing, free of charge, to stockholders upon request.

(4) The certificate must be signed by two officers designated by the board of directors with the corporate seal or a facsimile of same thereon.

(5) If the shares are signed by officers who no longer hold office, the shares are still valid.

(6) A certificate can be issued for a fraction of one share or more; the amount is infinite.

Form and Content of Certificate (Section 6.25, RMBCA)

(a) Shares may, but need not be, represented by certificates. Unless this act or another statute expressly provides otherwise, the rights and obligations of shareholders are identical whether or not their shares are represented by certificates.

(b) At a minimum each share certificate must state on its face:
   (1) the name of the issuing corporation and that it is organized under the laws of the state where organized.
   (2) the name of person to whom issued; and

(3) the number and class of shares and the designation of the series, if any, that the certificate represents.

(c) If the issuing corporation is authorized to issue different classes of shares or series within a class, the designation, relative rights, preferences, and limitations applicable to each class and the variations in rights, preferences, and limitations determined for each series (and the authority of the board of directors to determine variations for future series) must be summarized on the front or back of each certificate. Alternatively, each certificate may state conspicuously on its front or back that the corporation will furnish the shareholder this information on request in writing and without charge.

(d) Each share certificate (1) must be signed (either manually or in facsimile) by two officers designated in the bylaws or by the board of directors, and (2) may bear the corporate seal or its facsimile.

(e) If the person who signed (either manually or in facsimile) a share certificate no longer holds office when the certificate is issued, the certificate is nevertheless valid.

Shares Without Certificates (Section 6.26, RMBCA)

(a) Unless the articles of incorporation or bylaws provide otherwise, the board of directors of a corporation may authorize the issue of some or all of the shares of any or all classes or series without certificates. The authorization does not affect shares already represented by certificates until they are surrendered to the corporation.

(b) Within a reasonable time after the issue or transfer of shares without certificates, the corporation shall send the shareholder a written statement of the information required on certificates by Section 6.25(b) and (c) and, if applicable, Section 6.27 (referring to restrictions on transfer).

RIGHT TO VOTE

The right of shareholders to vote is a fundamental right. However, different classes of stock and different series of stock carry different rights as to voting, as well as the issues that the holders of the stock may vote on. Shareholders usually vote to elect directors and for structural changes in the corporation.

All statutes require an annual stockholders meeting. Notice of place, time, and date is required for annual as well as for special meetings of stockholders. Special meetings must also disclose the purpose of the special meeting in the notice. Federal proxy rules and some state statutes require the purpose of the meeting in all notices. Federal proxy rules apply to only a small number of corporations. The state statutes that require purpose stated in the annual meeting notice is only for structural changes such as to amend the certificate of incorporation, to sell substantial corporate assets, to form a merger, or for a dissolution.

Voting Requirements

Shareholders in publicly held corporations constantly change; therefore, notice of meetings is given to shareholders of record as of a specific date. **Beneficial stockholders** need not be given notice. **Beneficial stockholders** own shares but do not have the shares listed in their names for any of a number of reasons; consequently they are not stockholders of record. Often they are referred to as equity owners. For example, Ms. X owns 25 percent of the shares in Minisoft Corporation and they are listed in her name. She is a record holder of 25 percent of the shares issued and outstanding. Ms. X wants to purchase another 30 percent of the issued and outstanding shares giving her a controlling interest in the Minisoft Corporation, but, she prefers not to make this public. Ms. X purchases the 30 percent in the name of her married daughter. Only those who were shareholders of record as of a stated date may vote. The record date is usually fixed in the bylaws by the board of directors or by statute. If a record date is not set in any of these ways, it is the day or preceding day the notice is sent out.

(1) On ordinary matters, an affirmative vote of a majority of the shares represented at the meeting is necessary for action under most statutes. Some statutes require only a majority of those voting. In this case an abstention is a negative vote.

(2) For election of directors, a **plurality** vote is required. A plurality is the highest number of votes. For example, one director is to be elected. Mr. A receives 205 votes, Mr. B receives 206 votes, Mr. C receives 207 votes. Mr. C is elected. A **majority** of the vote is 50 percent plus one more vote.

(3) Structural changes, an amendment to the certificate, dissolution, sale of substantial assets, or merger usually requires two–thirds of the outstanding shares entitled to vote, rather than a majority of those present.

(4) Most statutes permit shareholders to act by written consent rather than at a meeting. Unanimous consent is usually required.

(5) Some states require cumulative voting for directors. Cumulative voting tends to favor minority stockholders. Some states allow corporations to have cumulative voting, if desired, but it has to be in the articles of incorporation.

(6) Most statutes require a majority of the shares entitled to vote to be a quorum. The corporation's articles of incorporation can set a higher or lower figure. Many statutes prohibit a quorum of less than one-third of the shares entitled to vote.

(7) Most statutes permit the setting of a higher vote to be placed in the certificate of incorporation. Some statutes say that an amendment to increase the vote can only be passed by the increased vote that the amendment is asking for.

Section 7.01, RMBCA, states that the annual meeting shall be held at the time stated or fixed in the bylaws. Failure to hold the annual meeting at the time fixed in the bylaws does not affect the validity of any corporate action.

Section 7.02, RMBCA, allows a special meeting of shareholders to be called by the board of directors or other parties authorized in the bylaws to call such meeting. Holders of at least 10 percent of all votes entitled to be cast can ask in writing for a special meeting. The articles of incorporation can fix a higher or lower amount with a maximum of 25 percent. Only the business listed in the notice can be conducted at special meetings.

Section 7.03, RMBCA, states that any shareholder, on application to the court, can ask for a meeting if an annual meeting was not held within six months after the end of the corporation's fiscal year or fifteen months after its last annual meeting.

Section 7.04, RMBCA, states that action can be taken without a meeting by a consent of all shareholders in writing. There must be unanimous consent for the action to be taken and it must be in writing.

Shareholders List for Meeting (Section 7.20, RMBCA)

(a) After fixing a record date for a meeting, a corporation shall prepare an alphabetical list of the names of all its stockholders who are entitled to notice of a shareholders' meeting. The list must be arranged by voting group (listing each voting group by class or series of shares) and show the address of and number of shares held by each shareholder.

(b) The shareholders' list must be available for inspection by any shareholder beginning two business days after notice of the meeting is given for which the list was prepared and continuing through the meeting at the corporation's principal office or at a place identified in the meeting notice in the city where the meeting is to be held. A shareholder, his agent, or attorney is entitled on written demand to inspect and copy the list during regular business hours and at his expense during the period it is available for inspection.

(c) The corporation shall make the shareholders' list available at the meeting, and any shareholder, his agent, or attorney is entitled to inspect the list at any time during the meeting or any adjournment thereof.

(d) If the corporation refuses to allow a shareholder, his agent, or attorney to inspect the shareholders' list before or at the meeting (or copy the list as permitted, if in good faith, and valid purpose) on application of the shareholder to the court in the county where the principal office is or its registered office, the court may summarily order the inspection or copying at the corporation's expense and may postpone the meeting for which the list was prepared until the inspection or copying is complete.

(e) Refusal or failure to prepare or make available the shareholders' list does not affect the validity of action taken at the meeting.

Voting Power of Shares

Each outstanding share, regardless of class, is entitled to one vote per share unless otherwise provided in the articles of incorporation (Section 7.21, RMBCA). The articles of incorporation may provide for multiple or fractional votes per share, may provide that some classes of shares are nonvoting on some or all matters, or that some classes have multiple or fractional votes per share while other classes have a single vote per share or different multiple or fractional votes per share, or that some classes constitute one or more separate voting groups and are entitled to vote separately on the matter.

The articles of incorporation may authorize the board of directors to create classes or series of shares with preferential rights, which may be voting or nonvoting in whole or in part (Section 6.02, RMBCA).

In the planning of a business venture, especially a closely held venture, multiple voting and nonvoting shares are a means of protecting financial interests of the founders. It is possible through these means to give persons with small financial contributions a large voting power within the corporation. It is customary, for example, to make classes of shares with preferential rights nonvoting, but the power to vote may be granted to those classes if **distributions** (dividends) are omitted for a specified period.

To Control Voting and/or Election of Directors

If one wants to be assured that minority shareholders or a group of minority shareholders will have representation on the board of directors, he or she should set up two or more classes of stock and provide that each class vote for and elect whatever number of directors he or she is looking to control, or a specified percentage of the board of directors. Then, issue each class or a majority of shares in each class to a different shareholder or group of shareholders. For example, Class One, Common Stock, shall have the power to elect three directors. Class Two, Common Stock, shall have the power to elect five directors (Section 703

New York Business Corporation Law explicitly allows this). Other statutes validate this by allowing one or more classes of stock with voting rights as stated in the certificate of incorporation. A class of stock may have voting power not in proportion to the investment of the class, or proprietary rights and no voting power, or voting power and no proprietary rights. Any combination can be used to accomplish the goal.

This system could be used where different shareholders invest different amounts in the corporation but both want equal voice in management.

HOW DIRECTORS ARE ELECTED

Every year at the annual stockholders' meeting directors are elected. If the board of directors consists of nine or more directors, most statutes permit the bylaws or certificate of incorporation to provide for the election to be divided into two groups where a portion of directors will be elected each year. If there are two groups, directors will be elected every other year for a two–year term. If there are three groups, directors will be elected every third year for a three–year term. Thus there will be staggered terms.

Staggered Terms for Directors (Section 8.06, RMBCA)

If there are nine or more directors, the articles of incorporation may provide for staggering their terms by dividing the total number of directors into two or three groups, with each group containing one-half or one-third of the total, as near as possible. In this event, the terms of directors in the first group expire at the first annual shareholders' meeting after their election, the terms of the second group expire at the second annual shareholders' meeting after their election, and the terms of the third group, if any, expire at the third annual shareholders' meeting after their election. At each annual shareholders' meeting held thereafter, directors are chosen for a term of two or three years to succeed those whose terms expire.

NONCUMULATIVE VOTING

If there is no cumulative voting, then it is sometimes referred to as straight voting. There is usually one vote per share; directors are elected by a **plurality** of the votes cast, by the shares entitled to vote in the election (Section 7.28, RMBCA). One vote per share is used unless otherwise provided in the articles of incorporation (such as in various classes and series of shares issued each with different voting rights). A **plurality** is the largest number of votes. A **majority** is 50 percent plus one vote. The certificate of incorporation and/or bylaws may require a higher percentage than a plurality for election of directors, but the higher requirement must be spelled out in the certificate of incorporation and/or bylaws. Shareholders do not have the right to cumulate their votes for directors unless the articles of incorporation so provide.

CUMULATIVE VOTING

In many states and under the RMBCA cumulative voting is allowed; i.e., it is permissible if so stated in the articles of incorporation. It is not mandatory. In a few states cumulative voting is mandatory. Cumulative voting will favor minority shareholders when all of the minority shareholders agree to vote all of their stock for the same director. To find out how many votes you have under cumulative voting, multiply the number of voting shares you have by the number of directors to be elected. You may then vote all for one director, or you may split up your votes. For example, you have 500 shares no par voting common stock. There are five directors to be elected. You multiply the number of voting shares which is 500 by the number of directors to be elected which is five, and you get 500 times five or 2,500 votes. In the absence of cumulative voting, a plurality of votes will win. For example, ten candidates are running to become directors; five are to be elected. The five with the most votes are elected unless the articles of incorporation call for a majority vote, or some other percentage, to elect directors.

Formulas for Minority to Elect One Director

Let us assume that corporation Green has 100,000 no par common voting shares outstanding. Five directors are to be elected. There is cumulative voting, and an individual wants to know how many shares he or she must own to elect one director. Take the number of outstanding shares and divide it by the number of directors to be elected plus one. Add one to that number and that is the number of shares needed to elect one director. For example, take the number of five directors, plus one, equals six, divide 100,000 by six, which comes to 16,666, add one, and 16,667 shares must be owned to elect one director. The formula would look like this:

$$\frac{\text{Number of shares outstanding}}{\text{Number of directors} + 1}$$

Add one to the above answer and that is the number of shares needed to elect one director.

To make it more costly for minority stockholders to win one seat on the board with cumulative voting, reduce the number of directors to be elected at one time. In the above example, 100,000 shares outstanding, five directors to be elected, 16,667 shares needed to be owned or 16⅔ percent of the outstanding stock. The election can be staggered so that three directors are elected one year and two the next. If three directors are to be elected, divide 100,000 by four, equals 25,000, plus one equals 25,001 shares needed to elect one director, or 25 percent of the outstanding stock. The same effect can be achieved by having different classes of stock with different voting rights. The same mathematics applies whether dealing with 100,000 outstanding shares or 10,000,000 outstanding shares. It can be easy or difficult depending on how the corporation articles are set up.

DEFECTIVE INCORPORATION

While the distinction of **de jure** and **de facto** corporations are no longer in modern statutes, the courts seem to follow the distinctions as a part of common law. A de jure corporation was one that was properly formed. A de facto corporation was one formed with a defect.

The following situations have occurred:

(1) The defendant was shown articles of incorporation duly executed months before investing in the corporation. He later invested and became a director and an officer believing the corporation had been chartered. He was told by the corporation's attorney that the articles of incorporation were filed. Because of a mix-up the articles were never filed. The court held the defendant not liable personally for corporate obligations. (Cranson v. IBM 234 MD. 477–1964).

(2) A defendant mails articles of incorporation, and then enters into a transaction in the corporate name. The letter is either delayed or returned by the secretary of state for corrections. Many state agencies follow the practice that receipt is the date of issuing the certificate; so that even though returned, when it is finally corrected, the certificate is issued as of the date of original receipt (backdated by the secretary of state).

(3) Liability has been escaped when a third party knew the certificate had not yet been filed but forced immediate signing of an agreement in the corporate name.

(4) Defendant represents that a corporation exists and enters into a contract in the corporate name. He knows no corporation exists because either he never filed or the articles were rejected and returned to him. Usually the third person assumed he was dealing solely with the corporation and did not rely on the personal assets of the defendant. A few courts will not impose personal liability. Most courts will impose personal liability.

(5) An inactive investor gives money to a promoter with instructions not to start or do business until incorporated. If the promoter does not wait for incorporation, the investor will not be held liable, but the promoter will be personally liable.

Liability for Preincorporation Transactions (Section 2.04, RMBCA)

All persons purporting to act as or on behalf of a corporation, knowing there was no incorporation under this act, are jointly and severally liable for all liabilities created while so acting.

LIMITED LIABILITY

It is the corporate form that provides limited liability. Without the corporation . . . personal liability exists. If a group has not done the things necessary to secure or retain de jure corporate status, then, they will not have corporate protection. They will be exposed to personal liability . . . (*McLean Bank v. Nelson*, 232 Va. 420 {1986}).

All persons who assume to act as a corporation without the authority of a certificate of incorporation issued by a state, shall be jointly and severally liable for all debts and liabilities incurred or arising as a result thereof. (Timberline Equipment Co. v. Davenport, 267 Or. 64 [1973])

Three requirements are typical for a de facto corporation. (1) A statute must be in existence whereby incorporation is legally possible, (2) A colorable attempt to comply with the statute has been made, and (3) There has been some actual use or exercise of corporate privileges.

ULTRA VIRES

Ultra Vires means that a corporation is acting beyond its powers granted by the state. Prior to modern statutes, the certificate of incorporation had to list each and every power the corporation was to have. If the power was not listed, the corporation could not do that act. If it did, it was an ultra vires act and could be upset by the courts for lack of power to perform same. Modern statutes have moved away from the ultra vires doctrine. Most states no longer require powers to be listed. Instead, there is a sentence inserted in the certificate of incorporation that grants the corporation the power to do all things necessary to carry on its intended business.

Ultra Vires (Section 3.04, RMBCA)

(a) Except as provided in subsection (b), the validity of corporate action may not be challenged on the ground that the corporation lacks or lacked power to act.

(b) A corporation's power to act may be challenged:
   (1) in a proceeding by a shareholder against the corporation to enjoin the act;
   (2) in a proceeding by the corporation, directly, derivatively, or through a receiver, trustee, or other legal representative, against an incumbent or former director, officer, employee, or agent of the corporation; or
   (3) in a proceeding by the Attorney General under Section 14.30.

(c) In a shareholder's proceeding under section (b)(1) to enjoin an unauthorized corporate act, the court may enjoin or set aside the act, if equitable and if all affected persons are parties to the proceeding, and may award damages for loss (other than anticipated profits) suffered by the corporation or another party because of enjoining the unauthorized act.

PIERCING THE CORPORATE VEIL

Piercing the corporate veil means removing the protection of the corporation and leaving the officers and directors personally liable on a joint and several basis. The courts will do this to prevent fraud, wrongdoing, and circumventing of the law. Generally, it is in closely held corporations and/or parent-subsidiary situations. In parent-subsidiary situations the court can make the parent corporation liable for the debts of the subsidiary corporation.

For example, Corporation X is in the business of manufacturing wood chairs. There are three stockholders and three directors. John is president, a director, and a stockholder. Frank is secretary, a director, and a stockholder. Tom is treasurer, a director, and a stockholder. The corporate bank account is with ABC bank. Corporation X leases the space it uses for manufacturing and offices. The lease is assignable. The corporation has been in business three years and is in financial difficulty. It owes suppliers $175,000, has accounts receivable of $35,000, and has other debts of $75,000.

John, Frank, and Tom, being all the directors, officers, and stockholders of Corporation X, attempt to obtain a loan from their bank. They are turned down for not having sufficient security. The tools and machines they use to manufacture are old, in need of repair, and were purchased secondhand. They are faced with a number of options. First, to obtain a lawyer and file for the bankruptcy protection and/or a Chapter Seven. The attorney wants a $2,500 retainer for the bankruptcy filing. Second, they could put more money of their own into the business as a loan. None of them have this financial ability. They have been taking one-half their normal salaries for the past two months to try and keep the business alive. Third, they could just close and wind up the business.

After considering the options above, they decide on a different course of action. They will form a new corporation and call it B Corporation. They will assign the lease to the new corporation. All of them will be officers and directors of the new corporation and keep the same titles. The bank account, although small, will be transferred from Corporation X to B Corporation. B Corporation will open an account in the same bank. They will continue with the same customers and just bill them from now on as B Corporation.

A creditor sues Corporation X and obtains a judgment. When the sheriff comes to Corporation X to levy against it on the judgment, he is told that Corporation X is out of business. They show the sheriff the sign that says B Corporation. The sheriff returns the execution as unsatisfied since Corporation X is no longer in business. The creditor tells his attorney that B Corporation is really Corporation X using another name. The attorney brings an action in court to pierce the corporate veil of B Corporation. After the hearing, the judge orders that B Corporation pay the judgment of Corporation X as B Corporation is really an extension of Corporation X. It has the same officers, same directors, same bank account, same furniture and equipment, and same customers. Therefore, the judge pierces the corporate veil and B Corporation is liable for all the debts of Corporation X. Any other decision would allow fraud to have taken place.

COMMINGLING OF CORPORATE FUNDS

Commingling corporate funds means to mix private funds with the funds of the corporation. A husband and wife, or two or more friends, or relatives, own all the stock in a small corporation they run. They use the corporate bank account to pay all corporate debts and to pay their personal mortgages on their houses and cars. They use the corporate account to pay all their personal bills. Occasionally, they deposit some of their personal funds into the corporate account to cover checks they wrote. This is commingling. If a judgment is rendered against the corporation and returned unsatisfied for lack of assets to levy upon, the judgment creditor can bring an action to pierce the corporate veil. If pierced by the court, the corporation and the stockholders, officers, and directors, would become personally liable jointly and severally for the judgment. One cannot commingle funds or assets with the corporation. Two corporations cannot commingle funds or their veils may be pierced by the court.

PROXY

A shareholder can vote shares either in person or by **proxy.** A proxy is an appointment from the shareholder, agent, or attorney-in-fact of the shareholder to vote or otherwise act for the shareholder by signing an appointment form or by electronic transmission. An electronic transmission must contain information from which one can determine that it was actually authorized by the shareholder. The appointment is valid for eleven months unless terminated sooner by the shareholder. A longer period can be specified in the appointment. The shareholder can revoke the proxy at any time prior to voting or acting by the proxy. (A form for a proxy can be found in Appendix F.)

Proxy voting is necessary in publicly held corporations as very often the shareholders' meeting is hundreds, or thousands of miles from where the shareholder is. The shareholder must travel to the shareholders' meeting at his or her own expense. Therefore, it can be economically unfeasible to attend meetings to vote.

Proxy Solicitation

Proxy solicitation is the method systematically used to contact shareholders to obtain their votes which they accomplish by executing the proxy form sent to them, returning it, and authorizing named persons to vote their shares either as stated in the proxy or by the shareholders' instructions.

Proxies (Section 7.22, RMBCA)

(a) A shareholder may vote his shares in person or by proxy.

(b) A shareholder, agent for the shareholder, or attorney-in-fact, may appoint a proxy to vote or otherwise act for him or her by signing an appointment form, or by an electronic transmission. An electronic transmission must contain or be accompanied by information from which one can determine that the shareholder, the shareholder's agent, or the shareholder's attorney-in-fact, authorized the electronic transfer.

(c) An appointment of a proxy is effective when a signed appointment form or an electronic transmission of the appointment is received by the inspector of election or the officer or agent of the corporation authorized to tabulate votes. An appointment is valid for eleven months unless a longer period is expressly provided in the appointment.

(d) An appointment of a proxy is revocable unless the appointment form or electronic transmission conspicuously states that it is irrevocable and the appointment is coupled with an interest. Appointments coupled with an interest include the appointment of:

    (1) a pledgee;

    (2) a person who purchased or agreed to purchase the shares;

    (3) a creditor of the corporation who extended it credit under terms requiring the appointment;

    (4) an employee of the corporation whose employment contract requires the appointment; or

    (5) a party to a voting agreement created under Section 7.31.

(e) The death or incapacity of the shareholder appointing a proxy does not affect the right of the corporation to accept the proxy's authority unless notice of death or incapacity is received by the secretary or other officer or agent authorized to tabulate votes before the proxy exercises his authority under the appointment.

(f) An appointment made irrevocable under Subsection (d) is revoked when the interest with which it is coupled is extinguished.

(g) A transferee for value of shares subject to an irrevocable appointment may revoke the appointment if he did not know of its existence when he acquired the shares, and the existence of the irrevocable appointment was not noted conspicuously on the certificate representing the shares or on the information statement for shares without certificates.

(h) Subject to Section 7.24 and to any express limitation on the proxy's authority stated in the appointment form or electronic transmission, a corporation is entitled to accept the proxy's vote or other action as that of the shareholder making the appointment.

Securities Exchange Act, 1934, Rule 14(a)

This section covers a series of proxy rules with respect to securities registered pursuant to the act. Securities registered under the act must abide by these proxy rules for solicitation. Shareholders are entitled to full disclosure with reference to matters they are being asked to approve, such as mergers, certificate amendments, or election of directors. You must receive a written proxy statement containing all pertinent information. No false or misleading information is permitted. The United States Supreme Court has ruled that a shareholder can bring either a direct or derivative action for violation of the Proxy Rules (*J.I. Case v. Borak*, 377 U.S. 426). Where a shareholder seeks to set aside or enjoin a transaction approved by the shareholders on the ground that the approval was solicited by a proxy statement that involved misstatements or omissions, he or she need do nothing more to prove causation than to prove materiality (*Mills v. Electric Lite Co.*, 396 U.S. 375). Material facts include "all facts which a reasonable shareholder might consider important" (512 F.2d 330).

SHAREHOLDERS RIGHT TO INSPECT BOOKS AND RECORDS

Some states require the shareholder to have held shares for at least six months prior to making a demand to inspect the books. A few states require the shareholder to own at least 5 percent of the outstanding shares prior to inspecting the books. The states with either of these requirements usually impose a penalty on the corporation for failure to allow the shareholder to inspect and make copies of the records. The penalty is in the form of a fine, and the fine is usually turned over to the stockholder. The amount of the fine varies from $50 per day to $200 per day for each day denied access to the records.

The RMBCA changes the above and grants inspection rights to all stockholders, without regard to the amount of stock owned as long as the demand is made in good faith and for a proper purpose. The penalty is also not in modern statutes. Obviously you cannot obtain trade secrets. You cannot expect to buy one share of Coca Cola and expect to obtain their formula. A good purpose means something concerned with your investment. You cannot obtain a list of the stockholders if you intend to resell it. That is not a good purpose.

Inspection of Records by Shareholders (Section 16.02, RMBCA)

(a) A shareholder of a corporation is entitled to inspect and copy, during regular business hours at the corporation's principal office, any of the records of the corporation described in 16.01(e) if he gives the corporation written notice of his demand at least five business days before the date on which he wishes to inspect and copy.

(b) A shareholder of a corporation is entitled to inspect and copy, during regular business hours at a reasonable location specified by the corporation, any of the following records of the corporation if the shareholder meets the requirements of subsection (c) and gives the corporation written notice of his demand at least five days before the date on which he wishes to inspect and copy.

   (1) excerpts from minutes of any meeting of the board of directors, records of any action of a committee of the board of directors while acting in place of the board of directors on behalf of the corporation, minutes of any meeting of the shareholders, and records of action taken by the shareholders or board of directors without a meeting, to the extent not subject to inspection under section 16.02(a);

   (2) accounting records of the corporation; and

   (3) the record of shareholders.

(c) A shareholder may inspect and copy the records described in Subsection (b) only if:

   (1) his demand is made in good faith and for a proper purpose;

   (2) he describes with reasonable particularity his purpose and the records he desires to inspect; and

   (3) the records are directly connected with his purpose.

(d) The right of inspection granted by this section may not be abolished or limited by a corporation's articles of incorporation or bylaws.

(e) This section does not affect:
  (1) the right of a shareholder to inspect records under Section 7.20 or, if the shareholder is in litigation with the corporation, to the same extent as any other litigant;
  (2) the power of a court, independently of this act, to compel the production of corporate records for examination.

(f) For purposes of this section, "shareholder" includes a beneficial owner whose shares are held in a voting trust or by a nominee on his behalf.

SCOPE OF INSPECTION RIGHTS

A shareholder's agent or attorney has the same inspection rights as the shareholder. There is the right to receive or make copies. The corporation may have a reasonable charge for copies (RMBCA 16.03). The corporation must furnish shareholders an annual financial statement (RMBCA 16.20). If the corporation indemnifies or advances expenses to a director under Section 8.51, 8.52, or 8.54, the corporation must report the same to the shareholders prior to the next shareholders' meeting (RMBCA 16.21).

Some corporations have a procedure that must be complied with prior to shareholders being permitted to inspect the books and records of the corporation. As long as the procedure is reasonable the shareholder must follow it to obtain permission to inspect. If the shareholder believes the procedure is dilatory or not in good faith, then, the remedy is an action to be brought to impose sanctions on the corporation. Sanctions would be fines for failure to permit inspection. The inspection must take place at the office of the corporation where the books and records are located. The inspection is during normal business hours. Shareholder may not see trade secrets or corporate sensitive matters. An example would be if the corporation was in merger talks, no information concerning the merger need be disclosed.

SUMMARY

Shareholders have a right to vote and a right to receive information from the corporation including an annual statement, financial statements, and profit and loss statements. The right to inspect the corporate books is an inherent right; however, the shareholder must show good faith and good cause for wanting to see and/or make copies of the records. Naturally, a shareholder cannot obtain trade secrets when inspecting the books. You cannot buy shares of Coca Cola stock for the purpose of trying to obtain their formula. That would not be good faith or a good purpose to inspect books and records. We discussed cumulative and noncumulative voting. We learned that cumulative voting favors minority stockholders, and, if all minority stockholders agree to vote all their shares for one director, they are almost totally assured of electing that one director. Directors are elected by a plurality of votes, not by a majority. Stockholders that cannot attend the annual stockholders' meeting can vote by appointing a proxy to vote on their behalf. When setting up the bylaws, you may want to consider the staggering of the election of directors. Also, if you act as a corporation without the benefit of a charter, you will incur personal liability. Different series of stocks can be issued carrying different kinds of voting rights. Piercing the corporate veil was discussed, removing the protection of the corporation and leaving officers and directors personally liable on a joint and several basis.

CASES

Inspection of Records

COMPAQ COMPUTER v. HORTON
Delaware Supreme Court, 1993
631 A.2d. 1.

Charles E. Horton had owned 112 shares of common Compaq stock since December 6, 1990. Compaq refused to permit Horton to inspect its stock ledger and other related materials.

On July 22, 1991, Horton and 78 other parties sued Compaq, 15 of its advisers, and certain management personnel in Texas. They allege that Compaq, its advisors, and certain personnel violated the Texas Deceptive Trade Practices Consumer Protection Act and the Texas Security Act. Plaintiffs also charge defendants with a continuing pattern of misconduct involving common law fraud, conspiracy, aiding and abetting, fraudulent concealment, and breach of fiduciary duty. All claims arise from the contention that Compaq misled the public as to the true value of its stock at a time when members of management were selling their own shares of Compaq stock. Plaintiffs seek individual damages.

On September 22, 1992, Horton, by counsel, delivered a letter demanding to inspect Compaq's stock ledger and related material for the period October 1, 1990, to June 30, 1991, to the extent that such information was available and in the control of Compaq. The purpose of the request was to allow Horton to communicate with other shareholders of Compaq, inform them of the pending shareholders suit, and ascertain if any of them would desire to become associated with the suit and assume a pro rata share of the litigation expenses.

On September 30, 1992, Compaq refused the demand, stating the purpose was not a proper purpose under section 220(b) of the General Corporation Law of the State of Delaware. In the Court of Chancery, Compaq conceded all technical requirements were met for the demand under the statute, but that the purpose was not proper for inspecting the records.

On November 12, 1992, the Court of Chancery ordered Compaq to permit Horton to inspect and copy the stockholder lists and related information listed in the demand letter. The Vice Chancellor ruled that even though the Texas litigation is neither derivative, nor brought for the benefit of Compaq, it concerns alleged corporate wrongdoing that affected the value of Horton's Compaq stock. Accordingly, it is a proper purpose related to his interest as a Compaq stockholder.

A shareholders' common law right to inspect the stock ledger is codified in 8 Del C Section 220(b) of the General Corporation Law. Under this section when a stockholder complies with the statutory requirements as to form and manner of making a demand, then the burden is on the corporation to prove the purpose is improper. If there is any doubt, it must be resolved in favor of the statutory right of the stockholder to have an inspection.

Horton alleges it is in the interests of Compaq's stockholders to know that acts of mismanagement and fraud are continuing and cannot be overlooked, and that a large filing of claims by individuals might well discourage further acts of misconduct, and in this context it is related to the interest of Horton as a stockholder.

A stockholder's right to inspect and copy a stockholder's list is not absolute. It is a qualified right depending on the facts presented (Loft, 156 A 172). Where litigation is brought against a corporation in good faith to redress supposed corporate wrongs, public policy would be on the side of those who have invested their money. Thus, a proper purpose may be stated in these circumstances even though no direct benefit flows to the corporation.

Compaq has failed to meet the burden of proving an improper purpose. Accordingly, the trial court concluded that plaintiff's desire to contact other stockholders and solicit their involvement in the litigation was a proper purpose reasonably related to one's interest as a stockholder. We agree and affirm.

Maximization of Shareholders' Wealth

DODGE v. FORD MOTOR CO.
204 Mich. 459, 170 N.W. 668 (1919)

This is one of the most famous of all corporation law cases. It concerns what is now known as corporate social responsibility.

Incorporated in 1903 with a capital of $150,000, the capital was increased to $2,000,000 in 1908. Henry Ford owned 58 percent of the Ford stock and controlled the board of directors. Two Dodge brothers owned 10 percent, and five other stockholders owned the balance. From 1908 on, it paid a regular annual dividend of $1.2 million, and between December 1911 and October 1915 it paid special dividends totaling $41 million. At the close of its 1916 fiscal year, Henry Ford, who controlled the board, declared it to be the settled policy of the company not to pay in the future any special dividends, but to put back into the business for the future earnings of the company, all other than the regular dividend of $1.2 million. "My ambition," declared Mr. Ford, "is to employ still more men and spread the benefits of this industrial system to the greatest possible number to help them build up their lives and their homes. To do this we are putting the greatest share of our profits back into the business." At the time of this announcement Ford had a surplus of $112 million, including $52.5 million in cash and $1.3 million in municipal bonds. The Dodge brothers then brought an action to compel a dividend equal to 75 percent of the accumulated surplus, and a restraining order for the proposed expansion. The trial court ordered Ford to declare a $19.3 million dividend, equal to half its cash surplus, minus special dividends paid between the complaint and July 1917. The Michigan Supreme Court affirmed this part of the trial court's decree.

Ford Motor Co. had a general policy to reduce the price of cars every year while maintaining or improving quality. The plan was to reduce the cost from $440 to $360 at a cost of $48 million.

Henry Ford felt the company made too much money and that a sharing with the public by reducing price ought to be undertaken. The fact that the company is organized for profit does not prevent the existence of implied powers to carry on with humanitarian motives and such charitable works as are incidental to the main business of the corporation.

We are not satisfied that the alleged motives of the directors, insofar as they are reflected in the conduct of business, menaces the interests of the shareholders. It is enough to say, perhaps, that the court of equity is at all times open to complaining shareholders having a just grievance.

No Charter—Personal Liability

TIMBERLINE EQUIPMENT CO. v. DAVENPORT
Supreme Court of Oregon, 1973
267 Or.64, 514 P.2d.1109

On January 22, 1970, Dr. Bennet signed articles of incorporation for Aero-Fabb Co. The original articles were not in accord with the statutes and, therefore, no certificate of incorporation was issued for the corporation until June 21, 1970, after new articles were filed. Leases were entered into for equipment and rental fees due for the period between January 22 and June 12. Dr. Bennet alleged as a defense that the rentals were to a de facto corporation and no personal liability should be on him. He also alleged that plaintiff was estopped from denying that he rented to a corporation.

The court held the principle of de facto corporation no longer existed in Oregon and that all persons who assume to act as a corporation without the authority of a certificate of incorporation issued by the Corporation Commissioner, shall be jointly and severally liable for all debts and liabilities incurred or arising thereof.

Evidence all supports that the finding that Dr. Bennet was a person who assumed to act for the organization, and the conclusion of the trial court that Dr. Bennet is personally liable, is hereby affirmed.

Inspection of Records

BERGMANN v. LEE DATA CORP.
Court of Appeals, MN, 1991
467 N.W. 2d. 636

Bergmann was an employee and shareholder of Lee Data Corp. After being fired for sexual harassment, he sued the company for defamation, emotional distress, and breach of contract. Bergmann sent interrogatories to the company asking about all charges of discrimination or sexual harassment that had been made against Lee's employees.

Two days later, as a shareholder, Bergmann requested to inspect the bylaws, charter, list of directors, list of shareholders, stock option records, information regarding sexual harassment, and discrimination complaints against Lee, the number of female and minority employees, and records relating to remedial actions taken to eliminate discrimination and sexual harassment. The stated purpose for the request was to identify and evaluate misconduct by Lee's officers. Lee sent Bergmann a list of shareholders and directors but refused to send the other material. Bergmann then sought injunctive relief to force Lee to comply. The trial court denied Bergmann's request.

A proper purpose is one reasonably related to the person's interest as a shareholder. Valuation of shares, determination of management competence, and communication with other shareholders concerning the corporation are proper purposes.

The corporation has the burden of establishing an improper purpose. The interests Bergmann is pursuing are not created by being a shareholder. Bergmann's request serves no purpose other than the personal interests of Bergmann. Lee alleged the actual purpose was to improve

Bergmann's position in the pending litigation by seeking documents concerning sexual harassment and discrimination.

Purely personal purposes are not reasonably related to interest as a stockholder. Decision affirmed.

WORDS TO KNOW

beneficial stockholder
commingling
commingling funds
cumulative voting
de facto corporation
de jure corporation
distributions

majority
nonassessable
piercing the corporate veil
plurality
proxy
ultra vires act

REVIEW QUESTIONS

1. What is an ultra vires act?
2. What is the duty of the board of directors with reference to shareholders?
3. How many different kinds of shares of stock can a corporation issue?
4. What is a series or class of stock?
5. When will a shareholder be personally liable for corporate debts?
6. In a public corporation, who receives notice of the annual stockholders' meeting?
7. How often and where must the annual shareholders' meeting be held?
8. Other than the annual meeting, when will shareholders have to approve the action of the board of directors?
9. Can shares of stock be issued without a stock certificate?
10. What is a majority? What is a plurality?
11. When is a majority vote necessary?
12. When is a plurality vote used?
13. How can you be assured of winning one seat on the board of directors?
14. Why would you want to stagger the election of the board of directors?
15. How do you stagger the election of the board of directors?
16. What is cumulative voting?
17. Who does cumulative voting benefit?
18. What is a de jure corporation? What is a de facto corporation?
19. If you act as a corporation without having a charter from a state, what is your liability?
20. What does piercing the corporate veil mean?
21. What does commingling of funds mean? What are the results of commingling?
22. What is a proxy? When is it used?
23. When does a shareholder have the right to inspect the books and records of the corporation?

Short Essays

1. You and five friends formed the XYZ Corporation ten years ago. You all have an equal stock ownership in the corporation, and the five of you are the sole officers and directors of the corporation. The present capitalization of the corporation is $1,000,000. You and the other board members are interested in selling stock to the public to raise $20 million to expand the business. The big concern is that you will have to issue shares, and you are all concerned about losing control of the board of directors. Is there anything you and your friends can do to solve this problem? You want to obtain the additional funds, and you do not want to lose control. Explain in detail.

2. Your corporation is a distributor of television sets. The Big T Corporation was one of your better accounts. They owe your corporation $700,000. A few months ago they offered to settle this debt with you for $100,000, advising that they are in serious financial trouble and owe a few million dollars. If they are unable to settle all their claims, they will have to close shop and go out of business. It is now six months later; and although you were willing to discuss the settlement proposal in detail with them, they kept putting you off saying they had to settle all claims to save the business. You then had your attorney bring suit against The Big T Corporation and you obtained a default judgment. Your attorney issued an execution to the Sheriff and has just advised you that the Sheriff said they are out of business. In the location is another business carrying on a similar business but their name is The Big Z. You have checked other locations and they are all now The Big Z. Making inquiries in the industry you have learned that the same officers and directors from The Big T are the officers and directors of The Big Z. What instructions can you give your attorney to aid in collecting this debt?

3. You are a minority shareholder in a corporation. The corporation has cumulative voting. Four directors are to be elected. You have 3,000 shares of common stock. The majority shareholders own 51,000 shares of common stock. All the minority shareholders combined own 49,000 shares. Is there any way that you can elect at least one director? Explain fully.

4. You are a minority shareholder. You would like to keep in touch with other minority shareholders. Is this a legitimate reason to ask for a copy of the stockholders' list from the corporate secretary? How do you go about obtaining a list of all shareholders?

5. You and five friends formed the XYZ corporation. You completed the certificate of incorporation and mailed it to the Secretary of State. While waiting for the charter to arrive by mail, you rent office space for the corporation and you execute the lease as president. You also buy furniture, office equipment, and the necessary ovens, etc., to run the business which is to be a retail bakery. You bill everything to the corporation. The cost is about $70,000. As president you sign all the orders. Two of your friends are bread and pastry bakers; they are two of the five who will be shareholders. Ten days after you send in the certificate of incorporation it is returned by the Secretary of State as it does not have all the information required by statute. When the two bakers learn that the corporation has not been chartered, they advise you they are going to take jobs with a bakery in town and will not be able to work for the corporation. After a few days you realize you cannot continue without bakers and are unable to hire any or convince any to invest money in the corporation. You close the office and retail store you rented. All the creditors are now suing you personally for the corporate contracts you signed for the leases, furniture, and equipment. Your defense is that there is no individual liability, and that the liability is the corporation's, if any. What would be the result?

CHAPTER

9

CAPITAL AND DISTRIBUTION

O BJECTIVES

After completing this chapter, you will be able to:

1. Know what a certified security is.
2. Know what an uncertificated security is and how it differs from a certified security.
3. Tell the difference between par value and no par value stock.
4. Explain what happens when a certified security is lost.
5. Know what treasury stock is and where it comes from.
6. List all the different kinds of dividends.
7. Explain what "distribution" means.
8. Tell who becomes liable if a dividend is improperly distributed.
9. Know if a shareholder can keep a dividend improperly declared and distributed.
10. Transfer a security.
11. List the warranties given when a security is sold.
12. List the warranties given when you seek transfer of a security.

13. Tell what statutes pertain to corporate capital and distribution.
14. Know the effects of a forged endorsement on a certificated security.
15. Explain the difference between the two definitions of bankruptcy.

INTRODUCTION

At one point in time the price of a share of stock was its par value. All shares carried a par value. Sometimes the stock could not be **issued** at par value. Issued means sold by the corporation. The purchase price is paid to the corporation. When the corporation sells stock for the first time it is called **equity capital** and the "**original issue.**" If the real value of the stock was less than par, then the corporation could not sell at par, and would sell at a lower price. When the corporation sold at a price below par it was called "**discount stock.**" If the real value was more than par, then the corporation would sell at above par value. **Bonus stock** was stock issued without payment, possibly as a bonus for purchasing another class of security. **Watered stock** was issued for property alleged to be equal or greater than the par value of the stock, but that actually was worth less than par. Discount and bonus stock could also be called watered shares. The term *watered stock* came from traders and ranchers who used to water their livestock before selling them to get them to weigh more.

CORPORATE LIABILITY

A shareholder obtaining watered stock from the corporation would not be liable for additional monies in a contract action, as all was paid pursuant to that contract. As a matter of corporation law, a recipient of watered stock was often liable to the corporation for the difference between par value and the lower payment made. If payment was in property to the corporation, the difference between the actual value of the property (usually the value was overstated to obtain the shares) and the par value of the stock would be the measure of damages. This same liability was from the stockholders to creditors.

LOW PAR STOCK

Today, par value is not the price for which the stock will sell at the original issue. It is only the price at or above for the first sale by the corporation (original issue). If the stock sells on the original issue for $15 and carries a $3 par value, it is called **low par stock**. After the first sale, there is no relationship between sales price and par value. A $3 par value can sell for $1 after the original issue. Statutes have usually been amended in most states to allow for the issuance of no par stock. In these states the watered stock issue is practically nonexistent, since watered stock is based on stock being issued for less than par value. Many states still allow par value stock as well as no par value stock. In these states there can be liability for watered stock as a result of bad planning or the improper use of high par values on stock. In all states a shareholder is liable for the price the shareholder agreed to pay for the original issue, and this can be enforced by the corporation as well as by creditors of the corporation.

CALIFORNIA AND THE RMBCA, REFERENCE PAR VALUE

California and the RMBCA eliminated the concept of par value for all practical purposes. Since shares do not need a par value under Section 6.21, RMBCA, there is no minimum price for the issuance of shares. Therefore, there is no watered stock and no liability for issuing shares below an arbitrarily fixed price.

Distributions (Section 1.40 (6), RMBCA)

(6) "**Distribution**" means a direct or indirect transfer of money or other property (except its own shares) or incurrence of indebtedness by a corporation to or for the benefit of its shareholders in respect of any of its shares. A distribution may be in the form of a declaration or payment of a dividend; a purchase, redemption, or other acquisition of shares; a distribution of indebtedness; or otherwise.

Section 1.40 (6) defines distributions to include all transfers of money or other property made by a corporation to any shareholder in respect to the corporation's shares, except mere exchanges in the unit of interest such as share dividends and share splits. A distribution includes the declaration or payment of a dividend, a purchase by a corporation of its own shares, a distribution of evidence of indebtedness or promissory notes of the corporation, and a distribution in voluntary or involuntary liquidation.

The term "indirect" in the definition of "distribution" is intended to include transactions like the repurchase of parent company shares by a subsidiary whose actions are controlled by the parent. It also is intended to include any other transactions in which the substance is clearly the same as a typical dividend or share repurchase, no matter how structured or labeled.

DIVIDENDS

Shareholders receive funds from a corporation in two ways. One is through dividends; the second is through repurchase of shares by the corporation. Corporate law and the remedies available to creditors have usually set limits on both of these distributions through the use of financial tests.

(1) Insolvency test—use of the **equity definition**, whether the corporation is capable of paying its debts on time (used by courts of equity); or the **bankruptcy,** definition liabilities exceed assets (used by the bankruptcy court). If either definition applies, the corporation is insolvent. In essence the equity definition says that anytime a business cannot pay its debts on time it can be declared insolvent; it is used by the court of equity and certified public accountants (CPA). The bankruptcy court uses the definition that one is insolvent when their liabilities are more than their assets. The New York Business Corporation Law, Section 510 does not permit a dividend to be declared if the corporation is insolvent. It also forbids a dividend if its payment would make the corporation insolvent. Dividends under this section can only be paid out of surplus capital. California statutes do not have provision for an insolvency test.

RMBCA, Section 6.40, retains restrictions on distributions built around both the traditional equity insolvency and balance sheet tests of earlier statutes. RMBCA has provision to hold directors personally liable for improper distributions (RMBCA 6.40 and 8.33). The Federal Bankruptcy Act insures the trustee or other representative in bankruptcy the ability to recover for improperly distributed creditors' funds.

(2) Balance sheet test—based on whether the corporation's assets exceed its liabilities plus its capital. In corporation accounting, equity has traditionally been divided into stated capital and surplus.

(3) Nimble dividend test—based on the corporation's current profits. Dividends paid out of current profits are called **nimble dividends**. Delaware General Corporation Law, Section 170, allows dividends to be paid out of surplus or out of current profits.

(4) Earned surplus test—based on corporation's accumulated profits. The RMBCA has dropped the earned surplus test, and most states that once followed it have also dropped it.

Earned Surplus consists of the corporation's undistributed net profits, income, gains, and losses, computed from its date of incorporation.

Surplus is the amount by which the net assets of a corporation exceed its stated capital.

Net assets equal the amount by which the total assets of a corporation exceed its total debts.

Stated capital is all of the consideration the corporation has received for its issued stock, excepting the amount allocated to capital surplus, but including any amount to stated capital transferred when a stock dividend was declared.

Capital surplus is the entire surplus of the corporation other than earned surplus. This may come from an allocation of part of the no par value stock, from any consideration in excess of par value stock, or from a reappraisal of corporate assets.

Dividend Payments

Generally there is one of four factors involved in dividend payments.

(1) Some corporations have dividend payout ratios developed over a long period of time which are used to maintain a dividend on a steady basis.

(2) Focusing on dividend changes, a $3 dividend is a major decision if last year's dividend was $1; but not that major a decision if last year's payout was $3. A lesser dividend would be a major decision.

(3) Corporations are fearful of making a dividend change that may not be continued in the future.

(4) Corporations like to keep payments steady (the same) or slowly rising. Short–lived earnings changes are unlikely to affect dividend payouts.

Therefore, dividend payments depend partly on current earnings and partly on last year's dividend. Dividends last year depend partly on earnings and partly on the previous dividend. When current earnings have increased steadily for a period of time, there would be the greatest probability for a dividend increase. Managers have to feel that the current windfall in earnings is going to be steady for the next few years to increase or begin a dividend payout.

Dividends anticipate future earnings so an announcement of a dividend cut will usually be followed by a falling (lower) stock price. Conversely, dividend increase announcements will usually be followed by a rise in the stock price. The dividend is a sign of future earnings: a rise in dividend causes a rise in stock price; a lower dividend causes a fall in stock price. **Market efficiency** dictates that all information available to investors is quickly reflected in stock prices. Stock splits, dividend announcements, etc., are all quickly reflected in the stock price because of market efficiency.

Dividends and other distributions are determined solely in the discretion of the board of directors as to when and if declared, as well as to amounts and frequency of payouts. Naturally, the distributions will take into consideration the bylaws, certificate of incorporation, state statutes, contract rights of stockholders, the corporation's working capital requirements, tax consequences, and shareholder expectations. Creditors are usually protected by contract rights incorporated in their lending instruments. Federal bankruptcy laws and state fraudulent conveyance acts also protect creditors.

Directors Liability for Declaring Improper Dividends or Distributions

A director is personally liable to the corporation if voting for or assenting to a distribution or dividend in violation of the statute or the articles of incorporation (RMBCA, Section 8.33[a]). Normally the director would be liable to the corporation and/or creditors, but the RMBCA sets the liability on the corporation. The damages that the corporation would receive equal the excess amount distributed from the amount that should have legally been distributed. A director would not be liable if acting in good faith, with due care, and reasonably believed to be acting in the best interests of the corporation (RMBCA, Section 8.30). A director can rely in good faith upon financial statements prepared by the corporation's officers, public accountant, or finance committee. These statements must be prepared pursuant to acceptable accounting practices and must be reasonable to rely on RMBCA, Section 6.40(d).

A shareholder receiving an improperly distributed distribution may be obligated to repay the money received to the corporation. It would depend on the good or bad faith of the stockholder. For example, was it known that the dividend or distribution was improper? Was the corporation insolvent at the time it was made, or did it make the corporation insolvent? If any of the above are affirmative, repayment will have to be made. Statutory liability of the directors does not relieve the stockholder from having to make repayment in the above circumstances. Most cases allow a stockholder who was in good faith without any knowledge of an illegal act to keep the dividend or distribution.

Liability for Unlawful Distribution (Section 8.33, RMBCA)

(a) A director who votes for or assents to a distribution made in violation of Section 6.40 or the articles of incorporation is personally liable to the corporation for the amount of the distribution that exceeds what would have been distributed without violating Section 6.40 or the articles of incorporation if it is established that he or she did not perform his or her duties in compliance with Section 8.30. In any proceeding commenced under this section, a director has all of the defenses ordinarily available to a director.

(b) A director held liable under subsection (a) for an unlawful distribution is entitled to contribution:

(1) from every other director who could be held liable under subsection (a) for the unlawful distribution; and

(2) from each shareholder for the amount the shareholder accepted knowing the distribution was made in violation of Section 6.40 or the articles of incorporation.

(c) A proceeding under this section is barred unless it is commenced within two years after the date on which the effect of the distribution was measured under Section 6.40 (e) or (g).

Kinds of Dividends

There are cash dividends, stock dividends, stock splits, property dividends, liquidating dividends, acquisition of shares, and redemption of shares. Kind, regularity, and amount, when declared and when paid are all determined by the discretion of the board of directors.

Cash Dividends   Cash dividends must be paid from legally available funds, and are generally paid on a regular basis and in regular intervals. The most common dividend amounts vary depending on the board of directors and the earnings of the corporation. There can also be a sporadic payment. Once a cash dividend is properly and lawfully declared, it is considered a debt owed by the corporation to the shareholders. Therefore, once declared, a cash dividend cannot be revoked without the consent of all stockholders. A stock dividend, however, can be revoked by the corporation prior to distribution.

Stock Dividend   Like a stock split, a stock dividend is not considered a distribution. The assets of the corporation are no less after a stock dividend. The interests of the shareholders are still the same. The legal results are similar to a stock split. For example, there are 100 shares issued and outstanding. You own 10 shares. The board of directors declares a 15 percent stock dividend. Before the stock dividend, you owned 10 out of 100 shares or 10 percent of the stock issued and outstanding. After a stock dividend of 15 percent, you get an additional 1.5 shares. You now have 11.5 shares out of 115 issued and outstanding shares. This is still 10 percent. An incorporation statute recognizing par value stock and stated capital would result in a transfer from surplus to stated capital of an amount equal to the par value of the stock dividend.

RMBCA, Section 6.23 (b), prohibits issuing a share dividend to a class of stock other than the one owned because it would dilute the equity of the other class. Therefore, a share dividend may not be issued to holders of another class unless (1) the articles of incorporation expressly provide for so issuing, (2) a majority of the votes entitled to be cast by the class to be issued approves the issue, or (3) the class to be issued includes no outstanding shares. This is to prevent dilution of the other class of stock unless the other class consents to it.

Stock Splits   Stock splits are used to lower the price of the stock and allow more individuals the opportunity of becoming stockholders at a lower price. If the stock were selling for $100 per share, and the board of directors declared a four for one stock split, every shareholder would receive three additional shares for each one held. Instead of owning one share for $100, the shareholder would now hold four shares at $25 each. The mathematics stays the same; each shareholder still has the same percentage of stock. The only change is more shares and a lower price. When the stock is low more people tend to buy it. The theory is that if you have stock in ABC Bread Company, you will buy that bread for yourself and family since you are an owner of that company. If the stock were $10 par value in the above four for one split, the par value will now be $2.50 per share. Unlike a dividend, a stock split is not a distribution. It entails no transfer of surplus to stated capital.

Property Dividends   Property dividends occur when the shareholder receives property instead of cash or stock. A cereal company at one time gave a property dividend of a case of breakfast cereal to each stockholder who had 500 shares. A whiskey company at one time distributed whiskey as a property dividend. Cash, however, is the usual dividend.

Liquidating Dividends   A distribution of capital assets to shareholders is referred to as a liquidating dividend in some jurisdictions. Statutes usually require that the shareholder be informed by the corporation that the dividend is a liquidating dividend. Normally a dividend is associated with the distribution of profits.

Acquisition of Shares   When a corporation acquires its own shares, they are either canceled or referred to as **treasury stock**. A corporation that is traded on an exchange or over the counter can acquire all of its outstanding shares and thereafter be a private corporation, closely held. This is referred to as going private. The shares so acquired would be authorized but unissued shares pursuant to the RMBCA. If the articles of incorporation prohibit the reissue of acquired shares, the number of authorized shares would be reduced by the number of shares acquired. In states not following the RMBCA the acquired shares would be considered treasury stock. The RMBCA changes this as follows.

Corporation's Acquisition of Its Own Shares (Section 6.31, RMBCA)

    (a) A corporation may acquire its own shares; shares so acquired constitute authorized but unissued shares.

    (b) If the articles of incorporation prohibit the reissue of acquired shares, the number of authorized shares is reduced by the number of shares acquired, effective upon amendment of the articles of incorporation.

    (c) The board of directors may adopt articles of amendment under this section without shareholder action, and deliver them to the secretary of state for filing. The articles must set forth:

        (1) the name of the corporation;

        (2) the reduction in the number of authorized shares, itemized by class and series; and

        (3) the total number of authorized shares, itemized by class and series, remaining after reduction of the shares.

The RMBCA eliminated the concept of treasury shares. The acquisition is viewed as a distribution of capital assets. If the articles of incorporation prohibit the reissue of acquired shares, the number of shares is reduced. If the corporation can reissue the shares, they are deemed authorized but unissued. A corporation can purchase its own shares only from earned surplus, or, if the articles of incorporation or shareholders approve, out of capital surplus. The corporation cannot acquire its own shares when insolvent or if it would render the corporation insolvent after the purchase (RMBCA 6.40).

Redemption of Shares   Redemption is the purchase by the corporation of its own shares, usually at its own option. Many states permit corporations to redeem preferred shares but not common stock. The RMBCA does **not** prohibit redemption of common shares or preferred shares. The articles of incorporation must expressly provide for the power of the redemption. A corporation cannot redeem or purchase its redeemable shares when insolvent or if it would render the corporation insolvent.

— STOP

LOST, DESTROYED, AND STOLEN CERTIFICATED SECURITIES

If a certificate is lost, destroyed, or stolen, the owner is entitled to a new one to replace the missing, destroyed, or stolen one, provided (1) the issuer is notified before the certificate is acquired by a **bona fide purchaser**. A bona fide purchaser is one who buys for value without notice of a defect, meaning that full value of the certificate is paid as consideration for its purchase and the buyer does not know the original was lost, stolen, or destroyed; (2) the issuer is then entitled to demand an indemnity bond prior to issuing the replacement certificate, costs to be paid by the party seeking the replacement certificate; and (3) the purchaser satisfies other reasonable requirements of the issuer such as an affidavit of the facts of how and where the certificate was lost, destroyed, or stolen. (Uniform Commercial Code, Section 8-405 [2]).

The issuer must be notified within a reasonable time after the loss, or the owner of the lost, destroyed, or stolen certificate may be deprived of a replacement if the corporation has registered the certificate to another prior to receiving notice of the lost, destroyed, or stolen certificate. [Uniform Commercial Code section 8-405 (1)].

Lost, Destroyed, and Stolen Certificated Securities (Uniform Commercial Code, Section 8-405)

(1) If a certificated security has been lost, apparently destroyed, or wrongfully taken, and the owner fails to notify the issuer of that fact within a reasonable time after he has notice of it, and the issuer registers a transfer of the security before receiving notification, the owner is precluded from asserting against the issuer any claim for registering the transfer under Section 8-404 or any claim to a new security under this section.

(2) If the owner of a certificated security claims that the security has been lost, destroyed, or wrongfully taken, the issuer shall issue a new certificated security or, at the option of the issuer, an equivalent uncertificated security in place of the original security if the owner:
   (a) so requests before the issuer has noticed that the security has been acquired by a bona fide purchaser,
   (b) files with the issuer a sufficient indemnity bond, and
   (c) satisfies any other reasonable requirements imposed by the issuer.

(3) If, after the issue of a new certificated or uncertificated security, a bona fide purchaser of the original certificated security presents it for registration or transfer, the issuer shall register the transfer unless registration would result in overissue, in which event the issuer's liability is governed by Section 8-104. In addition to any rights on the indemnity bond, the issuer may recover the new certificated security from the person to whom it was issued or any person taking under him or her except a bona fide purchaser, or may cancel the uncertificated security unless a bona fide purchaser or any person taking under a bona fide purchaser is then the registered owner or registered pledgee thereof.

Liability and Non-Liability for Registration (UCC, Section 8-404)

(1) Except as provided in any law relating to the collection of taxes, the issuer is not liable to the owner, pledgee, or any other person suffering loss as a result of the registration of a transfer, pledge, or release of a security if:
   (a) there were on or with a certificated security the necessary endorsements or the issuer had received instructions originated by an appropriate person (Section 8-308); and
   (b) the issuer had no duty as to adverse claims or has discharged the duty (Section 8-403).

(2) If a issuer has registered a transfer of a certificated security to a person not entitled to it, issuer on demand shall deliver a like security to the true owner unless:
   (a) the registration was pursuant to subsection (1);
   (b) the owner is precluded from asserting any claim for registering the transfer under Section 8-405(1); or

(c) the delivery would result in overissue, in which case the issuer's liability is governed by Section 8-104.

Effect of Overissue (UCC, Section 8-104)

(1) The provisions of this article, which validate a security or compel its issue or reissue, do not apply to the extent that validation, issue, or reissue would result in overissue; but if:

    (a) an identical security which does not constitute an overissue is reasonably available for purchase, the person entitled to issue or validation may compel the issuer to purchase the security for him or her and either to deliver a certificated security or to register the transfer of an uncertified security to him or her, against surrender of any certificated security he or she holds, or

    (b) a security is not available for purchase, the person entitled to issue or validation may recover from the issuer the price he or she or the last purchaser for value paid for it with interest from the date of his, her, or its demand.

(2) "Overissue" means the issue of securities in excess of the amount the issuer has corporate power to issue.

Endorsements; Instructions (UCC, Section 8-308)

(5) An instruction originated by an appropriate person is:

    (a) a writing signed by an appropriate person; or

    (b) a communication to the issuer in any form agreed upon in a writing signed by the issuer and an appropriate person.

If an instruction has been originated by an appropriate person but is incomplete in any other respect, any person may complete it as authorized; and the issuer may rely on it as completed even though it has been completed incorrectly.

(7) An "appropriate person" in subsection (5) means:

    (a) for an instruction to transfer or pledge an uncertificated security which is then not subject to a registered pledge, the registered owner, or

    (b) for an instruction to transfer or release an uncertificated security which is then subject to a registered pledge, the registered pledgee.

Issuer's Duty as to Adverse Claims (UCC, Section 403)

(4) An issuer is under no duty as to adverse claims with respect to an uncertificated security except:

    (a) claims embodied in a restraining order, injunction, or other legal process served upon the issuer if the process was served at a time and in a manner affording the issuer a reasonable opportunity to act on it in accordance with the requirements of subsection (5);

    (b) claims of which the issuer has received a written notification from the registered owner or the registered pledgee if the notification was received at a time and in a manner affording the issuer a reasonable opportunity to act on it in accordance with the requirements of subsection (5);

    (c) claims (including restrictions on transfer not imposed by the issuer) to which the registration of transfer to the present registered owner was subject and were so noted in the initial transaction statement sent to him or her; and

      (d) claims as to which an issuer is charged with notice from a controlling instrument it has elected to require under Section 8-402(4).

(5) If the issuer of an uncertificated security is under a duty as to an adverse claim, he, she, or it discharges that duty by:

      (a) including a notation of the claim in any statements sent with respect to the security under Sections 8-408(3), (6), and (7); and

      (b) refusing to register the transfer or pledge of the security unless the nature of the claim does not preclude transfer or pledge subject thereto.

(6) If the transfer or pledge of the security is registered subject to an adverse claim, a notation of the claim must be included in the initial transaction statement and all subsequent statements sent to the transferee and pledge under Section 8-408.

(7) Notwithstanding subsections (4) and (5), if an uncertificated security was subject to a registered pledge at the time the issuer first came under a duty as to a particular adverse claim, the issuer has no duty as to that claim if transfer of the security is requested by the registered pledgee or an appropriate person acting for the registered pledgee unless:

      (a) the claim was embodied in legal process which expressly provides otherwise;

      (b) the claim was asserted in a written notification from the registered pledgee;

      (c) the claim was one as to which the issuer was charged with notice from a controlling instrument it required under Section 8-402(4) in connection with the pledgee's request for transfer, or

      (d) the transfer requested is to the registered owner.

Assurance That Endorsements and Instructions Are Effective (UCC, Section 8-402)

(3) (b) In any case, a copy of a document showing the appointment or a certificate issued by or on behalf of a person reasonably believed by the issuer to be responsible, in the absence of the document or certificate, or other evidence reasonably deemed by the issuer to be appropriate. The issuer may adopt standards with respect to the evidence if they are not manifestly unreasonable. The issuer is not charged with notice of the contents of any document obtained pursuant to this paragraph except to the extent that the contents relate directly to the appointment or incumbency.

(4) The issuer may elect to require reasonable assurance beyond that specified in this section, but if it does so and, for a purpose other than that specified in subsection (3)(b), both requires and obtains a copy of a will, trust, indenture, articles of co-partnership, bylaws, or other controlling instrument, it is charged with notice of all matters contained therein affecting the transfer, pledge, or release.

INVESTMENT SECURITIES

Article 8 of the Uniform Commercial Code provides the statutory rules for investment securities and their transfer. Since a certificate of stock is a negotiable instrument, the rules for transfer are similar to Article 3 of the UCC covering negotiable instruments. Securities encompasses bonds, stocks, debentures, business trusts, voting trusts, **certificated securities** and **uncertificated securities.**

CERTIFICATED AND UNCERTIFICATED SECURITIES

A certificated security and an uncertificated security are shares, participation, or other interest in property of, or an enterprise of the issuer or an obligation of the issuer which is (a) represented by an instrument issued in bearer or registered form; (b) of a type commonly dealt in on securities exchanges or markets, or commonly recognized in any area in which it is issued as a medium for investment; and (c) either one of a class or series, or by its terms divisible into a class or series of shares, participation, interests, or obligations.

Ownership of a Security

The owner of a security can transfer it by sale, gift, or will, and can also pledge it, similar to the way any other property owned is transferred. There is usually a ready market for the sale of securities. A negotiable instrument is easy to transfer and generally liquid. It is intangible personal property and exists independently of a certificate. Uncertificated securities are registered by the issuer and maintained in ledgers.

Rights and Obligations of Certificated and Uncertificated Shareholders

RMBCA, Section 6.25, states that the rights and obligations of shareholders are identical whether or not their shares are represented by certificates.

Issuer Must Register a Transfer of Security Ownership When Requested

The issuer is under a duty to register certificated and uncertificated securities. This is necessary so that the owner receives dividends, notices, financial statements, reports, etc., from the corporation. The certificate is necessary to sell, transfer, or pledge the security. The transaction statement notice received with uncertificated securities is used as a certificate for selling, transferring, or pledging. The issuing corporation must register the transfer if: (1) The certificate is property endorsed (UCC 8-308). (2) Assurance, i.e., reassurance is given that endorsements are genuine and effective (UCC 8-402). (3) No adverse claims against issuer or same have been discharged (UCC 8-403). (4) Collection of taxes has been complied with. (5) The transfer is to a bona fide purchaser.

TRANSFER OF SECURITIES

In the absence of restrictions, shares of stock are freely transferable. Most incorporation statutes have no provision governing share transferability restrictions. The common law decides the validation of such restrictions. The Uniform Commercial Code, Section 8-204, provides that no restriction is valid against a person without actual notice of it unless the restriction is conspicuously noted on the share certificate or, for an uncertificated security, in the initial transaction statement.

The transfer is made by delivery of the certificate, endorsed in blank, in bearer form or by an "appropriate person." Uncertificated securities are transferred when the transfer is registered.

Transfer; Warranties

UCC 8-306(2) A seller of securities warrants to purchaser:

(a) The transfer is effective and rightful.

(b) The security is genuine and has not been materially altered.

(c) Seller knows of no fact that might impair the validity of the security.

UCC 8-306(1) A person who presents a certificated security for registration or transfer or for payment or exchange warrants to the issuer that he or she is entitled to the registration, payment, or exchange. But, a purchaser for value and without notice of adverse claims who receives a new, reissued, or re-registered certificated security of registration of transfer, or receives an initial transaction statement confirming the registration of transfer of an equivalent uncertificated security to him or her warrants only that he or she has no knowledge of any unauthorized signature (8-311) in a necessary endorsement.

Unauthorized or Forged Endorsement

A forged or unauthorized endorsement on a certificated security will not deprive the owner before the forged or unauthorized endorsement of title. In contrast, the purchaser of a security with a forged or unauthorized endorsement who sells it or transfers it to a bona fide purchaser breaches the warranty that the transfer is effective and rightful and, therefore, is liable to the purchaser for the value of the security at the time of sale (UCC 8-306(2)[a]). Neither party is owner as title cannot be transferred through a forged or unauthorized endorsement.

SUMMARY

Par value is the price at or above which the corporation must sell the original issue. After the first sale by the corporation, there is no longer any significance to the par value. A corporate distribution can be in the form of a cash dividend, property dividend, stock dividend, a purchase, redemption or other acquisition of shares, distribution of indebtedness, etc. A distribution is any transfer of dollars or property from the corporation to shareholders.

Shareholders receive funds from a corporation by dividends or repurchase of shares by the corporation. A corporation cannot issue a dividend if it is insolvent or if the dividend will make the corporation insolvent. There are two methods to determine insolvency. Equity definition is the accountants' definition that the corporation is unable to timely pay its obligations. The bankruptcy court's definition is that there are more liabilities than assets. Either definition can be used.

If the directors declare and distribute an improper dividend, the directors are personally liable to the corporation and creditors for that distribution. If the shareholder knew it was an improper distribution, then, the shareholder will have to reimburse the corporation. Various kinds of dividends can be declared; cash, property, stock, stock splits, and liquidation.

If a certificated certificate is lost, stolen, or destroyed, it can be replaced by the issuer as long as the requirements of the issuer are met. It is necessary to request a new certificate before a claim for transfer is made on that certificate. Stocks can be issued with a certificated security or noncertificated security. A noncertificated security is issued with a transfer agreement and has the same rights as a certificated security. The issuer cannot issue you a new certificate if it would be an overissue. The issuer can only issue the number of shares it has the power to issue; anything over is an overissue.

A certificated security is a negotiable instrument and can be transferred by the endorsement of an "appropriate party." When a seller transfers the security, the seller warrants that the transfer is effective and rightful. The security is the original not materially altered, and the seller knows of no facts to impair its validity.

CASES

Amount Available for Dividends—Balance Sheet Statute

RANDALL v. BAILEY
288 NY 280 (1942)

The issue in this case was whether the amount available for payment of dividends is limited to the differences between assets and liabilities as recorded on the corporation's balance sheet under generally accepted accounting principles, or the difference between the actual value of the corporation's assets and liabilities. If land and buildings are worth more than the book value listed on the balance sheet, can that extra value be used for dividends?

The Court held under New York's balance sheet statute, that dividends could be based on actual value rather than recorded balance sheet values. (Some other states with different balance sheet statutes have come to different rulings. Most states follow New York in this area.)

Restriction on Transferability

GALLAGHER v. LAMBERT
74 NY 2nd 562, 549 NY 2nd 945
New York Court of Appeals (1989)

Gallagher purchased an 8.5 percent interest in a close corporation owned by Lambert. The purchase was subject to a mandatory buy-back provision, that if the employment ended for any reason prior to January 31, 1985, the stock would be purchased by the corporation for book value. After that date the buy–back would be keyed to the company's earnings. On January 10, 1985, the corporation fired Gallagher.

Plaintiff's action based on an alleged breach of a fiduciary duty seeking a higher repurchase price was dismissed by the trial court and affirmed in the Appellate Division. This court affirms the decision of the trial court and Appellate Division in dismissing the action in summary judgment because there was no obvious breach of a fiduciary duty owed to plaintiff under the plain terms of the party's repurchase agreement.

Plaintiff did not and does not contest the firing. He seeks payment for his shares based on the post January 31, 1985, buy-back formula. The corporation refused and plaintiff sued, asserting eight causes of action. Only three claims, based on the alleged breach of fiduciary duty of good faith and fair dealing, are before us. The trial court denied defendant's motion for summary judgment on these claims stating that factual issues were raised relating to defendant's motive in firing plaintiff. The Appellate Division reversed and dismissed those claims and ordered payment at book value. That court granted leave and certified the following question to us "Was the order of this Court, which modified the order of the Trial Court, properly made?"

The parties negotiated a written contract with a buy-back provision. Plaintiff got what he bargained for, book value if employment ended prior to January 31, 1985. "A minority shareholder in a close corporation, by that status alone, who contractually agrees to the repurchase of his shares upon termination of his employment for any reason, acquires no right from the corporation or majority shareholders against at-will discharge." There is a difference in the duty a corporation owes to a minority shareholder as a shareholder from any duty it might owe him as an employee.

Plaintiff not only agreed to the buy-back formula, he helped write it, and he reviewed it with his attorney during the negotiation process before signing the agreement and purchasing the minority interest.

Accordingly, the order of the Appellate Division should be affirmed, with costs, and the certified question answered in the affirmative.

Statutory Restrictions on Distributions

NEIMARK v. MEL KRAMER SALES, INC.
102 Wis.2nd 282, 306 NW 2d 278
Court of Appeals of Wisconsin (1981)

Issue—Whether the trial court was correct in ordering specific performance of a stock redemption agreement upon death of the majority shareholder of the corporation.

Mel Kramer was founder and majority shareholder with 51 percent and his wife with 10 percent of the defendant corporation. Mel Kramer is deceased. His wife is president and a director. The plaintiff is vice president and a director. Two other directors are relatives of the wife. The plaintiff owns 29 percent, and a fourth shareholder owns 10 percent.

On June 22, 1976, the corporation and all shareholders entered into a stock redemption agreement. The agreement required the estate of the deceased shareholder to sell, and the corporation to buy, all of the deceased interest at $400 per share, less a specified credit. The agreement also gives the wife an option to sell her shares at the same time, same terms. The redemption price is $408,000, less a specifically provided credit of $50,000, making a net price of $358,000, to be paid $100,000 at closing, and the balance in five annual installments; first $43,200, and four remaining installments of $53,700 with 6 percent interest. The wife's net would be $80,000 if she took the option to sell, payable $40,000 in the sixth year and $40,000 in the seventh year, with interest

at 6 percent. The deceased's share of the initial payment of $100,000 was funded by life insurance payable to the corporation. It was reflected in the corporation retained earnings as of December 31, 1976.

The agreement also stated that if the corporation did not have sufficient surplus or retained earnings to purchase the deceased shareholder's stock, the parties would contribute the necessary capital to enable the corporation to lawfully redeem the shares, and the parties would be entitled to specific performance of the agreement.

After the death, the wife did not want the corporation to redeem the shares. Plaintiff insisted. A board of directors meeting was called and voted 3-1 against redemption, plaintiff being the one vote.

Plaintiff commenced an action seeking specific performance and alternatively money damages. First action was derivative on behalf of the corporation, second personal. The defendants counterclaimed saying plaintiff was only entitled to his ratable portion of the proceeds.

Subsequently, a third party offered to purchase the business for $1,000,000. Plaintiff conditioned his approval of the sale on the requirement that the deceased estate and wife receive proceeds equal only to the redemption price which was substantially lower than the tendered price.

The trial court dismissed plaintiff's personal claim, but ordered specific performance of the redemption agreement. The counterclaim was dismissed.

Statute prohibits acquisition by a corporation of its own stock if the corporation would thereby be rendered insolvent. The trial court's finding of fact was that performance of the stock redemption agreement would not render the corporation insolvent.

Additional statutory sections require the purchase be made out of earned surplus and cannot be made if insolvency is the result.

We vacate the judgment of the circuit court and remand for further proceedings. The circuit court is directed to apply the surplus cutoff test if it concludes specific performance as the remedy. If necessary, require the parties to contribute money as in the agreement to prevent insolvency.

WORDS TO KNOW

adverse claims

bankruptcy definition

bearer endorsement

blank endorsement

bona fide purchaser

bonus stock

capital surplus

certificated security

discount stock

distribution

earned surplus

equity capital

endorsement

issued

issuer

lost certificates

market efficiency

net assets

nimble dividends

original issue

overissue

property dividend

redemption

stated capital

stock dividend

stock splits

surplus

treasury stock

uncertificated security

watered stock

REVIEW QUESTIONS

1. Are shareholders ever liable for the return of a dividend distributed to them?
2. Explain low par value.
3. What is meant by distribution?
4. Explain earned surplus.
5. How does a corporation determine dividend payments?
6. What is the liability of all parties when an improper dividend is declared?
7. Name five different dividends a corporation can issue.
8. Explain treasury stock.
9. What does redemption of shares mean?
10. How do you obtain a replacement certificate if yours is lost, destroyed, or stolen?
11. What is a noncertificated security?
12. How is a noncertificated security issued?
13. Explain the difference in rights between a certificated and noncertificated security.
14. What is an endorsement?
15. What is a blank endorsement?

16. What does bearer mean?
17. What are the warranties given to transfer a certificated security?
18. What is the effect of a forged endorsement on a security?
19. What does original issue mean?
20. Explain overissue.

SHORT ESSAYS

1. Mark Corporation has a provision in its bylaws that says that no shareholder can sell his or her shares without first offering them for sale to the corporation. If the corporation refuses to purchase, then, the stock must be offered for sale to each of the directors in equal amounts. If any director refuses to purchase, then, that stock must be offered to the other directors. If the corporation refuses to buy, and all directors refuse to buy, then, the stock can be sold to anyone without restriction. The provision also states that a legend to this effect shall be conspicuously placed on all stock certificates issued by the corporation in the future and on all present shares of stock issued and outstanding. All stockholders have agreed to this provision. John Tom knew of this provision in the bylaws and purchased 500 shares from Frank Sam because his stock did not have the legend on it. Frank Sam was secretary of the corporation and forgot to place the legend on his stock although he placed the legend on all other shares issued. After purchase John Tom seeked a new certificate to be issued in his name. The corporation transfer agent refused. John Tom commenced an action to force the transfer agent to issue him a new certificate. State your decision and the reasons for that decision.

2. Al Smith is the receiver of ABC Corporation. John Thomas, a creditor of the corporation for the last three years, filed suit against all shareholders of ABC Corporation to recover dividends they have received for the last two years. The dividends were declared and distributed. As a result of the distribution the corporation became and still is insolvent. Who wins? Give reasons.

3. You are chairman of the board. The corporation manufactures chocolate. You believe that if you could quadruple the number of shares outstanding and increase the shareholders of the corporation, the new shareholders would buy the corporation's chocolate and thus increase sales. How would you go about accomplishing this?

4. You are a member of the board of directors. There are a total of five directors. The corporation is in the marketing business. Dividend payouts have been erratic over the past five years. Dividends starting five years ago were eighty cents. Four years ago one dollar and five cents. Three years ago sixty cents. Two years ago seventy–five cents. One year ago sixty cents. This year the corporation has made more money than in any of the previous five years. The cash position is excellent. There is enough in the required categories to pay a two dollar dividend. Next years business may not be as good as this year. What kind of a dividend policy would you like to see this company take? Explain your reasons.

5. You are chairman of the board. There are six other directors in addition to yourself. Business has been generally good over the past four years. Each year the board has declared a dividend and each year increased the dividend ten cents higher than the previous year. Last year the dividend was seventy cents. The vice president of finance is a new position, and the party in the position started five days ago. The corporation's certified public accounting firm terminated their relationship with the company six months ago as they were unable to get along with the controller of the corporation. He was replaced with the new position of vice president-finance. The new finance vice

president has prepared some financial information for the board, and he feels and has recommended that the dividend payout be suspended this year until he has had a chance to fully acquaint himself with the financial situation of the company. The board does not want to suspend the dividend. All the officers and department heads attended the last board meeting, and all stated that the corporation was doing better than last year in their opinion but they have no financial data to support their opinion. You have taken the sketchy financial information that has been presented to the board to a friend who is a bookkeeper at a large corporation. He looked over the information and said he sees no reason why you should not continue the dividend policy of the last few years. He attended the last board meeting as well and told the board the same thing. Acting on this information, in good faith, the board declared a dividend that was increased by the usual ten cents. It is now seven months later, and the corporation is in financial trouble. It looks as though the last dividend distribution has brought the company to the point of insolvency. The creditors are angry, and all are being paid late. The board is concerned and wondering if they have any personal liability in this situation as they feel they all acted in good faith. State your decision and explain the reasons for it.

6. Fred Thomas owns 100 shares of common no par stock in the Widget Corporation. The stock was issued to him as a certificated stock issue. Mr. Thomas was a cautious man and because of his elderly age, he just celebrated his 91st birthday, he signed the back of the certificate Fred Thomas. He did this so that his grandchild, Tom Sawyer, upon his death could pick up the certificate and own the stock. The certificate was kept in his night table drawer in the bedroom. He showed his grandchild the certificate many times, where he kept it, and that he wanted him as his only heir to have it after his death.

Mr. Thomas wrote in ink on a piece of paper in his own handwriting, that this is my Last Will and Testament, being of sound mind, I want my grandchild, Tom Sawyer, my only heir, to have the stock certificate in Widget Corporation. I keep the certificate in the night table drawer in my bedroom. This piece of paper was kept in the desk drawer which was the only drawer in the desk used by Fred Thomas in the kitchen.

When Fred Thomas died, the certificate was not in the night table drawer. The grandchild searched the complete house and could not find it. The piece of paper that was the will of M. Thomas was found in the desk drawer.

Mr. J. J. Carson has now presented the certificate to the transfer agent of the Widget Corporation and has asked them to issue him a new certificate in his name. The certificate that he is surrendering has the endorsements of Fred Thomas, Mary Kay, and J. J. Carson on the reverse side.

One hour after Mr. Carson delivered the certificate to the transfer agent, the grandchild came in and filed a claim saying the certificate was lost and demanded a new certificate in his name.

Mary Kay says Fred Thomas gave her the certificate as a gift. She worked for Mr. Thomas cleaning his house for three weeks before he gave her the gift. She has no other proof of this being a gift. J. J. Carson says he bought the certificate from Mary Kay for $9,000. He has a canceled check payable to Mary Kay for $9,000. The certificate is presently worth $9,800.

The grandchild claims the certificate was stolen. He claims the rightful owner to be Fred Thomas; and since he is the only heir of Fred Thomas, he should get the certificate. The grandchild says you cannot obtain title to stolen property. Mr. Carson says he bought it, and the certificate belongs to him.

State your decision and explain the reasons for it.

CHAPTER

10

SHAREHOLDER SUITS

OBJECTIVES

After completing this chapter, you will be able to:

1. Advise when an action is direct and when it is derivative.
2. Know when you can bring a derivative proceeding.
3. Explain the differences between a derivative and a direct proceeding.
4. List the requirements to commence a derivative action.
5. Know who are indispensable parties to a derivative action.
6. Explain when a demand on the board is necessary prior to commencing the action.
7. List the advantages and disadvantages of an investigative committee.
8. Know when a demand is excusable.
9. Explain when and where a trial by jury is obtainable.
10. Know what a contingency fee is.
11. Explain the "common fund theory."
12. Explain the "private attorney general principle."
13. Know what security for expenses means.
14. Bring the proceeding so that no security for costs is posted.
15. Explain indemnification.

16. Know what exclusive and nonexclusive statutes are.

17. Explain the steps necessary prior to settlement of a proceeding.

18. Define affidavit, depositions, interrogatories, and documents.

19. Know if a shareholder can object to a settlement.

20. Know what happens when a shareholder objects to a settlement.

INTRODUCTION

If wrongs done by officers, directors, and managers of the corporation could only be enforced by the corporation, many wrongs would never be corrected. Where the majority shareholders benefit from the breach of duty or care of the officers, directors, or managers, they would continue the same people in office or replace them with similar managers to continue the same breaches. If the majority of shareholders do not benefit from the breaches in public corporations, it is too difficult, expensive, time consuming, and practically impossible to organize the shareholders to remove the wrongdoers from office. The problem would be electing new directors who would be willing to sue, on behalf of the corporation, the old directors for their wrongs. To eliminate these obstacles and hold controlling stockholders and wrongdoing managers liable, the statutes permit shareholders to bring suit on behalf of the corporation. This type of lawsuit is called a derivative action.

There are two concerns with these actions. The derivative action has extraordinary procedural complexity, involving proper parties, jurisdiction, demand on the board, demand on the shareholders, right to sue, intervention, settlement, and dismissal. The second problem is a social one. Using a derivative action, a shareholder with a comparatively small investment in the corporation stock can force the corporation to expend a large amount of money and executive time to fight the lawsuit.

There are rules that must be adhered to prior to commencement of this action. There is a balancing act done by legislatures to make managers accountable for their wrongdoing and to prevent the knockout blow to the corporation with these actions.

The two methods to protect against managerial self dealings are the derivative action and the disclosure requirements of the securities acts.

DERIVATIVE ACTION

A **derivative action** is an action by a shareholder or shareholders for the benefit of the corporation. The reason it is called a derivative action is that the shareholder's right to bring the action derives from the corporation. It is an action in equity. A suit to enforce a corporate cause of action against officers, directors, managers, and/or third parties. To bring such an action the corporation must have a valid claim, and the corporation must have refused to bring the action after demand was made upon the corporation to commence an action. It is the plaintiff's right to bring an action on behalf of the corporation, using the merits of the corporation's claim. Any recovery of money or other relief goes to the corporation, not to the plaintiff or plaintiffs.

The complexity of the procedural matters in a derivative action make the defendant's motion to dismiss on procedural grounds the win or lose part of the action. If the plaintiff can survive the motion with the facts already known to the plaintiff, together with the material that can be developed through discovery, it will most often lead to a quick and substantial settlement without going into the merits of the case. The major problem for the plaintiff in this action is lack of information and the inability to obtain it until after defeating a motion to dismiss by the defendant.

Of course, if the defendant gets the case dismissed on procedural grounds, no other plaintiff can come forward because no one else would have the relevant facts necessary to proceed or because the statute of limitations has run.

Short of a stockholder selling their shares and interest in a corporation because of the wrongdoing of managers or third parties, is the right of shareholders to bring a derivative shareholder's action which is an action by a shareholder on behalf of and for the benefit of the corporation. Shareholder actions are basically of two types: (1) a derivative action or (2) a direct suit. To a lesser extent there is the class action.

Party That Can Bring a Derivative Action

The plaintiff must be a shareholder at the commencement of the action and must remain a shareholder during the pendency of the action. A few states have statutes defining a shareholder. New York Business Corporation Law, Section 626(a), states that the plaintiff in a derivative action must be a "holder of shares or of voting trust certificates . . . or of a beneficial interest in such shares or certificates."

When there is no statute defining a shareholder or when the statute is silent as to a definition, the courts usually define *shareholder* in a very expansive manner. To bring a derivative action:

(1) An unregistered shareholder will qualify. Record ownership is generally not required.
(2) Legal ownership is not required. **Equitable ownership** suffices. Equitable ownership includes stock owned even though it is held by a broker in a margin account in a street name; a pledgee; the beneficiary of a trust; a legatee; a surviving widow in a community property state where stock in the husband's name is held by a third party; and a person who has contracted to purchase stock.

Derivative Proceedings, Definitions (Section 7.40, RMBCA)

(1) "Derivative proceeding" means a civil suit in the right of a domestic corporation or, to the extent provided in Section 7.47, in the right of a foreign corporation.
(2) "Shareholder" includes a beneficial owner whose shares are held in a voting trust or held by a nominee on the beneficial owner's behalf.

(RMBCA, Section 7.47 provides that the law of the jurisdiction of incorporation governs foreign corporations, except as to stay of proceedings (7.43), discontinuance or settlement (7.45), and payment of expenses (7.46).

Standing (Section 7.41, RMBCA)

A shareholder may not commence or maintain a derivative proceeding unless the shareholder:

(1) was a shareholder of the corporation at the time of the act or omission complained of or became a shareholder through transfer by operation of law from one who was a shareholder at that time; and

(2) fairly and adequately represents the interests of the corporation in enforcing the right of the corporation.

Section 7.41, RMBCA, requires plaintiff to be a shareholder and, therefore, does not permit creditors or holders of options, warrants, or conversion rights to commence a derivative action. The language is clear that if plaintiff ceases to be a shareholder after commencement of the action, or a fair and adequate representative of the corporation, the action should be dismissed. Plaintiff must remain a shareholder throughout the proceeding and fairly and adequately represent the corporation.

Section 7.41(2) requires plaintiff to fairly and adequately represent the interests of the corporation rather than shareholders similarly situated.

Shareholder of a Parent Corporation

A shareholder in a parent company can bring a derivative action on behalf of a subsidiary, even though not a shareholder in the subsidiary.

Creditors and Derivative Actions

Without a statute allowing creditors to bring a derivative action, the rule that a shareholder must be a plaintiff in a derivative action implies that a creditor and/or a bondholder ordinarily has no right to bring a derivative action, *Brooks v. Weiser,* 57 FRD 491 Southern District, NY (1972).

If a corporation is insolvent, the directors owe fiduciary duties to the creditors whether or not there has been a statutory filing under bankruptcy laws. Therefore, it appears that creditors could bring an action against directors for violation of those duties.

In *Francis v. United Jersey Bank,* Supreme Court of New Jersey, 87 NJ 432.3 (1981), "Directors owe a duty to creditors even while the corporation is solvent." The court singled out bank depositors and persons for whom a corporation holds money in trust.

Some statutes give officers and directors the right to bring a derivative action (New York Business Corporation Law, Section 720(b)).

Indispensable Party to Derivative Action

The corporation is an **indispensable party** to the derivative action. After all, the lawsuit is based on protecting the corporation, and all benefits from the action go to the corporation, not to the plaintiffs. Therefore, one would assume that the corporation would be a party plaintiff. The decree must protect the defendants (officers, directors, managers, and possibly third parties) from any further suits by the corporation; this will only occur if the corporation is properly made a party to the action.

The usual practice in the United States is to make the beneficiary corporation a party defendant, although it is actually a plaintiff. The flexibility of the equity procedures allows a judgment to be entered in favor of one defendant against another defendant or defendants.

Difference between a Derivative and a Direct Action

A **derivative action** is brought by a shareholder on behalf of the corporation against the corporate managers (officers, directors, etc.) or third parties. The corporation is named as a party defendant. Any money award goes to the corporation. The three basic advantages of a derivative action are:

(1) to avoid a multiplicity of suits against the corporation by each injured shareholder,

(2) to protect the corporate creditors (multiplicity of suits could injure the financial position of the corporation), and

(3) to protect all shareholders as a corporate recovery benefits all equally.

A **direct action** is brought on the shareholders own behalf against either the corporation or its officers, directors, and managers. The award would go to the shareholder, <u>not</u> to the corporation.

A wrongful act that depletes or destroys assets of the corporation and affects the shareholder only by reducing the value of stock owned, gives rise to a direct action. If it affects the corporation, the remedy is a derivative action. If it affects the shareholder, the remedy is a direct action.

A wrongful act that does not deplete or divert the corporate assets and interferes with the rights traditionally either incident to stock ownership or inherent in the shares such as voting rights or pre-emptive rights, gives rise to a direct action by the injured shareholder. The right to vote is a basic right in most shares of stock and independent of any right the corporation has. Therefore, a direct action would be proper. Issuance of stock to perpetuate or shift control would be wrongful and give rise to a direct action. It affects the shareholder, not the corporation. Wrongs by controlling shareholders against noncontrolling shareholders would be a direct action. Suits to enjoin improperly authorized corporate actions are treated as direct actions. A suit to overturn a reorganization and merger was held to be a direct action, *Eisenberg v. Flying Tiger Line,* 451 F2d 267 (1971).

In many cases a wrongful act depletes corporate assets and interferes with rights inherent in shares. A direct action would not be precluded just because the facts could give rise to a derivative action and/or a direct action.

Proxy rule violations that interfere with the individual shareholders' voting rights are direct actions. Proxy rule violations that involve a breach of duty or care of management are derivative actions.

For example, the chairman of the board and two directors resign from a public company. The financial community is expecting a $100,000,000 loss. After the chairman and two directors leave, an audit is taken and the loss is $400,000,000. The stock drops from $40 a share to $3 a share. The shareholders cannot sue the directors or chairman directly as they were not technically injured. The corporation was. Therefore, the corporation has a right to sue. The remaining directors are not going to sue themselves, so the remedy is to allow the shareholders to bring the action on behalf of the corporation. This would be a derivative action.

Five Additional Areas That Give Rise to a Direct Action

(1) To inspect the books and records of the corporation.

(2) To force a dissolution of the corporation.

(3) To force the payment of a properly declared dividend.

(4) To enjoin an ultra vires act.

(5) To protect preemptive rights of shareholders.

Five Additional Areas That Give Rise to a Derivative Action

(1) To recover damages from management for an ultra vires act.

(2) To recover damages from management for a breach of duty or care.

(3) To recover damages from a third party.

(4) To enjoin wrongful issuance of shares.

(5) To recover for an improper dividend distribution.

Continuing Wrong Theory

A plaintiff can bring an action to challenge a wrong that began before he or she became a shareholder as long as the wrong continued after he or she became a shareholder. This is known as the continuing wrong theory.

Demand (Section 7.42, RMBCA)

No shareholder may commence a derivative proceeding until:

(1) a written demand has been made upon the corporation to take suitable action; and

(2) 90 days have expired from the date the demand was made unless the shareholder has earlier been notified that the demand has been rejected by the corporation or unless irreparable injury to the corporation would result by waiting for the expiration of the 90-day period.

RMBCA, Section 7.42, cases where the demand is excused under this section are rare. Therefore, most attorneys will give the demand rather than litigate that it should be excused. Although the section only requires the demand in writing, the demand should contain facts relating to share ownership and apprise the corporation of the action sought to be taken, and the grounds for the action. The best practice is to address the demand and to send copies to the board of directors, chief executive officer, and corporate secretary at its principal office. The reason is, if the action is against any one of them, you want to be sure the corporation will get the notice. If the corporation institutes an investigation into the allegations made in the demand or complaint, the court may stay any derivative proceeding for such period as deemed appropriate by the court (7.43). If the corporation at any time decides to assume control of the litigation, the shareholder's right ends unless it can be shown that the corporation will not diligently pursue the matter.

Derivative Action Without a Demand on the Board, New York State

***Barr v. Wackman,* Court of Appeals of New York, 36 NY 2d 371 (1975).** Plaintiff alleged a demand on the board would have been futile since the board of directors participated, authorized, and approved the challenged act; and members of the board are themselves subject to liability and, therefore, cannot be expected to vote to sue themselves. The court agreed a demand would have been futile.

Independent Committee to Investigate Basis for Derivative Action

When a majority of the directors are **interested** in the derivative action, i.e., they participated in the wrongdoing, the board can appoint a disinterested committee to consider whether the derivative action is in the best interests of the corporation. If the committee conducts an adequate investigation and finds that the action was not in the best interests of the corporation, the court can dismiss the action. If the board is disinterested, the board itself could conduct the investigation.

It is well established that demand need not be made on the board if a majority of the directors are interested, or where nominally disinterested directors are under the dominion and control of interested directors. However, the better practice is to file the demand and, if the board chooses, it can appoint a disinterested committee to investigate whether or not the action would be in the best interests of the corporation.

Decision by Disinterested Committee

A decision made by a disinterested committee appointed by the board of directors is usually beyond judicial review under the business judgment rule. The court, however, may inquire as to the disinterested independence of the members of the committee and to the appropriateness and sufficiency of the investigative procedures chosen and pursued by the committee, *Auerbach v. Bennett*, 419NYS 2d 920, Court of Appeals NY (1979).

A board of directors has the power to choose not to pursue litigation when demand is made upon it, so long as the decision is not wrongful. If the board determines the suit is detrimental to the corporation, the board's decision will prevail even when demand is excusable. "To allow one shareholder to incapacitate an entire board of directors merely by leveling charges against them, gives too much leverage to dissident shareholders." The court should inquire into the independence and good faith of the committee and the bases supporting its conclusions. The court should then apply its independent business judgment as to whether the motion to dismiss should be granted, *Zapata Corp. v. Maldonado*, 430 A2nd 779, Supreme Court of Delaware (1981).

Dismissal (Section 7.44, RMBCA)

(a) A derivative proceeding shall be dismissed by the court on motion by the corporation if one of the groups specified in subsections (b) or (f) has determined in good faith, after conducting a reasonable inquiry upon which its conclusions are based, that the maintenance of the derivative proceeding is not in the best interests of the corporation.

(b) Unless a panel is appointed pursuant to subsection (f), the determination in subsection (a) shall be made by:
   (1) a majority vote of independent directors present at a meeting of the board of directors if the independent directors constitute a quorum; or
   (2) a majority vote of a committee consisting of two or more independent directors appointed by majority vote of independent directors present at a meeting of the board of directors, whether or not such independent directors constituted a quorum.

(c) None of the following shall by itself cause a director to be considered not independent for purposes of this section:
   (1) the nomination or election of the director by persons who are defendants in the derivative proceeding or against whom action is demanded;
   (2) the naming of the director as a defendant in the derivative proceeding or as a person against whom action is demanded; or
   (3) the approval by the director of the act being challenged in the derivative proceeding or demand if the act resulted in no personal benefit to the director.

(d) If a derivative proceeding is commenced after a determination has been made rejecting a demand by a shareholder, the complaint shall allege with particularity facts establishing either (1) that a majority of the board of directors did not consist of independent directors at the time the determination was made, or (2) that the requirements of subsection (a) have not been met.

(e) If a majority of the board of directors does not consist of independent directors at the time the determination is made, the corporation shall have the burden of proving that the requirements of subsection (a) have been met. If a majority of the board of directors consists of independent directors at the time the determination is made, the plaintiff shall have the burden of proving that the requirements of subsection (a) have not been met.

(f) The court may appoint a panel of one or more independent persons upon motion by the corporation to make a determination whether the maintenance of the derivative proceeding is in the best interests of the corporation. In such case, the plaintiff shall have the burden of proving that the requirements of subsection (a) have not been met.

Demand on Shareholders

Rules for demand on shareholders prior to bringing a derivative action vary widely from state to state and among federal courts. Many jurisdictions do not require a demand on shareholders. California and New York intentionally omit any reference for need of a demand on shareholders, and thereby none is required.

In the states that require demand on shareholders, all agree that the demand is excused when a majority of the shareholders are wrongdoers. When the shareholders that are wrongdoers hold a controlling even though less than a majority of shares, demand will be excusable.

All states are in agreement that the demand is excused when it will be futile. Demand has been excused where only one shareholders' meeting was held in many years, and management had ignored earlier demands that such meetings be held, *Pioche Mines, et al., v. Dolman,* 333 F.2d 257, 9th Circuit (1964).

Cases are split on whether demand is excused because corporation has a large number of shareholders, or because management has refused to supply plaintiff with a shareholders' list.

Cases are also split as to excused or not where the alleged wrong could not be ratified by the shareholders. However, the majority rule is if the shareholders cannot ratify the wrongs, then this excuses the need for a demand on stockholders, *Mayor v. Adams,* 37 Del. Ch. 298 (1958).

Massachusetts holds that shareholders have power to preclude suit even when they do not have power to ratify, *S. Solomon & Sons Trust v. New England Theatres Operating Corp.,* 326 Mass. 99 (1950).

Right to Trial by Jury, Derivative Action

Traditionally a derivative action has been thought of as an equitable remedy and does not involve a trial by jury. The California Constitution does not have a right to a jury trial in a derivative action. A South Carolina statute likewise bars a right to a jury trial. In *Ross v. Bernhard,* 396 U.S. 531 (1970), however, the Supreme Court said that in a derivative action brought in federal court the parties have a right to a jury where the action would be triable by a jury if it had been brought by the corporation itself rather than by a shareholder. New York law allows a jury trial for a derivative action. There is a right to a jury trial under Alabama law.

Discontinuance or Settlement (Section 7.45, RMBCA)

A derivative proceeding may not be discontinued or settled without the court's approval. If the court determines that a proposed discontinuance or settlement will substantially affect the interest of the corporation's shareholders or a class of shareholders, the court shall direct that notice be given to the shareholders affected.

Counsel Fees for Plaintiff, Derivative Actions

All benefits accrue to the corporation in a derivative action. The action is brought for the benefit of the corporation although it is brought by a shareholder who actually does not directly gain from winning. Therefore, very few shareholders would finance an action for the benefit of the corporation without direct gain to the shareholder. Very few actions would occur if the law did not allow plaintiff's attorney to be compensated by a **contingency fee** payable out of the corporate recovery. A contingency fee is a fee paid the attorney if the attorney recovers a dollar award; the attorney receives a percentage of the award. If there is no recovery, there is no fee. The fee varies from 20 to 35 percent on recovery of less than $1,000,000 and 15 to 25 percent when the award is over $1,000,000. If an extraordinary amount of time was spent, the attorney can petition for additional compensation based on his or her hourly rate.

The award of fees to successful plaintiffs is justified by two theories: (1) **Common Fund theory**—Upon winning, plaintiff establishes a fund under control of the court. Many individuals besides the plaintiff may benefit from this fund. Counsel fees come from this fund. (2) **Private Attorney General** doctrine—Plaintiff's counsel fees should be awarded to encourage the initiation of private actions that vindicate important legal policies. This theory is important especially where the benefit is not pecuniary.

While success is a prerequisite to an award of counsel fees, a judgment is not. Counsel fees can be awarded even if a case is settled.

Payment of Expenses (Section 7.46, RMBCA)

Upon termination of the derivative proceeding, the court may:

(1) order the corporation to pay the plaintiff's reasonable expenses (including counsel fees) incurred in the proceeding if it finds that the proceeding has resulted in a substantial benefit to the corporation;

(2) order the plaintiff to pay any defendant's reasonable expenses (including counsel fees) incurred in defending the proceeding if it finds that the proceeding was commenced or maintained without reasonable cause or for an improper purpose; or

(3) order a party to pay an opposing party's reasonable expenses (including counsel fees) incurred because of the filing of a pleading, motion, or other paper, if it finds that the pleading, motion, or other paper was not well grounded in fact, after reasonable inquiry, or warranted by existing law or a good faith argument for the extension, modification, or reversal of existing law and was interposed for an improper purpose, such as to harass or to cause unnecessary delay or needless increase in the cost of the litigation.

Security for Expenses

The general American view and the rule of most states is that the losing party does not have to pay the expenses of the winning party, except for taxable costs, as docket fees, filing fees, and transcript fees. Security for expense statutes is usually not interpreted to have personal liability on the plaintiff for expenses. The liability is not more than the amount of the bond posted for expenses.

Avoiding Posting a Bond for Security

The shareholder looking to bring a proceeding against the corporate managers must try to find a way to do it in a state that is requiring a bond for security for costs in a manner where the bond is not necessary. Generally, a direct action does not require a bond. A derivative action does require a bond. The shareholder would have to frame the complaint so that it is a direct action and not a derivative action. A second possibility is to bring the proceeding under some federal law where no bond is required for costs, such as under Rule 10B-5 of the Securities Act or possibly under the proxy rules. Another answer is to go to a sister state that does not have a statute for security for costs in a derivative action.

Strategy to Avoid Posting a Bond or Reducing the Amount

Another possibility is to stay the effectiveness of an order to post the bond so that plaintiff can seek intervenors to help qualify under an exemption based on a percentage of dollar value of the shares held by plaintiff shareholders, *Baker v. MacFadden Publications,* 300 NY 325 (1950).

Another method is when the corporation moves for a bond to be posted, is to obtain an order for the corporation to produce a shareholders' list and thereafter seek a stay of the bond to solicit shareholders to join the proceedings. New York courts generally grant these motions. This move by the corporation to seek a bond from plaintiffs could be a double edged sword, as follows. A corporation moves for a bond for security; the plaintiff asks for a 60-day stay of the bond plus access to the shareholders' list to solicit help from other shareholders. The corporation is now in a terrible position. The stockholders are going to receive information of the misdeeds of the corporate managers, and the financial press will also receive this information. A proxy fight will be inevitable. Worse yet, the plaintiff's attorney has a list of shareholders that would be interested in further fighting the managers for their misdeeds in other lawsuits. As a result, it is not uncommon in New York for the corporation not to seek a bond for security for costs from shareholders.

Indemnification

There are three main reasons for a corporation to indemnify its directors: (1) To reinforce directors resisting unjust charges and to allow them to obtain competent legal counsel; (2) to attract responsible, competent people to serve on the board; and (3) to discourage shareholders' litigation of the harassment variety. **Indemnification** is the act of reimbursing. As an example; a director is sued for wrongdoing and a judgment is obtained against the directors for $100,000. The company would indemnify the director by giving her or him $100,000 to pay the judgment.

Just about every state has an indemnification statute. However, they differ widely in detail. Some only apply to officers and directors; some only cover directors; others include employees and agents. Some are **exclusive**, which means they prohibit any indemnification not consistent with the statute. Others are **nonexclusive**, which allows additional indemnification over and above that which is in the statute. In nonexclusive jurisdictions the charter and bylaws afford indemnification in excess of the indemnification authorized in the statute.

Many statutes require the officer or director to be successful in the proceeding to obtain the indemnification. The meaning of successful varies from state to state. Section 8.52, RMBCA, says the director must be "wholly successful, on the merits or otherwise." Delaware General Corporation Law, Section 145(c) and New York Business Corporation Law, Section 722(a) say the officer or director must be "successful, on the merits or otherwise." California Corporation Code, Section 317(d) says the officer or director must be "successful on the merits." These phrases are subject to various meanings. Where a claim is terminated against an officer without any payment, the officer is "successful, on the merits or otherwise," under the Illinois statute. Where a complaint is dismissed because of the statute of limitations, the defendants are "successful" under the New York and Delaware statutes.

If a complaint had four actions against a director and the director won three and lost one, the director would probably be "successful" under New York and Delaware statutes. Under the RMBCA's definition of "wholly successful" the director would not be considered "wholly successful." To be "wholly successful," the entire action would have to be disposed of without any liability.

Many statutes permit indemnification of an officer or director for fines and judgments as a result of violations of a civil or criminal statute. These are permitted where the violations were in good faith intending to further the corporation's interests.

Settlement of Derivative Actions

The action once commenced cannot be settled or dismissed without the approval of the court (Section 7.44, RMBCA and various state statutes).

The courts tend to rely on **affidavits, documents, depositions,** and answers to **interrogatories** when approving a settlement or dismissal. An affidavit is a sworn statement in writing. A document can be any piece of paper, a contract, letter, etc. A deposition is questions orally asked before a court reporter and answers taken down verbatim by the court reporter; the testimony is usually sworn to before a notary public who is usually the court reporter. Interrogatories are written questions that are submitted to the witness and the answers are written and sworn to.

Shareholders Who Object to a Settlement

Shareholders who object to a settlement of the action after receiving notice of the proposed settlement can object and enter the case. The objector becomes a party to the settlement proceeding although not to the original action. An objector can cross examine witnesses in the settlement hearings; obtain a reasonable adjournment to study the matter; and if appeal of the settlement decision is desired, even obtain discovery rights. If the objector is successful in improving the settlement, the attorney for the objector is entitled to counsel fees from the settlement. Therefore, the attorney for the objector drives the process since the objector has nothing to actually personally gain or lose; the attorney does. Very often the effort of the objector results in improving the settlement, and fees are paid to the attorney based on a percentage of the improvement of the settlement.

As far as a publicly held corporation is concerned, the plaintiff does not drive the case; the attorney for the plaintiff does as the attorney has a lot to win or lose. The attorney works for the fees to be earned in winning and has a substantial investment in time and disbursements. The plaintiff has little or no investment.

Class Actions

If many shareholders have the same claim against a corporation, they can join together and, rather than sue separately, sue as a class action. They can share expenses. The court only has to hear one case instead of many of the same case. If a corporation refused to pay a dividend that had been declared, it could be a class action or a direct action. Most jurisdictions have strict requirements that govern class actions.

(1) A judge must certify the class. All class members must have similar cases without any conflict of interest.
(2) A judge will not certify a class unless it is so large that individual suits would not be practical.

(3) Everyone eligible for the class must be personally notified. Shareholders must be willing to incur the expense to notify all who are eligible to join the class. Once notified, a shareholder has the option to join the class, sue individually, or do nothing. All who are eligible do not have to join for the class to be certified.

(4) Settlement must be approved by the court. Dismissal must be approved by the court.

SUMMARY

A derivative action is brought on behalf of the corporation for the benefit of the corporation. Any award goes to the corporation. To bring this action one has to be a shareholder and continue as a shareholder throughout the proceeding. If at any time the plaintiff ceases to be a shareholder, the action can be dismissed. Any time during the proceedings the corporation can decide to take over the action on behalf of the corporation, and the shareholder plaintiff is replaced by the corporation and is no longer a party to the action. A shareholder can be an equitable shareholder as well as an actual shareholder. Many states require the plaintiff shareholder(s) to post a bond for security. The action is brought against managers, officers, and directors who have committed wrongs that injured the corporation. The corporation is made a party defendant. The action is in equity. Equity allows a judgment to be issued in favor of a defendant corporation against other defendants. Some states permit a trial by jury, others do not. Prior to bringing the action a demand must be made on the board of directors to either bring the action themselves or permit the demanding party to do so. Upon receipt of the demand the board of directors can appoint a disinterested committee of directors to investigate the claim. If the committee appointed by the board of directors finds the action will not benefit the corporation or be in the best interests of the corporation, it can deny permission and have the corporation move to dismiss the complaint. If the court verifies the committee to have been disinterested directors, it will usually side with the board and dismiss the complaint.

The shareholder to avoid posting a bond for security for costs and to avoid having to serve a demand on the board of directors, may bring the action instead as a direct action. All benefits and monies recovered go to the shareholder plaintiff, not to the corporation. There are restrictions as to what matters bring about a direct action.

Many corporations indemnify their officers, directors, employees, and agents through insurance policies. Some states allow the corporation great leadway in indemnification; others limit what the corporation may indemnify and who it may indemnify.

Once the derivative action is commenced it cannot be settled or dismissed without approval of the court. Any shareholder objecting to a settlement becomes a party to the settlement proceeding but not a party to the actual proceeding.

CASES

Derivative Action or Direct Action

SAX v. WORLD WIDE PRESS, INC.
United States Court of Appeals, 9th Circuit (1987)
809 F2d 610

This was a diversity action. Plaintiff claims a direct action for damages as the conduct of defendants injured plaintiff personally. District court dismissed claim for damages and said under Montana law this is a derivative action, not a direct action. Court of Appeals affirmed the district court.

Defendant is a Montana corporation which manufactures gambling supplies and equipment. The individual defendants own more than half of the stock of World Wide. In 1972, World Wide hired Sax as general manager to create and open a plant in Great Falls, Montana. The oral employment agreement gave Sax an option to purchase up to 75,000 shares of World Wide stock. After Sax successfully started the business and acquired approximately 5 percent of World Wide's outstanding stock, World Wide breached the option agreement by refusing to sell him more stock. Sax terminated his employment in June 1976. After he left the company, Sax alleges the individual defendants conspired to deplete the assets of World Wide and depreciate the value of his stock, which deprived him of income. He alleges the conspiracy members illegally sold equipment and kept faulty records of inventory. They also sold equipment to their own corporation, Instant Ticket Factory, at less than fair market value. Sax also alleges the conspirators published false and fraudulent annual statements concealing their personal interests and conflict of interest.

Sax commenced a direct action as a shareholder seeking actual and punitive damages caused by the alleged wrongful conduct and conspiracy. The court dismissed the action reasoning that the alleged wrongful acts of the defendants did not injure Sax personally but rather damaged World Wide, and therefore the action must be brought derivatively.

Derivative or Direct Action—Seeking Injunction Not Dollars
EISENBERG v. FLYING TIGER LINE, INC.
451 F2d 267 (1971)

Plaintiff is seeking to overturn a merger and reorganization effected by defendant in 1969. Eisenberg claims a series of corporate maneuvers were intended to dilute his voting rights. Plaintiff alleges, defendant in July 1969 organized a wholly owned subsidiary, Flying Tiger Corporation (FTC). In August, FTC organized a wholly owned subsidiary, FTL Air Freight Corporation (FTL). The three Delaware corporations then entered into a plan of reorganization, subject to stockholder approval, by which Flying Tiger merged into FTL and only FTL survived.

Flying Tiger moved for an order to require Eisenberg to comply with New York Business Corporation Law, Section 627, which requires a plaintiff suing derivatively on behalf of a corporation to post security for the corporation's costs. The court granted the motion and gave Eisenberg 30 days to post security in the sum of $35,000. Eisenberg did not comply, his action was dismissed, and he appeals. The appellate court found the action to be personal and not derivative within the meaning of New York Business Corporation Law, Section 627, and therefore reversed the dismissal.

Actions to compel the dissolution of a corporation have been held to be representative, since the corporation could not possibly benefit therefrom. An action by a stockholder complaining that a proposed recapitalization would unfairly benefit holders of another class of stock was representative. Where a shareholder sues on behalf of himself and all others similarly situated to enjoin a proposed merger or consolidation, he is not enforcing a derivative right; he is enforcing a right common to all the shareholders which runs against the corporation.

Eisenberg's position is even stronger than it would be in the ordinary merger case. In routine mergers the stockholders retain a voice in the operation of the company, although a company other than their original choice. Here, however, the reorganization deprived him and other minority stockholders of any voice in the affairs of their previously existing operating company.

Demand on Board Prior to Bringing Derivative Action
BARR v. WACKMAN
Court of Appeals of New York (1975)
36 NY 2nd 371, 368 NYS 2d 497

Shareholders derivative action without first making a demand on the board of directors to initiate action on behalf of corporation or remedy the acts complained of. Plaintiff alleges a demand would be futile because the board of directors participated in, authorized, and approved the challenged acts; and its members are themselves subject to liability and, therefore, cannot be expected to vote to sue themselves.

Three of the defendants move to dismiss for failure to comply with New York Business Corporation Law, Section 626, which states, "The complaint shall set forth with particularity the efforts of plaintiff to secure the initiation of action by the board or the reasons for not making such efforts."

The certified question to the Court of Appeals and issue herein is, "Whether allegations of board participation in and approval of acts involving bias and self-dealing by minority directors and breach of fiduciary duties of due care and diligence by the remaining majority directors through their participation and approval, though there is no claim of self-dealing as to them, are sufficient to withstand a motion to dismiss for failure to make a demand."

The Appellate Court dismissed the motion having answered the certified question in the affirmative.

WORDS TO KNOW

affidavit	indemnification
common fund theory	independent committee
contingency fee	indispensable party
deposition	interested director
derivative action	interrogatories
direct action	nonexclusive statute
document	private attorney general theory
equitable ownership	security for costs
exclusive statute	settlement objection

REVIEW QUESTIONS

1. Explain a derivative action.
2. Explain a direct action.
3. What is meant by equitable ownership? Explain in detail.
4. Who would be an indispensable party in a derivative action?
5. When and for what reason is an independent committee used?
6. When would a director be considered interested?
7. Explain what indemnification means and why it exists.
8. Give the differences between an exclusive statute and a nonexclusive statute.
9. Is a demand on the board necessary prior to commencing a derivative action?
10. What does a demand served on the board say?

11. What parties do you need the approval of to settle a derivative action?

12. How can you avoid posting a bond for security for costs in a derivative action?

13. Explain what happens if a shareholder objects to a settlement.

14. When can an attorney for the shareholder have fees paid by other than the client?

15. What kind of action is a derivative proceeding?

16. When can you have a trial by jury in a derivative action?

SHORT ESSAYS

1. The issue is whether allegations of board participation in and approval of acts involving bias and self-dealing by a minority of directors and breach of fiduciary duty of care and diligence by the remaining majority directors through their participation and approval, though there is no claim of self-dealing as to them, are sufficient to withstanding a motion to dismiss for failure to make demand. Explain in detail.

2. Explain how you may try to avoid posting a bond for security for costs if you are considering bringing a derivative stockholders' action.

3. Can a corporation indemnify its officers, directors, employees, and agents? What, if any, restrictions are there to receiving this indemnification if allowed? Explain your answer in complete detail.

4. You are a shareholder in Executives, Inc. You were expecting to receive a financial statement showing the corporation has over $35,000,000 in assets. You also were expecting the corporation to show a very high profit this year and expected the board of directors to declare a dividend double what you received last year. You have just received the financial statement, and it shows the corporate assets down to $15,000,000. For the first time since you have owned these shares, about ten years, the board of directors has failed to declare a dividend. Friends who work at the corporation have told you that the seven directors have secretly formed another corporation and have been buying corporate assets at a price that is considerably lower than fair market value. You have also learned that these directors intend to leave the corporation as soon as they have all the assets they want. They are also taking all of the large customers to their new corporation. Prior to these events, your stock was worth about $330,000. At the present time you estimate your stock to be worth less than $50,000. It is possible that the corporation will be insolvent if this continues. You are concerned about the losses you personally are sustaining from these actions. What if anything can you do?

5. A group of shareholders brought a derivative stockholders' action against the ten directors of Zip Corporation. You have just been notified that an offer of $5,000,000 to settle the suit has been tendered, and the parties that commenced the action are in favor of the settlement. You have been a stockholder of Zip Corporation for twelve years and have carefully followed the corporation, its business, assets, and all avenues concerning the corporation. After studying the terms of settlement and all the financial matter submitted with the notice, and after doing your mathematics, you believe that a $10,000,000 to $15,000,000 offer would be more consistent with the facts. You are a retired corporation attorney but would like one more shot at a corporate case. What if anything can you do?

MERGERS, ACQUISITIONS, AND DISSOLUTIONS

OBJECTIVES

After completing this chapter, you will be able to:

1. Discuss what a merger is.
2. Know the different structures in obtaining an acquisition.
3. Explain a consolidation.
4. Know what a cash for assets purchase entails.
5. Know what a stock for assets purchase entails.
6. Explain appraisal rights.
7. Know what a stock market exception is.
8. Structure a statutory merger.
9. Know what a surviving corporation is.
10. Structure a short form merger.
11. Know the tax aspects of various merger combinations.
12. Know what a "type A" corporation is.
13. Structure a triangular merger.
14. Know what a reverse triangular merger is.
15. Know what advantages there are to a statutory merger.

16. Explain share exchanges.

17. Structure going private.

18. Know the various ways a corporation can be dissolved.

INTRODUCTION

Nonlawyers often refer to any business combination as a merger. To a lawyer a **merger** means two or more corporations pursuant to a formal written agreement incorporating specific statutory requirements of the jurisdiction and federal statutes, by which the stock of the seller (**transferor**) is converted into stock of the buyer (**survivor**). The survivor (buyer) then owns the assets of the seller (transferor). The buyer (survivor) is then liable for all the debts and liabilities of the seller (transferor). The seller (transferor) thereafter does not exist.

MERGER

A **merger** is two or more corporations coming together with the survivor keeping its name, as follows: Corporation "A" and corporation "B" plan to merge and thereafter will be known as corporation "B". Corporation "A" will no longer be in existence. Corporation "B" will have all of the assets and liabilities of "A".

CONSOLIDATION

In a **consolidation**, two or more corporations come together, and thereafter they are known as and by a new name. Corporation "A", "B" and "C" plan to consolidate and thereafter the corporation will be known as corporation "F". Corporation "F" will have all the assets and liabilities of corporations "A", "B", and "C". Corporations "A", "B" and "C" will no longer be in existence.

There are four other business combinations which are not mergers: cash for assets, cash for stock, stock for assets, and stock for stock.

BUSINESS ACQUISITIONS (OTHER THAN MERGER)

(1) *Cash for assets:*   **Cash for assets** is where one corporation purchases all of the assets of another corporation for dollars or some other consideration. The selling corporation is left with no assets and either goes into a new business venture or dissolves. Corporation "A" purchases substantially all of the assets of corporation "B" for cash or some other consideration.

(2) *Cash for stock:*   **Cash for stock** would be when one corporation purchases all of the stock or a majority of the stock of another corporation for cash or some other consideration. This leaves the selling corporation either as a subsidiary of the purchaser or a candidate for a future merger, consolidation or liquidation. Corporation "A" purchases at least a majority of the stock of corporation "B" for cash or some other consideration.

(3) *Stock for assets:*   **Stock for assets** is when one corporation purchases either all or substantially all of the assets of another corporation and for consideration issues shares of its own stock to the seller. The buying corporation can either assume all or some of the liabilities of the seller. Very often the seller will dissolve and distribute the shares it received to its stockholders as a liquidation dividend. Sometimes the directors and officers of the selling corporation join the buying corporation in some capacity as part of the transaction. Corporation "A" issues shares of its own stock to corporation "B" in exchange for substantially all of the assets of "B". Sometimes "A" will agree to assume the liabilities of "B". Sometimes "A" will agree to assume only the liabilities of "B" that "A" agrees to accept. Very often "B" will dissolve after the stock is received and then distribute it to its shareholders. This is agreed in advance so that a large block of the stock of "A" is not held by one corporation. Sometimes some of the officers and/or directors of "B" join "A" in some capacity.

(4) *Stock for stock:*   **Stock for stock** is a transaction between a corporation and the stockholders of another corporation. The stock of one corporation is exchanged for the stock of another corporation. To be beneficial to the corporation, all, or at least a majority of the shares of the other corporation must be obtained. With this method, formal approval of the directors, management or stockholders of the corporation being taken over is not required. Corporation "A" issues shares of its own stock directly to shareholders of corporation "B" in exchange for a number of shares of corporation "B". This would be at least a majority of the outstanding shares of "B". Thereafter, "B" becomes a subsidiary of "A". Sometimes "B" is either liquidated or merged into "A". In any event the assets of "B" are under the control of "A". This does not require approval of the management or the stockholders of "B" since the dealings were direct with the stockholders of "B". Sometimes part of the management of "B" will join "A".

SALE OF SUBSTANTIALLY ALL ASSETS OF A CORPORATION

1. In Regular Course of Business

It has been held that a sale of substantially all assets of a corporation in the ordinary course of business does not require the approval of shareholders. This type of sale does not prevent the continuance of the corporation. It would not have required unanimous shareholder approval at common law. Statutes covering the sale of substantially all assets were not designed to change the common law rule. Therefore, no shareholder approval is required.

2. Not in Regular Course of Business

If substantially all of the assets of a corporation are sold and the sale is not in the regular course of business, or if the selling corporation by the sale has rendered itself unable to carry on its business pursuant to its corporate charter, the sale or lease must be approved by the board of directors and also by a majority of the shareholders entitled to vote at a meeting called for this purpose (RMBCA 12.02). In most states **dissenting shareholders** of the selling corporation are given the right of appraisal pursuant to RMBCA, 13.02(a)(3). A **dissenting shareholder** is one that refuses to consent to and believes their investment is being adversely affected by any of the following corporate transactions: a merger, consolidation, cash for assets, cash for stock or stock for assets. Remedies usually include any one or all of the following depending on the jurisdiction: appraisal rights (determination of value of shares owned), equitable relief as an injunction to prohibit the transaction, or rescission if the transaction has already been completed.

Right to Dissent (Section 1302, RMBCA)

(a) A shareholder is entitled to dissent from, and obtain payment of, the fair value of his shares in the event of any of the following corporate actions:

(1) consummation of a plan of merger to which the corporation is a party: (i) if shareholder approval is required for the merger by Section 11.03 or the articles of incorporation and the shareholder is entitled to vote on the merger, or (ii) if the corporation is a subsidiary that is merged with its parent under Section 11.04:

(2) consummation of a plan of share exchange to which the corporation is a party as the corporation whose shares will be acquired, if the shareholder is entitled to vote on the plan;

(3) consummation of a sale or exchange of all, or substantially all, of the property of the corporation other than in the usual and regular course of business, if the shareholder is entitled to vote on the sale or exchange, including a sale in dissolution, but not including a sale pursuant to court order or a sale for cash pursuant to a plan by which all or substantially all of the net proceeds of the sale will be distributed to the shareholders within one year after the date of sale;

(4) an amendment of the articles of incorporation that materially and adversely affects rights in respect of a dissenter's shares because it:

(i) alters or abolishes a preferential right to the shares;

(ii) creates, alters, or abolishes a right in respect to redemption, including a provision respecting a sinking fund for the redemption or repurchase of the shares;

(iii) alters or abolishes a preemptive right of the holder of the shares to acquire shares or other securities; or

(iv) excludes or limits the right of the shares to vote on any matter or to cumulate votes, other than a limitation by dilution through issuance of shares or other securities with similar voting rights; or

(v) reduces the number of shares owned by the shareholder to a fraction of a share if the fractional share so created is to be acquired for cash under Section 6.04.

(5) any corporate action taken pursuant to a shareholder vote to the extent the articles of incorporation, bylaws, or a resolution of the board of directors pro-

vides that voting or nonvoting shareholders are entitled to dissent and obtain payment for their shares.

(b) A shareholder entitled to dissent and obtain payment for his shares under this chapter may not challenge the corporate action creating his entitlement unless the action is unlawful or fraudulent with respect to the shareholder or the corporation.

Appraisal Rights

Appraisal rights are a method to determine value. The question with statutes allowing appraisal rights for dissenting shareholders is whether or not the statute is exclusive as to remedy. Can one choose to take appraisal rights or obtain equitable relief in the form of an injunction or rescission? Does he or she have a choice? The answer is not always simple, as follows:

(1) Sometimes the statute by language says it is exclusive. Even then, the courts may say otherwise. An exclusive statute provision in Michigan was interpreted by the courts only to be exclusive in transactions that were accomplished in good faith.

(2) In the absence of explicit statutory language, it is clear that the availability of appraisal rights normally does not preclude attacks on any of the following grounds:
   (a) The transaction is illegal under corporation law and is not authorized by statute. *Eisenber v. Central Zone Property Corp.*, 306 NY 58 (1953).
   (b) Procedural steps required to authorize the transaction were not taken; therefore, it is not legal by corporation law. No notice to shareholders. *Starret Corp. v. Fifth Avenue, et al.*, 1 F.Supp 868 (SD NY).
   (c) There was fraudulent misrepresentation and violation of SEC proxy rules; therefore, the shareholder approval of transaction is improper.
   (d) It is clear from past decisions that availability of appraisal rights will preclude a shareholder from seeking to recover the money value of his or her shares under a nonstatutory remedy for which appraisal rights are available. *Schloss Associates v. Arkwin Industries*, 772 NYS 2d 605 (1985).
   (e) The general rule is that mere availability of appraisal rights does not preclude shareholders from injunctive relief or rescission for fraud and self-dealing.

Dissenters' Right to Appraisal

Generally most states allow dissenter's rights to appraisal when:

(1) dissenting shareholders of each corporation that is party to a consolidation.

(2) dissenting shareholders to a sale of substantially all assets not in the regular course of business so that the corporation can no longer function.

(3) dissenting shareholders of any corporation participating in a merger, except a short form merger where the parent owns 90 percent or more of the shares of the acquiring corporation. A few states have a provision for majority ownership or more. These statutes operate as cash out statutes where the dissenters get cash, not stock.

Stock Market Exception to Appraisal Rights

Many states have an exception to the right of dissenters to appraisal rights if an established market such as the New York Stock Exchange exists for the shares.

STATUTORY MERGER

Sections 11.01, 11.03, 11.05, 11.06, RMBCA, and Delaware General Corporation Law Sections 251, 259, 260 and 261 authorize statutory mergers. The procedures can be different in various states. After negotiations have been completed, a letter of intent is executed by the principals to the merger. This is a type of condensed draft of the formal agreement to be later agreed upon and executed. After the boards of both corporations and the shareholders of both corporations have approved the merger, articles of merger or a merger agreement are filed with the secretary of state. Securities of the survivor corporation are then exchanged for securities of the seller corporation. The selling corporation is no longer in existence as it has merged into the survivor corporation. Usually no deeds, bills of sale, or other documents of conveyance are necessary. By operation of law, the survivor has all of the assets and liabilities of the seller.

In the past all statutory mergers required a majority or two-thirds approval of the shareholders of each corporation as well as approval of the boards of each corporation. Today many states have statutes that have exceptions to shareholder approvals in short form mergers and small scale mergers.

Surviving Shareholder Approval Not Required

Section 11.03 (g), RMBCA, and Delaware General Corporate Law Section 251, as well as many other state statutes only require shareholder approval from the surviving (buyer) corporation if the transaction fundamentally alters the character of the enterprise or substantially reduces shareholder voting or profit distribution. As long as there is no increase in shares issued to the transferor (seller) in excess of 20 percent from the surviving corporation, no shareholder approval is necessary from the surviving corporation. This means no more than 20 percent additional shares can be issued for the transaction than there were before the transaction without shareholder approval. This 20 percent rule is consistent with the RMBCA, Delaware, and Michigan; there is a 15 percent in Pennsylvania and 18.5 percent in the New York Stock Exchange requirement.

Caution: This 20 percent or less rule in jurisdictions is only available as long as you do not modify or amend the articles of incorporation of the survivor corporation to be able to issue additional shares. You cannot amend the articles of incorporation to issue more shares without shareholder approval.

If you intend to issue more than the above 20 percent shares, you either need shareholder approval or must arrange the transaction in the form of a merger involving a subsidiary of the acquiring parent so no shareholder approval is necessary.

SHORT FORM MERGER

Most statutes have a provision for **short form mergers**. This is when a parent corporation acquires a subsidiary by merger. No vote of the subsidiary's shareholders or of the parent shareholders is required. The board of directors of both the parent corporation and subsidiary must authorize and approve the merger. There are no appraisal rights. The parent corporation by most statutes must own at least 90 percent of the stock of the subsidiary to qualify as a short form merger. If the parent corporation owns less than 90 percent of the subsidiary but over a majority of outstanding shares, the parent corporation can still force the merger as a cash out. The dissenting shareholders obtain appraisal rights and cash for their stock. Therefore, as long as a majority of the outstanding stock is owned by the parent corporation, the parent corporation can at any time force a merger and cash out. If the minority shareholders dissent on the price they are to receive for their shares, they can demand an appraisal. The minority shareholders cannot, however, force a cash out if the majority shareholders are not interested in a merger.

TAX ASPECTS OF CORPORATE ACQUISITIONS

Taxation consequences often determine how and why a combination will be structured in a particular manner. The major issue is whether the acquisition will be tax free, i.e., that taxes for the transferor (seller) will be postponed; the basis for the stock or property received will remain the same; and past operating losses for both companies can be carried forward to apply to future earnings of the transferee (buyer). (Internal Revenue Code Sections 351, 358, 361, 381, 382, et. al.).

The Internal Revenue Code provides three basic methods for a tax-free **reorganization**. Reorganization refers to one of the acquisition methods discussed below. The Code refers to "Type A", "Type B", and "Type C" reorganizations. These are congruent with statutory mergers or consolidation, stock for stock acquisitions, and stock for assets acquisitions.

- A **"Type A" reorganization** defined in Internal Revenue Code Section 368(a)(1)(A) is a statutory merger or consolidation. Consolidation can be voting stock, cash, or other consideration, such as notes, bonds, or nonvoting stock. If property other than stock or securities is used, there will be a taxable gain to transferor. However, under the continuity of interest doctrine, if 56 percent of the value of the transferred property is paid in stock or securities, it would qualify as a tax-free reorganization.

- A **"Type B" reorganization** defined in Internal Revenue Code Section 368 (a)(1)(B) is the acquisition by one corporation (transferee, buyer) from another corporation (transferor, seller) for all or part of its voting stock, or the voting stock of its parent corporation, or of another corporation, as long as the acquiring corporation has control of the acquired corporation immediately after the acquisition. The consideration paid by the acquiring corporation can only be voting stock. This is a stock reorganization. Control is defined as ownership of at least each class of stock issued and outstanding.

- A **"Type C" reorganization,** defined in Internal Revenue Code Section 368 (a)(1)(C), is acquisition by one corporation, in exchange for all or part of its voting stock, or of its parent, or of substantially all the properties of another corporation. The consideration must consist primarily of voting stock (in "Type B", solely of voting stock); other consideration can be used as long as 80 percent of the fair market value of all the property of transferor is paid in voting stock.

TRIANGULAR MERGERS

A triangular merger has the advantages of a merger without some of the disadvantages as follows. Corporations "A" and "B" want to merge. "B" corporation will be the survivor and the shareholders of "A" corporation will end up with 100,00 shares of "B" corporation stock. In a normal merger, "B" corporation would issue 100,000 shares of its stock to the shareholders of "A" corporation, and the shareholders of "A" corporation would issue all their shares to "B" corporation. Thereafter "A" corporation would disappear and "B" corporation would own all of the assets and liabilities of "A" corporation.

In a **conventional triangular merger,** the surviving corporation after the merger is completed controls all of the assets of the merged corporation but has none of the liabilities. The merged corporation thereafter disappears.

In a conventional triangular merger, "B" corporation forms a wholly owned subsidiary corporation known as "X" corporation. "B" corporation transfers 100,000 shares of its stock to "X" corporation. All of the stock of "X" corporation is then transferred to "B" corporation as consideration for the 100,000 shares of "B" corporation stock it received. Corporations "X" and "A" now engage in a merger and instead of "X" corporation giving its shares to "A" corporation's shareholders it gives 100,000 shares of "B" corporation stock to the shareholders of "A" corporation. "A" corporation gives all of its shares to "X" corporation. The end result is that the shareholders of "A" corporation get 100,000 shares of "B" corporation stock and "X" corporation owns all of the shares, assets and liabilities of "A" corporation. "B" corporation owns and controls "X" corporation which has all the assets of "A" corporation. The difference is that "B" corporation is in the same position as a statutory merger, BUT, now "B" corporation has none of the liabilities of "A" corporation, yet controls all of the assets of "A" corporation.

By statute in most major states, the surviving corporation can issue securities of any corporation, it need not be only from the surviving corporation.

The Internal Revenue Code, Section 368(a)(2)(D), permits a triangular merger to qualify as a tax-free "Type A" reorganization, if (i) substantially all of "A" corporation's properties are acquired by "X" corporation; and (ii) the merger would have qualified as a "Type A" reorganization if "B" corporation had merged directly with "A" corporation; and (iii) no stock of "X" corporation is used in the transaction to "A" corporation.

Reverse Triangular Merger

In a **reverse triangular merger,** the surviving corporation after the merger is completed controls all of the assets of the merged corporation but has none of the liabilities. The merged corporation does not disappear. A reverse triangular merger starts the same as a conventional triangular merger, except that instead of merging "A" corporation into "X" corporation, the subsidiary of "B" corporation, now we merge "X" corporation into "A" corporation. The shareholders of "A" corporation get the 100,000 shares of "B" corporation stock held by "X" corporation, and the shareholders of "A" corporation transfer their shares in "A" corporation to "B" corporation. The end result is that "X" corporation disappears. "A" corporation is still alive. All shares of "A" corporation are owned by "B" corporation and the shareholders of "A" corporation received 100,000 shares of "B" corporation. "B" corporation owns and controls "A" corporation and has none of the liabilities of "A" corporation. This is useful when "A" corporation has valuable contract rights, leases, licenses, or franchises and you do not want "A" corporation to disappear.

Under Internal Revenue Code Section 368(a)(2)(E), a reverse triangular merger will qualify as a tax free "Type A" reorganization, if (i) "B" corporation ends up with substantially all of the properties of "X" corporation and "A" corporation, and (ii) "X" corporation's voting stock is exchanged for at least 80 percent of "A" corporation's voting and nonvoting stock.

SHARE EXCHANGE

The newest combination is known as the **share exchange**. It is similar to the stock for stock exchange. The survivor issues stock in exchange for stock of the acquired corporation. However, in a stock for stock exchange, each shareholder of the acquired corporation makes their own decision whether or not to sell; there is no formal agreement by the acquired corporation. In the share exchange all shareholders of the corporation to be acquired vote on whether or not to engage in the exchange. If a majority of the corporation's outstanding shares approve of the exchange, ALL shareholders must surrender their shares unless they demand appraisal rights. Not too many states have statutes authorizing share exchanges. It is expected that many more states will be authorizing this kind of transaction in the future.

PUBLIC CORPORATION GOING PRIVATE

To accomplish this:

(1) The corporation itself can purchase its shares on the open market.

(2) The corporation can make a tender offer to all shareholders to purchase their interest.

(3) A majority shareholder can purchase the corporate shares on the open market.

(4) A majority shareholder can make a tender offer to all shareholders.

(5) A majority shareholder can form a new corporation, known as "A" corporation, own a majority of shares, and have institutional investors own the balance. It can sell bonds in corporation "A" to institutional investors (the same ones that have the stock), and use the cash to purchase the assets of the corporation they want to take private, corporation "B". The assets of corporation "B" will be the security for the bonds. This is a form of leverage buy out (LBO). **Leveraged buyout** is the purchase of a company, using the assets of the company, to raise a substantial amount of the purchase price.

(6) Set up a cash out purchase as discussed previously.

(7) Have the corporation set up another corporation and do a short form merger.

There are infinite combinations using the above to accomplish the purpose.

DISSOLUTION

Dissolution is the first step in terminating a corporation. The dissolution can be voluntary, involuntary, administrative or judicial. Dissolution, by itself, does not terminate the existence of a corporation. It is a three-part operation: (1) dissolution, (2) the windup of the corporation's affairs, and (3) the liquidation of its assets. After dissolution the corporation cannot carry on any business except the winding up and liquidation.

While corporations can have perpetual existence, there are many ways it can be terminated. Incorporation statutes usually provide for voluntary and involuntary dissolution. There are two types of involuntary dissolution: administrative and judicial.

Voluntary Dissolution

The board of directors passes a resolution to dissolve, and then a majority of the shares entitled to vote at a shareholders' meeting called specifically for the purpose of dissolution must approve the dissolution. Dissenting stockholders have no rights of appraisal. The only right would be to seek an injunction. The business must be wound up, liquidated, and the net proceeds distributed to shareholders within one year, RMBCA 13.002(a)(3).

Dissolution by Board of Directors and Shareholders (Section 14.02, RMBCA)

(a) A corporation's board of directors may propose dissolution for submission to the shareholders.

(b) For a proposal to dissolve to be adopted:
  (1) the board of directors must recommend dissolution to the shareholders unless the board of directors determines that because of conflict of interest or other special circumstances it should make no recommendation and communicates the basis for its determination to the shareholders; and
  (2) the shareholders entitled to vote must approve the proposal to dissolve as provided in subsection (e).

(c) The board of directors may condition its submission of the proposal for dissolution on any basis.

(d) The corporation shall notify each shareholder, whether or not entitled to vote, of the proposed shareholder's meeting in accordance with Section 7.05 RMBCA. The notice must also state that the purpose, or one of the purposes, of the meeting is to consider dissolving the corporation.

(e) Unless the articles of incorporation or the board of directors (acting pursuant to subsection (c)) require a greater vote or a vote by voting groups, the proposal to dissolve to be adopted must be approved by a majority of all votes entitled to be cast on that proposal.

Payment of Known and Unknown Claims in Dissolution

The dissolved corporation must notify known claimants where to send their claims, and the claims must be received no later than a fixed deadline. The deadline must be at least 120 days from the notice. If claimant fails to file a claim by the deadline, the claim is barred by Section 14.06(c), RMBCA. If the claim is filed and the corporation rejects the claim, the claimant must commence a proceeding to enforce the claim within 90 days of the rejection or the claim is barred Section 14.06(c)(2) RMBCA.

If the corporation publishes a notice under Section 14.07, a claimant who was not notified in writing is barred unless he commences a proceeding within five years after publication of the notice. (Publishing requires one time in a newspaper of general circulation stating where to file a claim and that the claim will be barred five years after publication unless filed.)

The directors are not trustees of the assets of a dissolved corporation, but they must make provision for paying all known claimants before distributing the remaining assets to shareholders.

Involuntary Dissolution There are two types of involuntary dissolution, administrative and judicial.

- Administrative dissolution for example, is when the state dissolves the corporation for failure to pay the state franchise fees, state taxes or other failure to comply with state laws concerning corporate filings.
- Judicial dissolution is when a court orders the corporation dissolved. The state courts can order a corporation to be dissolved and the assets divided between certain shareholders and/or creditors as a decision in a lawsuit.
  - Another judicial decision would be from the bankruptcy court, when creditors file an involuntary petition of bankruptcy. An involuntary petition if the debtor has twelve or more creditors can be filed by 3 or more unsecured creditors totaling over $10,775. If less than twelve creditors it can be filed by one or more totaling $10,775. The involuntary petition can only be filed under Chapter 11 (reorganization) or Chapter 7 (liquidation).

Administrative Dissolution The secretary of state can commence a proceeding to **administratively dissolve** a corporation for failure to pay franchise fees or any penalties imposed within 60 days after they are due; or if the corporation fails to file its annual report within 60 days after it is due; or if the corporation is without a registered agent or a registered office in the state for 60 days or more; or if the corporation fails to notify the secretary of state that its registered office or registered agent has changed, within 60 days of the change; or if the period of duration of the corporation has expired.

Judicial Dissolution The highest trial court of the state can dissolve a corporation by a proceeding by the attorney general if the corporation obtained its charter by fraud; or the corporation has continued to exceed or abuse the authority conferred upon it by law; or by a shareholder if it is established that the directors are deadlocked in the management of the corporate affairs, unable to break the deadlock, and irreparable injury to the corporation is threatened; or that the directors or those in control of the corporation have, are, or will be acting in a manner that is illegal, oppressive, or fraudulent; or the shareholders are deadlocked in voting for successor directors and have been for two consecutive annual meetings, and the director's terms have expired; or the corporate assets are being misapplied or wasted; or the corporation has admitted a claim is owed and due, but the corporation is insolvent or in a proceeding by the corporation to have its voluntary dissolution continued under court order and supervision.

Deadlock Causing Dissolution A **deadlock** arises on a given issue when there are equally divided shareholders at a shareholders' meeting, or an equally divided board of directors at a board meeting. Deadlock can also arise when a required supermajority is not obtained, or a veto is exercised. A number of statutes allow for involuntary dissolution on deadlock. The statutes are usually interpreted as being discretionary, not mandatory. Courts are very often reluctant to order a dissolution of a profitable corporation on the grounds of deadlock. However, profitable is not a bar to dissolution for deadlock, *Weiss v. Gordon*, 301NYS 2d 839 (1969). In a close corporation, deadlock would be grounds for dissolution even if the corporation was profitable. However, courts will generally order a mandatory buyout of the interest of the minority shareholder rather than order dissolution of a profitable corporation. The courts believe it is against the public interest to dissolve a profitable corporation.

SUMMARY

There is a difference between a merger and a consolidation. A merger is when the surviving corporation retains its name, and the other corporation or corporations disappear. In a consolidation, all corporations disappear and a new name comes out of the consolidation. There are different ways to purchase an acquisition: cash for stock, cash for assets, stock for stock, and stock for assets. Each one has advantages and disadvantages. The major thing with a merger or acquisition is you get the assets and liabilities. It can be structured so that you get control of the assets and no liabilities. A purchase of substantially all assets in the regular course of business can be accomplished without approval of shareholders if structured properly. Often dissenting stockholders have a right of appraisal of their shares and purchase of them at the appraised price. Statutory mergers can be accomplished without the consent of either corporation's shareholders. The surviving corporation is the one left after the merger or consolidation. There are tax implications of various acquisitions and the Internal Revenue Code setting up "Type A", "Type B", and "Type C" acquisitions. Triangular mergers can leave you with the assets of a merger candidate but no liabilities. We discussed going private and the means by which to reacquire stock. Finally, we covered the dissolution of a corporation; voluntary, involuntary, administrative, and judicial dissolutions; and lastly payment of claims.

CASES

Sale of Substantially All Assets

KATZ v. BREGMAN
Delaware Court of Chancery (1981)
431 A2d.1274

Plaintiff Katz is the owner of approximately 170,000 shares of common stock of the defendant, Plant Industries, Inc., on whose behalf he brought this action, for his own benefit as a stockholder and benefit of all record owners of Plant Industries, Inc. Plaintiff wants to enjoin the proposed sale of Canadian assets of Plant Industries, Inc. to Vulcan Industrial Packaging, Ltd. At common law the sale of substantially all assets of a corporation required unanimous vote of the shareholders.

Defendant Bregman is the CEO of Plant Industries, Inc., and the complaint alleges that Bregman for the last six months has disposed of several unprofitable subsidiaries of the defendant. Mr. Bregman then proceeded on a course to dispose of Plant National Ltd., the corporation's entire business in Canada and the only profitable income producing business for the last four years for defendant. The purpose of the sale is to raise cash and improve the defendant's balance sheet. Bregman refused to negotiate with another company interested in buying the defendant plant, saying that the board cannot ethically negotiate with two at the same time.

Plaintiff relies on two points for injunctive relief. First, that the sale of substantially all of the assets not only requires the approval of the board of directors of Plant National, but also a resolution approved by a majority of the shareholders.

Breach of fiduciary duty of the board is sustained as a result of their failure to negotiate with the other corporation to possibly obtain a better deal. Defendants concede that Plant National represents 52.4 percent of their net income for 1980. In 1978 the Canadian operation made a profit of $2,900,000 while the United States operation profit was $700,000. In 1979 Canadian profit was $3,500,000 while the United States operation lost $334,000.

The principal business of Plant Industries has not been to buy and sell industrial facilities, but rather to manufacture steel drums for use in bulk shipping. The proposal to manufacture plastic drums after the sale is a radical departure from Plant's historically successful business. The court, therefore, concludes that this sale is for substantially all of Plant's assets. Accordingly, an injunction should be issued preventing the consummation of the sale at least until a majority of the shareholders entitled to vote at a meeting of shareholders has approved the sale. The shareholders meeting must be on at least 20 days notice.

Claims Against Dissolved Corporation That Arose Prior to Dissolution

PENASQUITOS v. BARBEE
812 P.2d 154 (Cal. 1991)

Penasquitos graded, prepared, and owned lots with one family homes on them. The homes were constructed by Crow Pacific. They were all in one subdivision. Several owners of the homes brought suit against both Penasquitos and Crow Pacific for construction defects.

Both of the corporations dissolved before the homeowners discovered the defects. The corporations both defend by saying they are dissolved and therefore do not exist and cannot be sued.

The question is whether the homeowners can sue on claims that arose for defects discovered after the corporations dissolved.

California's statutes permit suits against dissolved corporations for claims that arose after dissolution. Common law treated dissolution of a corporation similar to the death of a person. Once dead or dissolved, claims **abated,** i.e., no longer viable or in existence. California abandoned the common law concerning corporate dissolution in 1929 with the Civil Code Section 399. Section 1905 subdivision (b) now says that when the certificate of dissolution is filed, "the corporate existence shall cease, except for the purpose of further winding up if needed." A corporation which is dissolved continues to exist to wind up affairs, prosecuting and defending actions by and against it. RMBCA 14.07(c) permits claims against a dissolved corporation whether they arose before or after dissolution as long as suit is commenced within five years from the date of the certificate of dissolution.

Assets for Stocks

HARITON v. ARCO ELECTRONICS, INC.
Supreme Court of Delaware
41 Del.Ch. 74, 188 A2d 123

This is a stock for assets reorganization. Seller Arco will receive 283,000 shares of stock of the buyer. The buyer is Loral. The seller will then dissolve and stock of buyer will be distributed to shareholders of seller. The seller is a Delaware corporation, and the sale is pursuant to section 271, Delaware Corporation Law. The buyer is a New York corporation. A Reorganization Agreement and Plan was entered into between the parties. This accomplishes the same result as a merger of the seller into the purchaser. The issue is whether the sale is legal.

The seller, Arco, called a special meeting of shareholders for the purpose of voting on this plan; 80 percent of the shareholders entitled to vote approved the sale. Plaintiff who did not vote at the meeting now sues to enjoin the consummation of the plan on the grounds that (1) it was illegal, and (2) it was unfair. Defendant moved for summary judgement and dismissal of the complaint. The vice chancellor granted the motion and plaintiff appeals.

Plaintiff says the result here is the same as a merger of Arco into Loral. In a true sale of assets, the stockholders of seller retain the right to elect whether the selling company shall continue as a holding company. The stockholder of the seller is forced to accept an investment in a new enterprise without the right of appraisal granted under the merger statute. This is in effect a de facto merger.

We now hold the reorganization and the mandatory plan of dissolution and distribution is legal under Section 271. The framers of the plan may either use the merger route where appraisal will be available, or the stock for assets plan where no appraisal rights are available. Judgment is affirmed.

WORDS TO KNOW

acquisitions
administrative dissolution
appraisal rights
cash for assets
cash for stock
consolidation
deadlock
dissolution
involuntary dissolution
judicial dissolution
merger
reorganization
reverse triangular merger
right to dissent

share exchange
short form mergers
statutory mergers
stock for assets
stock for stock
survivor
tax aspects
transferee
transferor
triangular merger
"Type A"
"Type B"
"Type C"
voluntary dissolution

REVIEW QUESTIONS

1. What is a merger?
2. What is a triangular merger?
3. Explain a consolidation.
4. What is meant by appraisal rights?
5. What is the stock market exception?
6. What is an administrative dissolution?
7. How would you take a public corporation private?
8. Explain share exchanges.
9. What is a surviving corporation?
10. Explain what deadlock means.
11. Set up a stock for assets acquisition; explain the advantages, if any.
12. How do you accomplish a statutory merger?
13. Explain the dissolution process.
14. What claims, if any, is a corporation liable for after dissolution?
15. Explain a sale of substantially all corporate assets. Who requires notice?
16. What is the tax aspect of a "Type A" transaction?

17. What is a judicial dissolution? When does it happen?

18. How do you structure a voluntary dissolution?

19. What is the tax aspect of a "Type B" transaction?

20. What is the tax aspect of a "Type C" transaction?

21. Set up a reverse triangular merger. Why is it used?

22. What is meant by a plan of reorganization?

SHORT ESSAYS

1. Corporation A, a New York corporation, has 200 shareholders and would like to accept the offer it received from corporation B, a Delaware corporation, to purchase all of its assets for 300,000 shares of stock B corporation, the purchaser. Structure the transaction in as many different ways as you can, listing the advantages and disadvantages of each method.

2. Corporations A, B, and C in some manner would like to become associated in a business venture. They have all agreed to call the new venture "Z". What advice would you give and how would you structure the transaction?

3. Corporation B is a Delaware corporation and was engaged in building houses in Georgia. Business was bad and about two years ago the ten stockholders agreed to dissolve the corporation. The corporation was thereafter voluntarily dissolved. Five people that bought houses from B corporation have serious problems. Their houses began to sink about six months ago. What, if any, remedy is there?

4. Corporation A agrees to sell all its assets to Corporation B in exchange for 200,000 shares of stock in Corporation B. Corporation A also agrees it will distribute the 200,000 shares of stock in B Corporation to the shareholders of A Corporation, and thereafter dissolve A Corporation. A corporation also agrees to call a shareholders' meeting to approve the plan.

At the meeting of shareholders called specifically for the purpose of approving this sale, 80 percent of the shareholders voted to approve the sale. Z was not at the meeting and did not vote.

Z now brings a proceeding (1) to enjoin the consummation of the sale, and (2) that the sale was unfair. Z says that this is actually a merger. A Corporation transfers all of its assets to B Corporation in exchange for the 200,000 shares of B Corporation stock and thereafter A Corporation dissolves. "Z" says that as a dissenter to the merger he is entitled to appraisal rights. Decide and give reasoning.

WHAT ARE INSIDER AND TENDER OFFERS?

OBJECTIVES

After completing this chapter, you will be able to:

1. Know what an insider is.
2. Know what a prospectus is.
3. Explain what an issuer is.
4. Discuss the secondary market.
5. List the problems for short swing profits.
6. Explain transaction causation.
7. Tell the difference between loss causation and transaction causation.
8. Explain a tender offer.
9. Define a white knight.
10. Define a raider.
11. Define a target.
12. Explain a lock up.
13. Define crown jewels.
14. Explain a standstill.
15. Define junk bonds.
16. Explain what an LBO is.

INTRODUCTION

Various states have their own securities laws regulating the sale of securities and prohibiting fraud in the sale of securities within their state. The laws are referred to as **Blue Sky Laws.** Most of these laws require the registration of securities and regulate brokers and dealers in the state.

The major federal statutes are the Securities Act of 1933 which concerns itself mainly with the issuance of securities. The Securities Exchange Act of 1934 deals mainly with the trading in issued securities, generally referred to as secondary transactions. The dollar volume of secondary issues greatly exceeds the original issues.

The Securities and Exchange Commission is an independent quasi-judicial administrative agency referred to as the SEC. It administers both the 1933 and the 1934 Acts. The SEC has five commissioners appointed by the President of the United States with the consent of the senate. The term of office is five years with staggered terms, one commissioner's term expires each year. It is said to be an independent agency since it is run by commissioners with stated terms of office that cannot be terminated without cause. The SEC issues its own rules that have the same force and effect as statutes. The SEC can seek injunctions in the Federal District Court against violators of its rules. It can also recommend that the Justice Department bring criminal prosecutions against violators of its rules. The agency can also issue orders censuring, suspending, or expelling broker dealers, investment advisers, and investment companies. The Securities Enforcement Remedies and Penny Stock Reform Act of 1990 gave the SEC power to issue cease and desist orders and to impose administrative civil penalties up to one half million dollars. The Private Securities Litigation Act of 1995 amends the Securities Exchange Act of 1933 and the 1934 Act against **aiders and abetters** who are people who intentionally and knowingly provide substantial assistance to a person who violates the statute. If you desire to sell, or issue securities, you must comply with federal and state laws.

The SEC provides guidance in the use of electronic media to deliver information to the SEC required by the Federal Statutes and Rules. Electronic media is defined as fax, electronic mail, audiotapes, videotapes, CD-ROM, and computer networks. Electronic delivery must provide notice, access, and evidence of delivery comparable to that provided by paper delivery. Contact the SEC for further information and guidance prior to using these media for filings.

SECURITIES ACT OF 1933

Designed to provide investors with:

(1) material information concerning securities offered for sale to the public, and

(2) to prohibit misrepresentation, fraud, deceit, and other practices in the sale of securities, whether or not they are required to be registered.

The Securities Act of 1933 is sometimes referred to as **The Truth in Securities Act.** It requires that before any security can be offered for sale to the public a registration statement must first be filed with the SEC and that statement must become effective prior to any sale being made. There are some exemptions to the filing of this registration statement. The registration statement must disclose financial and other information about the

issuer and those who control it, so that potential investors can decide on the merits of the security prior to purchase. The issuer is the corporation selling the security. Potential investors must also be furnished a **prospectus** containing important data set forth in the registration statement which is much more detailed than the registration statement. A prospectus is a brochure offering securities for sale to the public. The act prohibits fraud in all sales of securities in interstate commerce and the mails, even if the securities are exempt from registration requirements of the act. Civil and criminal penalties can be imposed for violations of the act.

SECURITIES EXCHANGE ACT OF 1934

The Securities Exchange Act of 1934 extends protection to investors trading in securities that are already issued and outstanding. The act also requires disclosure requirements on publicly held corporations and regulates tender offers and proxy solicitations.

The act deals principally with the **secondary distribution** of securities. After the original issue of stock has been sold, sales from the original purchasers to new purchasers are transacted in what is called the secondary market. The act prohibits fraudulent and manipulative practices and establishes rules for operation of markets. It provides protection for all holders of securities listed which are on national exchanges, as well as for holders of equity securities of companies traded over the counter, whose corporate assets exceed $5,000,000 and whose equity securities include a class with 500 or more shareholders. Companies must register such securities and are subject to the reporting requirements, short swing profit provisions, tender offer and proxy solicitation rules, as well as internal record keeping requirements and control of the Foreign Corrupt Practices Act. An over-the-counter issuer may terminate registration when its equity holders number less than 300, or when the issuer has fewer than 500 shareholders and assets of less than $5,000,000 at the end of each of the last three years. Issuers of securities, whether registered or not, must comply with the antifraud and antibribery provisions of the act.

WHO IS AN INSIDER?

Securities Exchange Commission Rule 10b-5 case law, defines an **Insider** as including officers, directors, employees, agents, underwriters, accountants, attorneys and consultants, as well as people who receive material, nonpublic information from insiders or others. Basically, if you received nonpublic material information from your mechanic on a company that is traded, and he received that information from someone else who received it from an insider, you would be considered an insider. If you acted on the information, you would have the liabilities of an insider. An insider has material information not available to the general public. An insider who fails to disclose this material information before trading on the information becomes liable under the rule.

Short-Swing Profits Section 16(b) Securities Exchange Act of 1934

If any insider purchases stock within six months of a prior sale of the stock by an insider, or if the insider sells stock within six months of purchase, the corporation is entitled to recover any and all profit the insider accumulates from these purchases and/or sales. Losses cannot be offset from profits. An action to recover said profit can be brought by the corporation whose stock was traded by the insider or by any shareholder of the corporation traded in the name of and for the benefit of the corporation, in the event the corporation fails to bring the action within sixty days of the shareholders' request. This is pursuant to Section 16(b) of The Securities Exchange Act of 1934. This act imposes express liability on insiders and any person owning more than 10 percent of the stock of a corporation listed on a national stock exchange or registered with the SEC, may commence the action on behalf of the corporation for all profits resulting from their short-swing trading in such stock.

Securities Exchange Act of 1934, Rule 10b-5

It shall be unlawful for any person, directly or indirectly, by the use of any means or instrumentality of interstate commerce, or of the mails or any facility of any national exchange,

(a) To employ any device, scheme, or artifice to defraud,

(b) To make any untrue statement of a material fact or to omit to state a material fact necessary in order to make the statements made, in the light of the circumstances under which they were made, not misleading, or

(c) To engage in any act, practice, or course of business which operates or would operate as a fraud or deceit upon any person, in connection with the purchase or sale of any security.

Under this section any investor injured, as a result of insider trading, can bring an action in the investor's name for damages sustained. The award, if any, goes to the plaintiff, investor. Under Section 16(b) Securities Exchange Act of 1934 the award goes to the corporation.

Securities Exchange Act of 1934 (Antifraud Provision), Section 10

It shall be unlawful for any person, directly or indirectly, by the use of any means or instrumentality of interstate commerce or of the mails, or of any facility of any national securities exchange

(a) To effect a short sale, or to use or employ any stop-loss order in connection with the purchase or sale, of any security registered on a national securities exchange, in contravention of such rules and regulations as the Commission may prescribe as necessary and appropriate in the public interest or for the protection of investors.

(b) To use or employ, in connection with the purchase or sale of any security registered on a national securities exchange or any security not so registered, any manipulative or deceptive device or contrivance in contravention of such rules and regulations as the Commission may prescribe as necessary or appropriate in the public interest or for the protection of investors.

Discussion: Section 16(b) and Rule 10b-5 Securities Exchange Act of 1934

Note: Section 16(a) . . . "a beneficial owner of 10 percent of any class of equity security, or an officer or director, must report the amount of all equity securities of the issuer of which he is the beneficial owner." Any changes must also be reported. This provides a means for bringing to light violations of 10b-5 and 16(b).

Section 16(b) Short Swing Profits and Rule 10b-5 both concern the problem of insider trading and both may sometimes apply to the same transaction. However, they differ in a few instances:

(1) Rule 10b-5 applies to ALL securities. Section 16(b) applies only to registered securities.

(2) In Rule 10b-5, an insider is anyone possessing material information about a corporation that is not general public knowledge, and one who trades on this information prior to it being disclosed to the general public. In Section 16(b), an insider is a director, officer, or owner of more than 10 percent of a corporation's stock and is limited to those persons.

(3) Rule 10b-5 applies to insider trading only when such information is not disclosed. Section 16(b) does not require that the insider possess material that is nonpublic information; liability is strict.

(4) Rule 10b-5 has no time limitations. Section 16(b) applies only to transactions occurring within six months of each other.

(5) Rule 10b-5 allows injured investors to recover damages on their own behalf. Section 16(b) allows a shareholder to bring an action on behalf of the corporation. However, the proceeds recovered, if any, go to the corporation.

Antifraud Provision, Section 10(b) and Rule 10b-5 Securities Exchange Act of 1934

Rule 10b-5 applies to securities transactions by any person. An affirmative duty to disclose material information has traditionally been imposed on directors, officers, controlling stockholders, and insiders. Courts have consistently held that insiders must disclose material facts known to them because of their position or otherwise which are not known to persons with whom they deal, and which, if known, would affect their investment judgment. Failure to disclose constitutes a violation of the antifraud provision. If, on the other hand, disclosure prior to a purchase or sale would be improper or unrealistic under the circumstances, one should forego the transaction.

The obligation of disclosure rests on two principles. First, the existence of a relationship giving access, directly or indirectly, to information intended to be available only for a corporate purpose and not for the personal benefit of anyone; and, second, the inherent unfairness involved when a party takes advantage of such information knowing it is unavailable to those with whom he is dealing.

There is a justifiable expectation that all persons trading in the securities marketplace and exchanges have equal access to material information. Thus, anyone in possession of material inside information must either disclose it to the investing public or must abstain from trading. Cady, Roberts & Co., 40 SEC 907 (1961).

Causation and Reliance: Rule 10b-5

Causation and reliance are required elements of a private action under Rule 10b-5. However, they have sometimes proven to be elusive or even illusory in practice.

Case law has distinguished between loss causation and transaction causation. **Transaction causation** means there must be a relationship between the defendant's violation of the rule and the plaintiff's purchase or sale. To show a Rule 10b-5 violation, a private plaintiff must prove a causal connection between a defendant's misrepresentation and the plaintiff's injury, *Basic Inc. v. Levinson*, 485 U.S. 224 (1988). This is a connection showing that, but for the violation, the plaintiff's purchase or sale would not have occurred. The violation may have been the proximate cause for the purchase or sale. At most, the plaintiff may have to prove defendant's misstatement or misconduct was a substantial factor in causing the loss. Another example is if the misstatement affected an investment decision.

The meaning of **loss causation** is that the defendant's wrongful act not only must have caused the plaintiff to buy or sell a security, it must also have been the cause of the plaintiff's loss on the security. Otherwise, the defendant is becoming an insurer against market risks. For example, plaintiff bought a security as a result of the wrongful action of defendant. The stock went down not because of the wrongful action but because the market crashed. In this circumstance, the defendant would not be held liable.

On the **reliance** issue, once the plaintiff has shown that the defendant omitted to disclose a material fact that he was obligated to disclose, the burden is on the defendant to prove the plaintiff would have made the same decision and investment even if disclosure had been made. People who trade within a reasonable time after a material misrepresentation is made will have almost always relied on the misrepresentation. As a practical matter, reliance will be presumed and the burden will shift to the defendant to show plaintiff did not rely on the misrepresentation. Misrepresentation cases are similar to omission cases; once plaintiff makes a showing of materiality, the burden shifts to the defendant to show reliance did not occur.

Case Law Under Rule 10b-5 Securities Exchange Act of 1934

Blue Chip Stamps v. Manor Drug Stores, 421 U.S. 723 (1975). Plaintiff alleged that defendant's misrepresentation caused him to refrain from purchasing a stock, to his loss. The court rejected the claim. Only a person that actually bought and sold securities, only a buyer and seller, could bring a private action under Rule 10b-5.

Ernst & Ernst v. Hochfelder, 425 U.S. 185 (1976). The court held that scienter was a necessary element in a Rule 10b-5 case.

Santa Fe Industries v. Green, 430 U.S. 462 (1977). Minority shareholders were being involuntarily cashed out through a short-form merger which alleged the price to be paid for their shares was too low. However, facts on how the valuation took place were disclosed to the shareholders. The court said deception and manipulation are required in a Rule 10b-5 case. Fully disclosed information will not give rise to a Rule 10b-5 case.

SEC v. Texas Gulf Sulphur, 401 F2d 833 (1969). A corporation, even if it does not trade, that makes misstatements may be liable under Rule 10b-5.

Backman v. Polaroid Corp., 910 F2d 10 (1990). If a corporation makes a statement that is misleading (inaccurate) when made, even though not intentionally, and it later learns the statement was misleading, it is under a duty to correct the statement if the statement would still be likely to be material to investors.

Greenfield v. Heublin, Inc., 742 F2d 751 (1984). If a corporation voluntarily makes a public statement that is correct when issued, the corporation has a duty to update the statement if it becomes materially misleading in light of subsequent events.

Elkind v. Ligget & Myers, Inc., 635 F2d 156 (1980). A corporation may so involve itself in the preparation of statements about the corporation by outsiders, such as analysts reports or earnings projections, that it assumes a duty to correct material errors in those statements.

State Teachers Retirement Board v. Fluor Corp., 654 F2d 843 (1981). A corporation may be under a duty to correct erroneous rumors resulting from leaks by the corporation or its agents.

Suggested in dictum in various cases: Nondisclosure by a corporation may violate Rule 10b-5 if no valid corporate purpose requires nondisclosure.

Lampf, Pleva et al. v. Gilberson, 501 U.S. 350 (1991). A private action cannot be brought more than one year after discovery of the facts constituting the cause of action, or more than three years following accrual of the cause of action. Tolling of the statute of limitations because of efforts by defendant to conceal knowledge of his wrong from discovery is inapplicable under the one and three year structure.

Elements Needed for a Rule 10b-5 Private Action Securities Exchange Act of 1934

Recovery of damages under Rule 10b-5 requires proof of the following elements:

(1) Plaintiff must be a buyer and seller of securities with a loss.

(2) There must be an omission of facts (nondisclosure) or misstatement of facts.

(3) The omission or misstatement of facts must be material. A misstatement or omission is material if a reasonable investor would have deemed it important.

For example, change in a dividend, earnings, asset value, tender offer, or a new contract; or finding oil, etc.

(4) The omission or misstatement must have been deceptive or manipulative.

(5) Scienter must be present (intentional, knowing wrongdoing). Remember, the rule imposes an affirmative duty of disclosure. Therefore, an intentional nondisclosure is scienter.

(6) Reliance on the omission or misstatement by the plaintiff. Buying and selling shows reliance.

(7) Plaintiff must have sustained a loss.

Securities Exchange Act of 1934, Section 20A

In 1988 Congress adopted the Insider Trading and Securities Fraud Enforcement Act (ITSFEA). Section 20A was added to the Securities Exchange Act of 1934 as ITSFEA. If trading on the basis of misappropriated information violates Rule 10b-5, then under Section 20A a private action can be brought on the basis of such trading. There is a civil liability upon anyone violating the act by purchasing or selling a security while in possession of material nonpublic information. Any person who sold or purchased the same class of security as improperly traded may bring a private action against the trader to recover damages for the violation. Damages may not exceed the profit gained or loss avoided by the violation. The action must be brought within five years after the date of the last transaction that was a violation. **Tippers** and **tippees** are jointly and severally liable by trading on inside information. A tipper is someone who gives financial advice to buy or sell a security. A tippee is the person getting the advice.

Civil Penalties for Insider Trading

In addition to a private action for damages by a private person, the U.S. Government can bring a civil action for penalties. The maximum penalty that can be imposed by the U.S. District Court is the greater of $1,000,000 or three times the profit gained or loss avoided as a result of the violation, whichever is larger. Civil penalties are payable to the U.S. Treasury. The SEC is authorized to award bounties of up to 10 percent of any penalty recovered for information leading to the imposition of such penalty. An action to recover a penalty hereunder must be brought within five years after the date of the violation. Liability also extends to any person aiding or abetting in committing such violation.

TENDER OFFERS

A **tender offer** is an offer from a person, corporation, or group composed of infinite business combinations, designed to participate in the management of the corporation or to fully take over a corporation by purchasing a percentage of its outstanding shares or a majority of its outstanding shares. The more stock one owns in a corporation, the greater the amount of participation by that party, culminating with full control. A person may only want a few seats on the board of directors. If he or she owns enough shares he or she can talk with management to have him or her or his or her designates elected to the board. If it is not amicably resolved the person may enter into a proxy fight or tender offer to buy or control enough shares to fully control the corporation, and then elect board members and officers that the person wants; old management loses their positions. The basics are simple. He or she notifies all shareholders that he or she will buy up to 52 percent but no less than 41 percent of the outstanding shares. He or she now owns 10 percent. The stock is selling for $15 per share. He or she offers to buy up to 52 percent at $26 per share and place a short time limit on the offer. If he or she does not have the minimum amount of stock tendered for sale, he or she can withdraw the tender and quit, extend the tender time, or can modify the price offered. He or she is always in full control. The reason to buy this way is that if the person went into the marketplace to buy this large an amount of stock, he or she would run the price up on each purchase made. Then, if it became too expensive, he or she would be stuck with a lot of stock which he or she may not be able to sell very quickly, and thus take a huge loss. The tender offer eliminates all these problems, and maintains full control at all times. Naturally, all of the above must be accomplished in compliance with the federal statutes and SEC rules.

Terminology with Tender Offers

target The corporation whose shares are being accumulated by the bidder. The company the bidder wants to either take over or obtain board seats for.

raider The person or group desiring to purchase shares in the target to obtain board seats or control. Actually the bidder.

white knight Management may not be happy with the present bidder, so it seeks offers from other corporations that may be friendlier to management's plan to take over the corporation. The friendly one is called a white knight.

lock-up A favored bidder is given an option to acquire selected assets or stock of the target at a favorable price under certain conditions, usually that result in the unfriendly bidder being defeated. It is used to protect a friendly bidder against an unfriendly bidder.

crown jewels The giving or selling of a lock-up option to a white knight for the most desirable business of the target, or at least the business the raider is most interested in. This is done in hopes of discouraging the raider.

standstill A method to amicably stop a potential proxy fight or tender offer. Management agrees with a stockholder who has accumulated a sizeable amount of its stock for the stockholder not to accumulate any more stock; not to sell any of its shares without first offering them to the target; not engage in a proxy contest or tender offer; and vote its stock in a designated manner. It is therefore a standstill. In return, the corporation offers representation on the board, possibly stock options, and an agreement to register the stock under the Securities Act on demand.

junk bonds A bond with a high risk of default which is below investment grade, usually has a high yield, and is used to finance a leveraged buyout. By having a diversified portfolio of junk bonds, there is a degree of safety for the investor.

fair-price provisions A fair-price provision requires a supermajority, usually 80 percent of the shareholders, to approve a merger with an acquirer who owns a specified number of shares, usually 20 percent. This provision discourages purchasers from accumulating large blocks of stock, and seeks to prevent an acquirer from obtaining control at a low price.

no-shop clause The board of directors enters into an agreement for merger, possibly with a white knight, and agrees it will recommend the merger to its shareholders and will not shop around for a better deal.

leveraged buyout The use of debt to finance a purchase. Mortgages, loans, junk bonds, sale of some assets of the corporation to be purchased, leases, contracts, and options, signed on condition that the buyout takes place, all to raise cash for the purchase.

Toehold Acquisitions, Tender Offers, and the Williams Act, Sections 13(d), 14(d), and 14(e), Securities Exchange Act of 1934

The Williams Act and its amendments, which added sections 13(d), 14(d), and 14(e) to the Securities Exchange Act of 1934, regulate the toehold share acquisitions and tender offers, in a great number of respects.

Toehold Acquisitions A person or group that has acquired a beneficial ownership of 5 percent of any class of security registered under Section 12 of the act must file a schedule 13(d) within ten days of the acquisition (Section 13[d]). Schedule 13(d) includes the purchaser's identity and background; the amount and sources of the funds used for the purchase; any plans with respect to extraordinary transactions for the corporation whose stock has been acquired; and any contract arrangements or understandings with other persons regarding the corporation's securities. Person herein means group or otherwise.

Tender Offer within the Williams Act is based on the following eight factors:

(i) whether the purchasers engage in active and widespread solicitation of shareholders,

(ii) whether the solicitation is made for a substantial percentage of the issuer's stock,

(iii) whether the offer to purchase is made at a premium over the prevailing market price,

(iv) whether the terms of the offer are firm rather than negotiable,

(v) whether the offer is contingent on the tender of a fixed number of shares,

(vi) whether the offer is open for a limited period of time,

(vii) whether the offerees are under pressure to sell their stock, and

(viii) whether a public announcement of a purchasing program preceded or accompanied a rapid accumulation of large amounts of the target's securities.

Schedule 14D   requires any person making a tender offer for 5 percent or more of the shares of a company to file a Schedule 14D. This form must disclose extensive matters as to the offer; identity of bidder; past dealings between bidder and corporation; the bidder's source of funds; the bidder's purpose and plans for the corporation; the bidder's contracts, understandings, and relationships concerning securities of the corporation; and any arrangements between the bidder and those holding important positions with the corporation.

Regulation of the Terms of Tender Offers   regulated by 14(d), of the act, and Rules 14d and 14e.

(1) A tender offer must remain open for at least 20 days;

(2) must be open to all security holders of the class;

(3) shareholders must be permitted to withdraw tendered shares during the first 15 days of an offer, or after 60 days if the shares have not been purchased by then;

(4) if tender offer is oversubscribed, the offeror must purchase on a pro rata basis from among the shares deposited during the first 10 days, or such longer period as the bidder may designate;

(5) if the tender price is increased, the higher price must be paid to all tendering shareholders, even those that tendered at a lower price, and the offer must remain open at least 10 days after notice of the increase is first published.

Obligations of the Target's Management   Rule 14e-2 requires the target company, no later than 10 days from the date the tender offer is first published, to give its shareholders a statement disclosing that the target either:

(1) recommends acceptance or rejection of the tender offer;

(2) expresses no opinion and is remaining neutral toward the tender offer; or

(3) is unable to take a position with respect to the tender offer.

The statement must include the reason for the position or for the inability to take a position.

Tender Offers by Issuers   Section 13(e) of the act and Rule 13e says that corporations that tender for their own stock are subject to obligations similar to those imposed on outside bidders under rules 14d and 14e.

Antifraud Provision   Section 14(e) of the act prohibits material misstatements, misleading omissions, and fraudulent manipulative acts in connection with a tender offer or any solicitation in favor of or in opposition to a tender offer.

SUMMARY

Securities regulation statutes are referred to as Blue Sky Laws. The major federal statutes are the Securities Act of 1933, the Securities Exchange Act of 1934, and the Rules of the Securities and Exchange Commission (SEC). The SEC administers both acts. The 1933 act was referred to as The Truth in Securities Act. The 1934 act deals principally with secondary distribution of securities.

An "insider" is a director, officer, controlling stockholder, or anyone having non-public material information concerning a traded corporation. A person having this information cannot trade without first making a public disclosure of the information. An "insider" who trades violates the act and can be civilly liable to the federal government, civilly liable to any other trader that lost money on the stock, and have criminal liability as well. Short swing profits refers to profits made within six months by one possessing material information which is nonpublic.

A shareholder holding over 10 percent of a stock is subject to the regulations and must file a form stating the number of shares owned, where the funds came from to purchase the shares, and other information. After that, any increase or decrease in holdings must be reported.

Toehold acquisition occurs when one owns 5 percent of the issued and outstanding class of shares of a corporation traded. As soon as one has 5 percent, he, she, or it must record the information on a form and file it with the SEC. The form tells why the shares were purchased, the intentions of the investor, where the funds came from to make the purchase, and other information. Any change in holdings, an increase or decrease, must be reported. Civil and criminal liability exists for violators.

A tender offer is for one who wishes to obtain one seat or more on the board of directors or to take full control of the corporation. An offer is made to all shareholders which is higher than market price. The offer is open for a period of time stated in the offer, together with the conditions of the offer. Anyone making false or misleading statements concerning a tender offer has civil and criminal liability.

Anyone losing money as a result of someone violating the act has a civil lawsuit as long as the party lost money, bought and sold a security, the violator omitted or misstated material information in his possession which was nonpublic, or deceived or manipulated a person with scienter, and after reliance upon the information by the party led to a loss in the value of the security.

CASES

Federal Mail Fraud

CARPENTER v. UNITED STATES
Supreme Court of the United States, 1987
484 U.S. 108

Kenneth Felis and R. Foster Winans were convicted of violating Rule 10(b) and Rule 10b-5 of the Securities Exchange Act of 1934. They were also convicted of violating federal mail and wire fraud statutes. Petitioner Carpenter, who was convicted of aiding and abetting, was Winans' roommate.

The Court of Appeals affirmed the District Court, certiorari to the U.S. Supreme Court.

In 1982, Winans, a reporter for the *Wall Street Journal*, started writing a daily column "Heard on the Street." In the column, positive and negative information was given concerning selected stocks and recommending buying or selling of selected stocks. The perceived quality and

integrity of the column had the potential of affecting the price of the stocks it reviewed. Testimony showed the column had an impact on the market and did affect prices.

The policy and practice of the *Wall Street Journal* was that prior to publication, the contents of the column were confidential information. Despite this rule that Winans was familiar with, he, Brent (a co-conspirator that pleaded guilty and was a witness for the government), and Felis, who were both connected with Kidder Peabody Brokerage in New York City, entered into a scheme to give them advance information on the column and timing as to publication schedules. This permitted Brent, Felis, and another conspirator, Clark, to buy and/or sell on the probable impact of the column. Profits were shared. All agreed that only truthful information would be in the column to protect its purity. Over a four-month period and 27 columns, the conspirators made $690,000 in profits.

The court reasoned that the scheme's sole purpose was to buy and sell securities at a profit based on advance information on the contents of the column. They were, therefore, in possession of non-public material information and traded on that information which is a violation of Section 10(b) of the Securities Exchange Act of 1934 and Rule 10b-5 of the SEC. As to the mail and wire fraud convictions, the court found they had fraudulently misappropriated "property" within the meaning of the mail and wire fraud statutes and that the revelation injured the *Wall Street Journal*. The judgment of the Circuit Court of Appeals is affirmed.

Insider Trading

GOODWIN v. AGASSIZ
Massachusetts Supreme Judicial Court, 1933
283 Mass 358, 186 NE 659

The defendant, in May 1926, purchased through brokers on the Boston Stock Exchange 700 shares of stock in Cliff Mining Company which up to that time the plaintiff had owned. Agassiz was president and a director of the company. He had certain information material to the value of the stock which plaintiff did not have. Plaintiff contends that such purchase without disclosure to him of that knowledge was a wrong against him. Plaintiff seeks recovery of losses suffered by him in selling his shares and requests an accounting, rescision of the sale, loss of the profits, or redelivery of the shares. Plaintiff was a member of the Boston Stock Exchange.

The knowledge plaintiff claims defendant had was that an experienced geologist, in March 1926, formulated a theory in writing as to the possible existence of copper deposits under the properties of Cliff Mining. The region was known as the mineral belt in northern Michigan. The defendant felt the theory had value and should be tested, but agreed with his board of directors that, before starting to test it, options should be obtained on adjacent land which was in the copper belt, and that no mention of this theory should be made until these options were secured. It was believed that if this theory became public, the price of the stock would rise and the option price for adjacent land would also rise. Pursuant to the agreement, the defendant bought many shares through agents on the Boston Stock Exchange. The defendant then released information to the press that they were ceasing exploration in this area. Plaintiff read the article, and it prompted him to sell his shares. The plaintiff says he would not have sold if he knew of the geologist's report. He did not know the buyer was the president of the company.

The Lower Court ruled that there was no fiduciary duty requiring such disclosure by defendant to plaintiff and dismissed the bill. On appeal, the question is whether the bill should have been dismissed.

The Supreme Judicial Court found that the only knowledge defendant had that plaintiff did not have was the existence of a geologist's theory that there may be possible copper deposits. There was no opinion that copper would be found at a particular location. No facts say they were under an obligation to disclose the theory. The corporation was not injured by nondisclosure. Plaintiff was not a novice; plaintiff was a member of the Boston Stock Exchange. The judgment was affirmed and the Bill dismissed. This was the common law, the majority rule of the day. The 1933 and 1934 acts addressed this exact problem. What would the decision have been after the acts?

Misleading Press Release and Trading and Tipping

SECURITIES AND EXCHANGE COMMISSION v. TEXAS GAS SULPHUR CO.
United States Court of Appeals, 2nd Circuit, 1968
401 F2d 833, 394 U.S. 976

The action was against the defendant for a misleading press release, and against certain officers and employees based on their trading and tipping. The case came about as a result of an important mineral discovery by TGS. Four defendants were members of the geological group that made the discovery: Molison, vice president, mining engineer, who headed the exploration; Holyk, chief geologist; Clayton, engineer and geophysicist; and Drake, a geologist. Other defendants were Stephens, president; Fogarty, executive vice president; Kline, vice president and general counsel; and Coates, a director.

In March 1957 aerial geophysical surveys were taken over 15,000 square miles led by Molison and a vice president. The exploration indicated an average copper content of 1.15 percent, and zinc 8.64 percent. There was enough reason to obtain additional land nearby. All were instructed to keep these findings secret. The drilling was unusually good, and it excited the interest and speculation of those who knew about it. Additional land was acquired and drilling commenced. Defendants and persons receiving "tips" from them purchased TGS stock and calls. In 1956 TGS issued stock options to the defendants and others. At this point neither the TGS stock option committee nor the board of directors had been informed of the valuable results of the drilling, presumably because of the ongoing land acquisition program which required confidentiality. This knowledge would have been material to investors.

The Court held all transactions in TGS stock and calls were made in violation of Rule 10b-5. Insiders cannot act until the material nonpublic information they have is made public, and the public has had an opportunity to act on it. It was improper for all who took the options that knew of the material information that was not disclosed. Those defendants violated the acts.

Insider Trading—Target Company

CHIARELLA v. UNITED STATES
United States Supreme Court, 1980
445 U.S. 222, 100 S.Ct. 1108

The question is whether a person who learns from the confidential documents of one corporation that is planning an attempt to secure control of a second corporation violates Section 10(b) of the 1934 act if he fails to disclose the impending takeover before trading in the target company's securities.

The petitioner is a printer by trade. In 1975 and 1976 he worked as a markup man in a New York composing room of Pandick Press, a financial printer. Documents that petitioner handled included five announcements of corporate takeover bids. When delivered to the printer, the names of the companies were concealed by blank spaces. The true names were sent to the printer on the night of the final printing. The petitioner, however, was able to figure out the names before the final printing from other information in the documents. Without disclosing this information, petitioner purchased shares in these companies and sold them immediately after the announcements were made public. Petitioner made a profit of more than $30,000 in 14 months.

In January 1978, petitioner was indicted on 17 counts of violation of Section 10(b) of the Securities Exchange Act of 1934 and SEC Rule 10(b)-5. The petitioner was convicted on all counts. The Court of

Appeals affirmed the lower court's decision, and we now reverse.

The District Court charged the jury that the jury can convict if it found he willfully failed to inform sellers of target company securities that he knew of the forthcoming takeover bid that would make their shares more valuable. Nothing in the statute says whether silence may constitute a manipulative or deceptive device. Case law shows that a corporate insider and the stockholders of his corporation give rise to an obligation to disclose. The party failing to disclose must be under a duty to disclose. A purchaser of stock who has no duty because he is neither an insider nor a fiduciary has no obligation to reveal material facts. The jury charge failed to specify any duty. Reversed by a vote of 5-4. Chief Justice Burger and three others dissented.

WORDS TO KNOW

Blue Sky Laws
crown jewels
deceptive
insider
issuer
junk bonds
leverage buyout
lock-up
loss causation
manipulative
private action
prospectus
raider

Rule 10b-5
scienter
secondary market
Section 10(b)
short swing profits
standstill
target
tender offer
transaction causation
Truth in Securities Act
white knight

REVIEW QUESTIONS

1. What federal statutes govern securities?
2. What is an insider?
3. Explain statute 10(b) of the 1934 Act.
4. Explain SEC Rule 10b-5.
5. Explain Section 16(b) of the act.
6. What is a tender offer?
7. Who makes a tender offer?
8. Are tender offers regulated?
9. Does a state have a right to regulate securities?
10. Explain short swing profits.
11. What does a private action refer to?
12. Explain the antifraud provision in the 1934 Act.
13. Does the federal government have a right to civil penalties for violation of the acts?
14. What criminal sanctions does the federal government have for violators of the acts?
15. Explain secondary distribution.
16. Explain a toehold acquisition.

17. What is a white knight?
18. What does crown jewels refer to?
19. What does raider refer to?
20. What does target refer to?
21. Explain junk bonds.
22. What does lock-up refer to?
23. What is an LBO?
24. Explain transaction causation.

SHORT ESSAYS

1. Give an explanation of all of the elements necessary prior to bringing a civil action to recover losses under the Securities Exchange Act of 1934.

2. Mr. X is a proofreader for a printer that prints various kinds of financial material. A client is preparing a notice to all shareholders of their intentions to make a group of tender offers to purchase a few corporations. All the information and details are in the copy that Mr. X is working with, except the names of the target companies. They will be supplied the night before the final press run. Mr. X, however, has, he believes, figured out the names of the target companies. Mr. X goes out and buys stock in all target companies. Ten months later, the announcement of the tender offers is made public. The shares all advance in price. Mr. X sells these shares at a profit of over $100,000. Has Mr. X violated any laws?

3. Mr. Smith has just started writing a financial newsletter that he sells to subscribers. He has been quite successful and has approximately 500 subscribers. The local newspaper has now asked him to write a weekly article for them assessing the value of various stock market security investments. Mr. Smith intends to write the weekly reviews for about six months to build readership, and then he will begin an investment program by purchasing shares in corporations that he reviews, prior to the reviews appearing in print, and then sell the securities, hopefully at a profit, as they advance in price as a result of his reviews becoming public. What legal considerations should he consider?

4. Mr. Thomson is a janitor at a major corporate headquarters facility. At night he empties all wastebaskets, dusts the desks and furniture, and vacuums and cleans the offices. He works the executive floor where the president, CEO, CFO, executive vice president, and general counsel all have their offices. They very often leave papers and files on their desks as well as folders with documents inside. Lately, Mr. Thomson has begun to read the papers on the desks and look in some folders. He believes he can use some of the information he has access to for investing purposes, as he will know what others do not. Mr. Thomson has no real savings. He contacts his brother-in-law who has a good job and asks him to loan him $5,000. When asked what he wants the money for, he tells his brother-in-law his plan to buy some stocks from the information available to him and then sell them after they have gone up. His brother-in-law suggests giving him $25,000 on condition that they be fifty-fifty partners. Mr. Thomson will buy and sell the stocks, and they will split the profits. After ten months, this has earned each of them $35,000 in net profit. What suggestions do you have concerning this venture?

PUBLIC DISTRIBUTION OF SECURITIES

OBJECTIVES

After completing this chapter, you will be able to:

1. Explain a best efforts deal.
2. Know what a firm underwriting is.
3. Explain a strict underwriting.
4. Define a security.
5. Define an offer.
6. Explain what an exemption is.
7. Know what a stop order is.
8. Explain what an underwriting syndicate is.
9. Know the reason for a market out clause.
10. Explain transactional disclosure.
11. Know what a prospectus is.
12. Explain a registration statement.
13. Know what a broker is.
14. Explain who an issuer is.
15. Know what an underwriting entails.
16. Explain the civil and criminal sanctions under the securities acts.

INTRODUCTION

Public distribution of securities is generally governed by the Securities Act of 1933 and in small part by the Securities Exchange Act of 1934. To a lesser extent it is governed by state laws, known as Blue Sky Laws. The act defines many key terms in a way that is different from ordinary business usage. Some of the terminology of the act is as follows:

Issuer   An issuer is a corporation that **issues** its own stock or bonds. Issue means sells. Section 2(a)(4) of the Securities Act of 1933 defines issuer to mean, every person who issues or proposes to issue any security. The definition is extended in Section 2(a)(11) of the Act to include, an **issuer** as any person directly or indirectly, controlling or controlled by the issuer, or any person under direct or indirect common control with the issuer.

Controlling   The terms **controlling,** controlled, controlled by, and under control with, mean the possession, direct or indirect, of the power to direct, or cause the direction of the management and policies of a person, whether through the ownership of voting securities, by contract, or otherwise. Securities Act of 1933 Rule 405.

Underwriter   In ordinary usage, an **underwriter** markets securities for an issuer or controlling person. As defined in Section 2(a)(11) of the Securities Act of 1933, an underwriter is any person who has purchased from an issuer with a view to, or offers or sells for an issuer in connection with, the distribution of any security.

Dealer   In ordinary usage, a dealer is a person who buys and sells securities on his or her own behalf, taking title to the securities until sale. A **dealer** is defined under Section 2(a)(12) of the Securities Act of 1933 as any person who engages either for all or part of his time, directly or indirectly, as agent, broker, or principal, in the business of offering, buying, selling, or otherwise dealing or trading in securities issued by another person.

Broker   In ordinary usage, a **broker** is a person who buys or sells securities on behalf of others, never taking title to the securities. Under Section 3(a)(4) of the Securities Exchange Act of 1934, a broker is defined as any person engaged in the business of effecting a transaction in securities for the account of others. Under Section 2(a)(12) of the Securities Act of 1933, the term *dealer* is defined to include brokers.

Registration Statement   To register securities under the act, a **registration statement** must be filed giving certain business and financial information about the issuer and the security. The act requires certain securities to be registered with the SEC prior to transfer or sale.

Prospectus   In ordinary usage, a prospectus is a document that describes the issuer, security, and terms of offering. Under Section 2(a)(10) of the Securities Act of 1933, a prospectus is defined as any **prospectus,** notice, circular, advertisement, letter or communication, written, or by radio or television, which offers any security for sale or confirms the sale of any security.

Brief Description of the Securities Act of 1933

The Securities Act of 1933 is sometimes referred to as the truth in securities law, or the Act, or the Securities Act. The law has two basic objectives: (1) to require investors to be provided with material information concerning securities offered to the public for sale; and (2) to prevent misrepresentation, deceit, and other fraud in the sale of securities. This is accomplished by registering offers, sales, stocks, bonds, indebtedness, limited partnerships, and trusts to name a few. Registration requires disclosure of financial information about the issuer and parties involved, as well as background information on the parties. The object is to supply enough information so the investor can make an informed decision. Some transactions qualify for exemption.

REGISTRATION

Registration requires but does not guarantee the accurate disclosure of material facts in the prospectus and registration statement. False and misleading statements can lead to fines, imprisonment, or both. If such misleading or false information can be proven, the party suffering a loss by purchase and sale of the securities can bring a civil action in the federal or state court against the issuing company, its directors, its officers, its underwriters, its controlling interest, sellers of the securities, and others.

The SEC does not approve or disapprove registrations on the merits of the investment. They only require full and accurate disclosure. The investment can still be risky, a poorly managed company and/or an unprofitable company. Price, promoters, and underwriting commissions or profits have no bearing on registration. They must be disclosed. There must be full disclosure of all material facts.

The Registration Process

The SEC has special forms for different kinds of companies desiring registration. Disclosure requirements vary. Disclosure of the following information is usual.

(1) Kind of business and list of the properties owned by the corporation and controlled by the registrant.
(2) Description of the capital securities of the corporation and the security to be offered with whatever provisions there are in the security and its overall relationship to the capital structure.
(3) Full disclosure as to the management of the corporation.
(4) The independent public accountant's certified financial statements.

The financial information, registration statements, and prospectus become public information upon filing. After filing, securities may be orally offered for sale or by summaries of the information filed, pursuant to SEC rules. The securities cannot be sold until the effective date of the registration. Most registration filings become effective 20 days after filing, or 20 days after filing the last amendment. It is within the discretion of the SEC to advance the effective date based on public information of the security and the ease of understanding the information contained in the registration statement. If information is incomplete or inaccurate, the registrant must file an amendment to correct it. The SEC can suspend the effectiveness of a registration statement if it finds any information to be misleading, inaccurate, or incomplete. The SEC can hold a hearing to develop facts by evidence if it feels there is a deliberate attempt to conceal or mislead. The hearing determines if a stop order will be made to suspend effectiveness or refuse it. If an amendment is filed correcting the reason for the stop order, the stop order will be lifted.

Exemptions to Registration

The following securities are exempted from registration:

(1) Private offerings to a limited group of persons or institutions who do not propose to redistribute the securities and have the information that registration would disclose.

(2) Intrastate offerings. Restricted to the state where the corporation is organized and doing business.

(3) Offerings of less than certain amounts pursuant to regulations of the SEC. Usually $5,000,000.

(4) Municipal, state, federal, and other government units. Banks, charities, and carriers subject to the Interstate Commerce Act.

(5) SBICs (small business investment companies) pursuant to regulations of the SEC. Under $5,000,000.

(6) Regulation A permits domestic and Canadian companies to be exempt.

(7) Regulation D for certain companies to issue under $1,000,000, with minimal federal restrictions and extensive disclosure requirements.

Notification to the SEC is necessary for exemption plus an offering circular with basic information as required by the SEC.

HOW TO TAKE A SMALL BUSINESS PUBLIC

Section 5 of the Securities Act of 1933 requires filing a registration statement before securities can be offered for sale. They cannot be sold until the registration statement becomes effective. There are two parts to the registration statement:

Part I: The prospectus that must be furnished to all purchasers. The issuer, the company, must have all essential facts regarding the business in the printed prospectus, financial information and management information. The prospectus must be made available to anyone offered or purchasing the security.

Part II: Additional information which is available from the SEC. This is available in copy form for a copying fee.

Some of the additional items required are:
• Expenses of Issuance and Distribution.
• Indemnification of Directors and Officers.
• Recent Sales of Unregistered Securities.
• Exhibits and Financial Statement Schedules.
• Undertakings.

The S-1 form is the basic registration form. It requires among other items:

(a) A description of company business.

(b) A list of its properties.

(c) Any material transaction between the company and its officers and directors.

(d) A list of all competitors.

(e) The salaries and payments to all officers and directors, and background information on each.

(f) A list of any pending legal proceedings and summaries of same.

(g) A plan for distributing the securities.

(h) The use that the proceeds are needed for.

The items above are prepared in narrative form together with certified financial statements. If significant risk factors exist about the success of the company, they must be prominently set forth in a place where they will be seen. Such as: (1) short business experience for the company or its management. (2) Economic conditions are not good for the industry. (3) Lack of market for the securities. (4) Large dependence on key personnel. For example, if a formula is involved and it is tricky to prepare and known only by one person, that would be a risk that must be set forth. If that person died, the business would no longer exist.

TYPES OF UNDERWRITING

There are three basic types of **underwriting.** Underwriting is when a person or firm purchases shares from the issuer for resale to the public, or offers to sell for an issuer in connection with the distribution of shares.

(1) *Strict, also known as standby or old-fashioned:* Only used in the United States in connection with offerings to existing stockholders by means of warrants or rights. The underwriter for a fee agreed to take whatever was not sold to the public by a specified date. Insurance companies, investment trusts, institutions, and large investors would use this method to obtain large blocks of shares at reduced prices. It aids the underwriter as a back-up to assure full distribution.

(2) *Firm Commitment Underwriting:* Takes away the risk from the issuer of not selling by reason of poor market conditions. It almost guarantees the issuer of receiving a specified amount of money by a specified date from the underwriting. Typically, the issuer would sell the entire issue to a group of securities firms; they would then sell to a larger group of dealers who, in turn, would sell to the public. Naturally, the corporation is going to pay higher fees (or sell its initial sale to the group at a discount) for this kind of underwriting.

   An **underwriting syndicate** is sometimes used as the name of the group. A **market out clause** provides that the underwriting group can terminate the agreement before the date of public offering and settlement date to the corporation, if the corporation or any subsidiary sustains an adverse change, or if trading in the securities is suspended, or if government restrictions on trading come into effect, or if a banking moratorium is declared, or if it is in the judgment of the manager of the group that economic, political, financial, or international conditions, or other adverse conditions exist that, in the judgment of the managing underwriter, makes it impractical to market at the specified public offering price.

(3) *Best Efforts Underwriting:* Unless the company is well established and a known commodity, the corporation is going to be offered a best efforts deal. Instead of the securities house buying the issue from the company and then reselling it as a principal, it sells it for the company as an agent and receives commissions for sales. This is really merchandising and not truly an underwriting.

WHAT IS A SECURITY?

In normal usage a security is a stock or bond. Section 2(a)(1) of the Securities Act of 1933 defines **security** as any note, stock, bond, debenture, evidence of indebtedness, certificate of interest, or participation in any profit sharing agreement, investment contract, and any interest or instrument commonly known as a security.

The courts generally broadly construe the word *security* to include schemes, and narrowly to exclude arrangements whose name suggests a security but whose economic realities do not.

WHAT IS A SALE? (REFERENCE TO SECURITY)

Sale is defined in Section 2(a)(3) of the Securities Act of 1933 to include every contract of sale or disposition of a security or interest in a security, for value. Use of "include" rather than "means" shows the broadness of this definition. Courts have interpreted the term to include ingenuous methods employed to obtain money from members of the public to finance ventures, regardless of the name the scheme uses to attempt to avoid the act.

A transfer of securities need not be voluntary to be a sale under the act. Mergers and stock for assets are sales under Rule 145 of the Securities Act of 1933. Rule 145 is applicable only if no exemption is available. It does not cover stock for stock exchanges.

Section 3(a)(9) of the Securities Act of 1933 says this title shall not apply to any security exchanged by the issuer with its existing security holders exclusively where no commission or other remuneration is paid or given directly or indirectly for soliciting said exchange. This overlaps with Rule 145, Securities Act of 1933.

WHAT IS AN OFFER TO SELL?

An offer to sell, offer for sale, or offer, is defined under Section 2(a)(3) of the Securities Act of 1933 to include every attempt or offer to dispose of, or solicitation of an offer to buy, a security or interest in a security, for value.

Section 5(a), Securities Act of 1933

Unless a registration statement is in effect as to a security, it shall be unlawful for any person directly or indirectly

(1) to make use of any means or instruments of transportation or communication in interstate commerce or of the mails to sell such security through the use or medium of any prospectus or otherwise; or

(2) to carry or cause to be carried through the mails or in interstate commerce, by any means or instruments of transportation, any such security for the purpose of sale or for delivery after sale.

You cannot use a prospectus to offer to sell or to sell securities without a registration statement, Section 5(c) Securities Act of 1933.

Limited Offering Exemptions—Private Offers

Regulation D, SEC, and Sections 4(2) and 3(b) of the Securities Act of 1933 streamline requirements for private offers and sales of securities. The regulation establishes three exemptions from registration in Rules 504, 505, and 506, Securities Act of 1933.

Rule 504 Securities Act of 1933

Rule 504 provides an exemption for non-reporting companies, unless they are blank check issuers, for sales of securities up to $1,000,000.

(1) The sale of up to $1,000,000 of securities in a 12-month period is permitted;

(2) No limitation is placed on the number of persons purchasing securities;

(3) The offering may be made with general solicitation or general advertising;

(4) The securities received in the offering are not restricted securities; and

(5) A Form D notice must be filed with the SEC headquarters within 15 days after the first sale of securities under this rule.

Unlike Rules 505 and 506, Rule 504 does not mandate that specific disclosure be provided to purchasers. However, sufficient information must be provided to meet the full disclosure requirements under the antifraud provisions of the securities laws.

Rule 505 Securities Act of 1933

Rule 505 provides a limited offering exemption for sales of securities totaling up to $5,000,000 in any 12-month period. This rule contains restrictions regarding accredited investors. Accredited investors are:

(1) Banks, insurance companies, registered investment companies, business development companies, small business investment companies;

(2) Employee benefit plans where investment decisions are made by a bank, insurance company, or registered adviser;

(3) Any employee benefit plan with total assets in excess of $5,000,000.

(4) Charitable organizations, corporations, or partnerships with assets in excess of $5,000,000.

(5) Directors, executive officers, and general partners of the issuer;

(6) Any entity where all equity owners are accredited investors;

(7) Natural persons with a net worth of at least $1,000,000;

(8) A natural person with an income in excess of $200,000 in each of the two most recent years, or joint spousal income of $300,000 for the last two years with a reasonable expectation of the same income in the current year.

(9) Trusts with assets of at least $5,000,000, not formed to acquire the securities offered and whose purchases are directed by a sophisticated person.

There is no specific information needed to be furnished accredited investors. Non-accredited investors must be advised of and furnished with, upon request, all material information furnished to accredited investors, as well as the following specific information:

(1) The issuer must be available to answer questions by prospective purchasers about the offering and issuer;

(2) The offering may not exceed $5,000,000 and may not be made by general solicitation or general advertising;

(3) The issuer may sell to an unlimited number of accredited investors and up to 35 non-accredited investors;

(4) Securities are restricted and may not be resold for up to two years. Investors must be informed of this restriction. The issuer must take steps to be sure investors will not resell.

(5) The issuer is not required to file any offering materials with the SEC; 15 days after the first sale in the offering, the issuer must file a notice of sales on Form D. Notice also has an undertaking that must be furnished the SEC. Upon staff's request, any information furnished non-accredited investors must be disclosed to the SEC.

Rule 506 Securities Act of 1933

To be exempt under this rule:

(1) There can be no ceiling on the amount to be raised;

(2) There is no general solicitation or general advertising permitted.

(3) The issuer may sell to an unlimited number of accredited investors and to 35 non-accredited investors. All non-accredited investors must be sophisticated, that is have sufficient experience in business and financial matters to be able to evaluate an investment.

(4) No specific information is required for accredited investors. Non-accredited must be advised and furnished upon request with all material information furnished to accredited investors, and any specific information.

(5) Securities sold are restricted for two years.

(6) The issuer must file notice 15 days after the first sale on Form D.

MECHANICS OF REGISTRATION

The registration process begins with filing a registration statement. Forms S-1, S-2, and S-3 are the basic forms and there are other forms for special situations.

The registration statement must describe the securities to be registered; the kind of business enterprise, its size, earnings, financial history, and capital structure; underwriters and underwriters' commissions; names of all who participate in management, control, and direction of the business, their security holdings, and their remuneration including options and payments to promoters made in the last two years or intended to be made in the future; acquisitions of property not in the ordinary course of business; interests of directors, officers, and principal shareholders; any legal proceedings pending, expected, or threatened; and the reason for the need for the proceeds and how they will be applied. Financial statements certified by an independent accountant must accompany the statement.

Incomplete or inaccurate statements can be cause for the Commission to reject the statement. Issuer is notified by informal letter as to in what respects the statement fails to comply with the regulations. The registrant can then file an amendment to correct the problems. If the SEC feels a deliberate attempt has been made to conceal or mislead the Commission, it can order a hearing to determine if a stop order should be issued. The minimum time from filing to the effective date is 20 days.

After Registration

The 1934 Act requires periodic disclosure by issuers registered under the act. Issuers must file an annual 10-K report which includes financial information and statements, must annually distribute a proxy statement or the equivalent containing information on remuneration of directors and officers and conflict of interest transactions, and must timely file 8-K reports whenever certain material events have occurred. The 1933 Act only requires **transactional disclosure** which is public distributions. A uniform S-K Form under Uniform Regulation covers both acts, rather than requiring separately filing under each.

Duties and Prohibitions When in Registration

The operation of Section 5 of the Securities Act of 1933 imposes limitations and responsibilities on the underwriters and dealers participating in the offer and sale of the issue of the securities prior to and after the filing of a registration statement.

Before Filing a Registration Statement   Offers to buy and offers to sell are unlawful. Preliminary negotiations and agreements between the issuer and the underwriter who is to make distribution and/or their agents are exempt under Section 2(a)(3) Securities Act of 1933. Financing negotiations can be carried on; but neither the issuer nor underwriter can offer the securities to dealers or investors, and it is unlawful for dealers to offer to buy the securities at this point. No selling can be done, and dealers cannot seek to be included in the selling group prior to registration. Any publicity about the issuer, proposed offering, or securities may be construed as an unlawful offer to sell. Therefore, an underwriter should not announce that it will be the underwriter; this could bring offers to buy that are illegal. Stock exchanges require certain announcements; Rule 135 permits a brief announcement of proposed rights, proposed stock exchange offerings, and offerings to employees as not constituting an offer in violation of the act.

After Filing but Before the Effective Date   After the registration but before the effective date, oral offers to sell the securities can be made, but no written offers can be made, except by a statutory prospectus. The tombstone advertisement is permitted at this time. Underwriters or dealers expecting to participate in the distribution have limitations on customer contact by the antifraud provisions of the act. Written material other than a statutory prospectus or tombstone advertisement may not be used. The dealer may orally solicit indications of interest or offers to buy from customers, and issue opinions as to whether or not these securities will be good investments. If the dealer will recommend the security, the dealer should have copies of the prospectus for information purposes. To accelerate the effective date, the issuer must show all possible actions to make information contained in the registration statement and statutory prospectus available to dealers who may participate in the distribution. No contracts of sale may be made at this time. The purchase price cannot be paid or received, and offers to buy can be canceled.

After the Effective Date   After the effective date oral offerings can continue and sales may be consummated. A copy of the final statutory prospectus must be delivered with any written order, or confirmation, or upon delivery of the security, whichever is first. Care needs to be taken to see that no information is false or misleading in the prospectus because time has elapsed since it was drawn. If the offering continues, the prospectus must be current and not misleading or false. All dealers trading in the registered security must use the prospectus for sales.

LIABILITY UNDER THE SECURITIES ACT

There are four basic provisions for liability under the Securities Act of 1933, Sections 17(a), 12(a)(2), 12(a)(1), and 11.

(1) *Section 17(a):* Section 17(a) is an antifraud provision. There is no private right of action under this section. It regulates sellers and offers. Rule 10b-5 was modeled after section 17(a). Rule 10b-5 regulates sellers and buyers. It does not regulate offers. There is a private right of action under Rule 10b-5.

(2) *Section 12(a)(2):* Section 12(a)(2) is an antifraud provision similar to Section 17(a). It provides for liability to injured buyers. It regulates both buyers and sellers. It does not depend on Section 5 for a violation. A person wrongfully selling an unregistered security is liable to the buyer. It requires privity of contract. The recovery of buyer is limited to the purchase price unless the security has been sold. If the buyer resold the security, the buyer is entitled to damages. Damages are the difference between the purchase price and the selling price (there can only have damages if the security was sold at a lower price than was paid for it). No reliance is necessary on the omission or misstatement. The buyer need not show reliance on misstatement or omission. The buyer must show a false statement or omission, and need not show the seller was at fault. This is a negligence standard with the burden of proof on the seller.

(3) *Section 12(a)(1):* Privity is required. Recovery is the same as in 12(a)(2). There is no reliance needed on a misstatement or omission violation of Section 5. The buyer must show it was sold in violation of Section 5. The seller does not have to make a false statement or omission of material facts.

(4) *Section 11:* Liability is limited to false statements in the registration statement. No reliance is necessary on false statements. The damages for the buyer is no more than the price paid unless the security was sold; then the buyer is entitled to damages totaling the difference between the purchase price and the selling price, and is not limited to the purchase price. There is strict liability for the issuer. The burden of proof is on the seller. The buyer can also bring action under Section 10b-5 for misrepresentations or omissions.

BLUE SKY LAWS

Section 18 of the Securities Act of 1933 says, "Nothing in this title shall affect the jurisdiction of the securities commission (or any agency or office performing like functions) of any State . . . over any securities or any person, . . ." Under this section state and federal regulations have survived side by side.

All states have securities regulations called Blue Sky Laws. Many securities are not registered under federal regulations because of exemptions. Many of the Blue Sky Laws are much stricter and broader in disclosure requirements than the federal act.

Three basic methods of regulation employed by states are fraud, dealer registration, and securities registration. Most states use all three methods. The methods, procedures, and standards vary greatly from state to state.

(1) *Fraud Method:* Certain areas are described as fraud and are grounds for criminal sanctions, suspension of trading, or both. The state administrator usually has broad powers to investigate. However, the powers are generally not used in the absence of a complaint or suspicious circumstances. Therefore, it is not always effective if not used with another method or methods.

(2) ***Dealer Registration Method:*** Before trading within the state, dealers (includes brokers, issuers, and salespeople) must register. The nature of information and the kind required to be disclosed on the registration form vary widely from state to state.

In many states registration may be denied or revoked for cause, and the administrator often has great latitude and discretion in determining who will be registered in the state.

(3) ***Security Registration Method:*** Trading in and dealing in securities is unlawful until registration has been completed in accordance with statutory procedures. This is sometimes referred to as **merit regulation** because the state administrator can deny registration on the ground that the security lacks merit even though full disclosure has been made. Under federal statutes the SEC does not pass on merit, just full disclosure. These statutes vary widely from state to state. Generally the states look for and try to restrict the sale of unseasoned, speculative securities attempting to be sold in the state.

A few other methods of state regulation:

(a) ***Qualifying Approach:*** Trading in non-exempt securities is unlawful until there has been an affirmative administration determination that the issue meets statutory standards in the state as fair, just, and equitable. Unsafe issues have broader standards. In most states, cheap stock, promotional stock, and options are limited to a percentage or amount that the administrators deem reasonable.

(b) ***Notification Approach:*** Registration by notification becomes effective after a designated period unless the administrator takes action to stop it. The administrator can still review the application based on merit criteria.

(c) ***Coordination Approach:*** This is similar to the notification approach, but it is only available for issues registered under the Federal Securities Act. Information to the state administrator is basically copies of the federal registration statement. The state registration becomes effective on the same date as the federal registration. The administrator can still review for merit during the waiting period.

Federal Securities Act is a reference to the Securities Act of 1933 and Securities Exchange Act of 1934. All Blue Sky Laws are state attempts to regulate the securities business in their state. The wide variety of legislation in the area has led to the Uniform Securities Act which three fourths of the states have adopted some parts of. The Uniform Securities Act encompasses all of the above six methods.

ANTIFRAUD PROVISIONS

Section 10(b) of the 1934 Act and Rule 10b-5 make it unlawful for any person using the mails or facilities of interstate commerce in connection with the purchase or sale of any security to:

(a) employ any device, scheme, or artifice to defraud;

(b) make any untrue statement of a material fact;

(c) omit to state a material fact without which the material is misleading; or

(d) engage in any act, practice, or course of business that operates or would operate as a fraud or deceit upon any person, in connection with the purchase or sale of any security.

MISLEADING PROXY STATEMENTS

Damages, recission, and attorneys' fees can be recovered when anyone distributes a materially false or misleading proxy statement. Liability is to the shareholder who suffered a loss in purchasing or selling relying on the proxy statement (case law).

FRAUDULENT TENDER OFFERS

Section 14(e) of the 1934 Act applies even if the target company is not subject to the act. It is unlawful for any person to make any untrue statement of a material fact; to omit to state any material fact; or to engage in any fraudulent, deceptive, or manipulative practice in connection with any tender offer.

CRIMINAL SANCTIONS

Section 32 of the 1934 Act imposes criminal sanctions on anyone willfully violating any provision of the act (except the antibribery provision) or the rules and regulations of the SEC. For individuals, conviction imposes a fine not over $1,000,000, or imprisonment not over ten years, or both. The exception for someone who proved no knowledge of the act is that there is no imprisonment. For a corporation the fine cannot exceed $2,500,000.

SUMMARY

Public distribution of securities is basically governed by two federal acts: The Security Act of 1933 and The Securities Exchange Act of 1934. To a lesser extent, state laws, known as Blue Sky Laws, govern securities. You must check the official meaning of words under the acts as their meanings are different than ordinary meanings. The 1933 Act is sometimes known as the Truth in Securities Law and was designed to prevent fraud, misrepresentation and deceit, and to provide the investor with material information needed to make an informed decision as to investments. The acts require full disclosure. For giving false information there are civil and criminal penalties.

The SEC does not approve a registration on merit. It looks for full disclosure and truthful disclosure. There are different forms to fill out for different businesses seeking registration. Twenty days after registration it becomes effective unless rejected by the SEC or if a stop order is issued. If needed, corrections and/or amendments can be filed; the effective date is 20 days from the last amendment filing.

There are certain exemptions available for registration. There are different kinds of underwriting: strict underwriting, firm commitment and best efforts deal. Each has advantages and disadvantages. Market out clauses can be placed in the underwriting agreement.

CASES

What Constitutes a Security?

REVES v. ERNST & YOUNG
Supreme Court of the United States, 1990
494 U.S. 56, 110 S Ct. 945

This case presents the question whether certain demand notes issued by the Farmer's Cooperative of Arkansas and Oklahoma are "securities" within the meaning of Section 3(a)-10 of the Securities Exchange Act of 1934. We conclude that they are.

To raise money to support its general business operation, the Co-Op sold promissory notes payable on demand by the holder. The notes were uncollateralized and uninsured. They paid a variable rate of interest that was adjusted monthly to keep it higher than the rate paid by local financial institutions. The Co-Op offered the notes to both members and non-members, marketing the scheme as an "investment program." Advertisements for the notes appeared in each Co-Op newsletter and read in part, "Your Co-Op has more than $11 million dollars in assets to stand behind your investments. The investment is not Federally insured but it is . . . safe . . . secure . . . and available when you need it." Despite these assurances the Co-Op filed for bankruptcy in 1984. Over 1,600 people held notes worth a total of $10 million.

Petitioners, a class of holders of the notes, filed suit against Arthur Young & Co., the firm that had audited the Co-Op's financial statements (the predecessor of Ernst & Young). Petitioners alleged the defendant failed to use generally accepted accounting practices in its audit, especially to the valuation of one of the assets, a gasohol plant. This was alleged to have been done to inflate the assets and net worth. Petitioners allege if the plant was treated properly in its audits, they would not have purchased the notes because the Co-Op's insolvency would have been apparent. Therefore, the antifraud provisions of the 1934 Act were violated.

The fundamental purpose of the acts is "to eliminate serious abuses in a largely unregulated securities market." The best way to achieve this goal is "to define the term 'security' as broadly as possible, to include many types of instruments that our commercial world would use to fall within the ordinary concept of a security."

There is no risk-reducing factor to suggest that these instruments are not in fact securities. The argument that they are payable on demand fails, as common stock can also be converted readily to cash on demand. We conclude they are securities.

Exemption

SEC v. RALSTON PURINA CO.
Supreme Court of the United States, 1953
346 U.S. 119

We must decide whether Ralston Purina's offerings of treasury stock to its "key employees" are within the exemption of not involving a public offering Section 4(1) of the 1933 Act. Complaint by the commission to enjoin the unregistered offering was dismissed by the District Court and affirmed by the Court of Appeals.

Ralston is staffed by over 7,000 employees, and since 1911 company policy was to encourage stock ownership by its employees. Between 1947 and 1951 Ralston sold $2 million of stock to employees without registration and in so doing used the mails. Parties taking advantage of the offer to buy these securities were electrician, artist, bakeshop foreman, chow loading fireman, copywriter, stock clerk, mill office clerk, credit trainee, production trainee, stenographer, and veterinarian. The buyers lived in over fifty widely scattered communities in various states. The lowest salary bracket of those purchasing was $2,700 in 1949, $2,435 in 1950, and $3,071 in 1951. No records were kept as to how many employees were solicited; the estimated number was 500 in 1951. The company claims exemption as all offerees were "key employees." That an offering to all of its employees would be public is conceded.

Blue Sky Laws and statutory antecedents of federal legislation have made one thing clear—to be public, an offer need not be open to the entire world. *SEC v. Sunbeam,* 95 F2d 699.

The act is designed to protect investors by promoting full disclosure of information necessary to make an informed decision. The question should be, did the particular class being offered the security need protection? An offering to those who can fend for themselves is a transaction "not involving any public offering."

The Commission has consistently interpreted the provision of exemption not to apply when a large number of offerees is involved. We agree some offerings may come under the exemption as to executives who have access to the same information as required in the registration process. Absent that showing, employees are no different than the investing public and entitled to the protection of the act.

Reversed.

WORDS TO KNOW

best efforts	merit regulation
broker	prospectus
controlling	registration statement
dealer	security
exemption	stop order
firm underwriting	strict underwriting
issuer	transactional disclosure
issues	underwriter
market out clause	underwriting syndicate

REVIEW QUESTIONS

1. What is an issuer?
2. Who is an underwriter?
3. Explain what a broker is.
4. What is the use of a registration statement?
5. What are the principal federal acts governing securities?
6. Explain the meaning of Blue Sky Laws.
7. Explain the antifraud provision.
8. Explain a stop order.
9. What are the various exemptions?
10. Explain a best efforts underwriting.

11. What is a security?
12. What is a sale?
13. What is an offer?
14. When and why is a market out clause used?
15. Explain a firm underwriting.
16. What is a registration statement, and what is its use?
17. What is and when is a prospectus used?
18. What kind of liability is there under the acts?
19. Are there any civil lawsuits permitted under the acts? By whom and for what?
20. If there is a state and federal regulation covering securities, which do you follow?
21. What is the maximum amount of an underwriting permitted under federal regulation?

SHORT ESSAYS

1. If an employer desires to sell stock to his employees, and has 5,000 employees, can this be accomplished with an exemption? Explain in detail.

2. An employer has 500 employees, assets of $1,000,000, sales of $5,000,000, and six family members who own the only class of issued and outstanding stock. Which of the federal acts cover this situation?

3. Jones, Inc., sold a small issue of common stock: 500,000 shares at $10 per share. Tom Investor bought 500 shares at $10 per share. It is now three years later and the stock is selling at $18 per share. Tom Investor just learned that the prospectus and the registration statement had false and misleading information in it. What kind of civil action does Tom Investor have?

4. Mr. Friend is president and chairman of the board of a corporation that is looking to sell $15,000,000 in common stock in a public offering. The corporation has $90,000,000 in assets, and yearly sales of $195,000,000. He is not sure of the kind of underwriting commitment he should seek. What do you think and why?

CERTIFICATE OF INCORPORATION
OF
(name of corporation)

First: The name of the corporation is (insert name of corporation).

Second: The registered address of the corporation in the State of Delaware is (insert address)   . The name of its registered agent at such address is (insert name).

Third: The purpose of the corporation is to engage in any lawful act or activity for which corporations may be organized under the general Corporation Law of the State of Delaware.

Fourth: The total number of shares for which the corporation shall have authority to issue is 3,000 shares of capital stock, no par value. (Insert whatever stock you desire the corporation to have power to issue.)

Fifth: The name and mailing address of the incorporator is (insert name and address).

Sixth: The board of directors of the corporation is expressly authorized to make, alter, or repeal bylaws of the corporation. The stockholders may make additional bylaws and may alter, repeal, or modify any bylaw whether adopted by them or otherwise.

Seventh: Elections of directors do not have to be by written ballot unless provided otherwise in the bylaws of the corporation.

The undersigned incorporator herein acknowledges that the foregoing certificate of incorporation is the act and deed of said incorporator and that the same is true.

_____

(Signature of Incorporator)

Appendix B
FORM OF MINUTES OF ORGANIZATION MEETING

MINUTES OF ORGANIZATION MEETING
OF THE BOARD OF DIRECTORS
OF
(name of corporation)

An organization meeting of the board of directors of (Place name of corporation here) was held at the offices of the corporation, (insert address of corporation)   , on the   (place date here)   day of (place month here)   , 20   , pursuant to a written Waiver of Notice signed by all of the directors named in the Certificate of Incorporation fixing the time and place aforesaid.

The following directors were present in person:

(List names of directors named in Certificate of Incorporation, from one to infinite).

1.

2.

3.

4.

5.

Upon motion duly made and carried,   (list name)   , was elected temporary chairman and   (list name)   was elected temporary Secretary of the meeting.

The chairman reported that the original Certificate of Incorporation was filed in the office of the secretary of state of the state of   (insert state)   , on   (insert date), 20   . That the state tax and other fees incident to the filing thereof had been paid to the state of   (insert state)   , and that a certified copy of the Certificate of Incorporation has been filed for record on   (insert date), 20   , in the office of the county clerk in and for the county of   (insert county of main office).

The secretary then presented a certified copy of the Certificate of Incorporation, and, on motion duly made, seconded and unanimously carried, it was ordered that said copy be inserted in the Minute Book of the Corporation following the minutes of this meeting. The secretary presented and read the Waiver of Notice of this meeting, duly signed by all of the directors as aforesaid, which waiver, on motion duly made, seconded, and unanimously carried, was ordered to be inserted in the Minute Book of the Corporation following the minutes of this meeting.

The secretary presented a form of bylaws for the regulation of the affairs of the Corporation, which was read article by article and unanimously adopted. Upon motion duly made, seconded, and unanimously carried, it was ordered that the said bylaws as adopted be inserted in the Minute Book following the minutes of this meeting.

Upon motion duly made, seconded, and unanimously carried, the following persons were elected to the offices set opposite their respective names, to hold such offices until their successors shall be duly elected and qualified:

President	(Name)
Treasurer	(Name)
Secretary	(Name)

Upon motion duly made, seconded, and unanimously carried, the following resolution was adopted,

IT IS HEREBY RESOLVED, that the treasurer, be and hereby is, authorized to open a bank account in the name of the Corporation in the   (name of bank)   , for the deposit of funds of the corporation, and in this connection the bank resolution form contained in the certificate of said bank attached hereto as Exhibit A, is hereby adopted, and that (1) all checks, drafts, notes, bills of exchange, acceptances, undertakings, and other instruments or orders of payment, transfer, or withdrawal of monies in the amount of One Thousand Dollars ($1,000.00) or less for whatever purpose and to whomever payable shall be the signature of any one of the following:

(Name)

(Name)

and (2) all checks, drafts, notes, bills of exchange, acceptances, undertakings, and other instruments for payment, transfer, or withdrawal of money in excess of One Thousand Dollars ($1,000.00) for whatever reason and to whomever payable shall require the signature of any two of the following:

(Name)

(Name)

(Name)

(Name)

The chairman then reported that the Corporation has received the offer of (insert name of subscriber), to purchase   (number)   shares of the common stock of the Corporation for the purchase price of ($) per share. Thereupon, upon motion duly made, seconded and unanimously carried, the following solution was adopted:

IT IS HEREBY RESOLVED, that the appropriate officers of this Corporation be, and they are hereby, authorized and directed to accept the offer of   (name)   to purchase   (number)   of shares of the common stock of the Corporation for the price of (\$), such consideration to be allocated to the stated capital account on the books of the Corporation, and

IT IS FURTHER RESOLVED, that the appropriate officers of this Corporation be, and they are authorized and directed to execute and deliver certificates evidencing such shares in exchange for the said purchase price.

There being no further business, on motion duly made, seconded, and unanimously carried, the meeting was adjourned.

_____
(Secretary)

All present at meeting sign here:

1.
2.
3.
4.
5.
6.
etc.

Note: The purchase of the above shares was by subscription. If more than one person subscribed to buy shares, list them in the paragraph.

Note: If you want only one signature on checks regardless of amount, change the form. If you want two or more signatures for whatever amount or amounts you desire, change the form.

Appendix C
FORM OF BYLAWS

BYLAWS
OF
(name of corporation)
ARTICLE I
Stockholders

Section 1.1 *Annual Meeting.* An annual meeting of stockholders shall be held for the election of directors at such date, time, and place within the state of incorporation (if a Delaware corporation it would say within or without the State of Incorporation) as may be designated by resolution of the board of directors from time to time. Any proper business may be transacted at the annual meeting.

Section 1.2 *Special Meetings.* Special meetings of stockholders for any purpose may be called at any time by the board of directors, or by a committee of the board of directors, if said committee by resolution of the board, has power to call a special meeting.

Section 1.3 *Notice of Meetings.* Whenever stockholders are required or permitted to take any action at a meeting, a written notice of the meeting shall be given stating the place, time, and date of the meeting, and in the case of a special meeting, the purpose or purposes for which it is called. Unless otherwise provided by law, the certificate of incorporation or these bylaws, the written notice of any meeting shall be given not less than ten nor more than sixty days before the date of the meeting, to each stockholder entitled to vote at such meeting.

If mailed, such notice shall be deemed to be given when deposited in the mail, postage prepaid, directed to the stockholder at his address as it appears on the records of the corporation.

Section 1.4 *Adjournments.* Any meeting of stockholders, annual or special, may be adjourned from time to time to reconvene at the same or some other place, and notice need not be given of any such adjourned meeting if the time and place are announced at the meeting at which the adjournment is taken. At the adjourned meeting the corporation may transact any business which might have been transacted at the original meeting. If the adjournment is for more than thirty days, or if after the adjournment a new record date is fixed for the adjourned meeting, a notice of the adjourned meeting shall be given to each stockholder of record entitled to vote at the meeting.

Section 1.5 *Quorum.* Except as otherwise provided by law, the certificate of incorporation, or these bylaws, at each meeting of stockholders the presence in person or by proxy of the holders of shares of stock holding a majority of the votes which could be cast by the holders of all outstanding shares of stock entitled to vote at the meeting shall be necessary and sufficient to constitutue a quorum. In the absence of a quorum, the stockholders present may by majority vote adjourn the meeting from time to time in the manner provided in Section 1.4 of these bylaws until a quorum shall attend. Shares of its own stock belonging to the corporation or to another corporation, if a majority of shares entitled to vote in the election of directors of such other corporation is held, directly or indirectly, by the corporation, shall neither be entitled to vote nor be counted for quorum purposes; provided, however, that the foregoing shall not limit the right of the corporation to vote stock, including but not limited to its own stock, held by it in a fiduciary capacity.

Section 1.6 *Organization.*   Meetings of stockholders shall be presided over by the chairman of the board, if any, or in his absence by the vice chairman of the board, if any, or in his absence by the president, or in his absence by a vice-president, or in the absence of the foregoing persons by a chairman designated by a chairman chosen at the meeting. The secretary shall act as secretary of the meeting, but in his presence the chairman may appoint any person to act as secretary of the meeting.

Section 1.7 *Voting: Proxies.*   Except as otherwise provided by the certificate of incorporation, each stockholder entitled to vote at any meeting of stockholders shall be entitled to one vote per share of stock held, which has voting power on the question. Each stockholder entitled to vote at a meeting of stockholders may authorize another person or persons to act for him by proxy, but no such proxy shall be voted or acted upon after three years from its date, unless the proxy provides for a longer period of time. A duly executed proxy shall be irrevocable if it states that it is irrevocable as long as provided so by law. A stockholder may revoke any proxy not irrevocable by attending the meeting and voting in person, or by filing an instrument in writing, revoking the proxy with the secretary of the corporation. Voting at a stockholders meeting need not be by written ballot, and need not be conducted by inspectors of election, unless so determined by the holders of shares of stock, having a majority of the votes which could be cast by the holders of all outstanding shares of stock entitled to vote thereon which when present in person or by proxy at such meeting. At all meetings of stockholders for the election of directors, a plurality of the votes cast shall be sufficient to elect. All other elections will be decided by a majority of the votes which could be cast by the holders of all shares of stock entitled to vote thereon which are present in person or by proxy.

Section 1.8 *Fixing Date to Determine Stockholders of Record.*   In order that the corporation may determine the stockholders entitled to notice or to vote at any meeting of stockholders or any adjournment thereof, or to express consent to any corporate action in writing without a meeting, or entitled to receive payment of any dividend or other distribution or allotment of any rights, or entitled to exercise any right in respect of change, conversion or exchange of stock or for the purpose of any other lawful action, the board of directors may fix a record date, which record date shall not precede the date upon which the resolution fixing the record date is adopted and which record date: (1) determination of stockholders entitled to vote at any meeting of stockholders or adjournment thereof, shall unless otherwise required by law, not be more than sixty nor less than ten days before the date of such meeting; (2) in determination of stockholders entitled to express consent to corporate action in writing without a meeting, shall not be more than ten days from the date upon which the resolution fixing the record date is adopted by the board of directors; and (3) in the case of other action shall not be more than sixty days prior to such action.

If no record date is fixed: (1) the record date for notice of or to vote at a meeting of stakeholders shall be at the close of business on the day next preceding the day on which notice is given, or if waived, at the close of business the next day preceding the day on which the meeting is held; (2) the record date for determining stockholders entitled to express consent to corporate action in writing without a meeting when no prior action of the board of directors is required by law, shall be the first date on which a signed written consent is delivered to the corporation in accordance with applicable law. Or if prior action of the board is required, shall be the date the board adopts the resolution and (3) the record date for determining stockholders for any other purpose shall be at the close of business on the day on which the board of directors adopts the resolution hereto.

Section 1.9 *List of Stockholders Entitled to Vote.* The secretary shall prepare and make, at least ten days before every meeting of stockholders, a complete list of stockholders entitled to vote at the meeting, in alphabetical order, and showing the address of each stockholder and the number of shares registered in the name of each stockholder. This list shall be open to examination by any stockholder for any purpose during normal business hours for a period of at least ten days prior to any meeting; this shall be available at the place specified for the meeting. The list shall also be available at the time of the meeting and be available to any stockholder attending. Upon the willful neglect or refusal of the directors to produce said list at any meeting for election of directors, they, the directors, shall be ineligible for election to any office at said meeting. The corporate stock ledger shall be the only evidence as to who shall be eligible to inspect the ledger, or to vote in person or by proxy.

Section 1.10 *Action by Consent of Stockholders.* Unless otherwise restricted by the certificate of incorporation, any action required or permitted to be taken at any annual or special meeting of the stockholders, may be taken without a meeting, and without prior notice, and without a vote, if, consent in writing, setting forth the action so taken, shall be signed by the holders of outstanding stock having not less than the minimum of votes that would be necessary to authorize or take such action at a meeting at which all shares entitled to vote were present and voted. Prompt notice of the taking of this corporate action without a meeting by less than unanimous written consent shall be given those stockholders who have not consented in writing.

ARTICLE II
Board of Directors

Section 2.1 *Number, Qualifications.* The board of directors shall consist of one or more members, the number thereof to be determined from time to time by resolution of the board of directors. Directors need not be stockholders.

Section 2.2 *Election; Resignation; Removal; Vacancies.* The board of directors shall initially consist of the persons named as directors in the certificate of incorporation, and each director so elected shall hold office until the first annual stockholders meeting or until his successor is elected and qualified. At the first annual meeting of stockholders and at each annual meeting thereafter, the stockholders shall elect directors each of whom shall hold office for a term of one year or until his successor is elected and qualified. Any director may resign at any time upon written notice to the corporation. Any newly created directorship or any vacancy occurring in the board of directors for any cause may be filled by a majority of the remaining members of the board of directors, although majority is less than a quorum, or by a plurality of the votes cast at a meeting of stockholders, and each director so elected shall hold office until the expiration of the term of office of the director whom he has replaced or until his successor is elected and qualified.

Section 2.3 *Regular Meetings.*   Regular meetings of the board of directors may be held at such places within or without the state, and at such times as the board of directors may from time to time determine, and if so determined notices thereof need not be given.

Section 2.4 *Special Meetings.*   Special meetings of the board of directors may be held at any time or place within or without the state whenever called by the president, any vice-president, secretary, or by any member of the board of directors. Notice of a special meeting of the board of directors shall be given by the person calling the meeting at least twenty-four hours prior to the special meeting.

Section 2.5 *Telephonic Meetings Permitted.*   Members of the board of directors, or any committee designated by the board, may participate in a meeting thereof by means of conference telephone or similar communications equipment by means of which all persons participating in the meeting can hear each other, and participation in a meeting pursuant to this bylaw shall constitute presence in person at such meeting.

Section 2.6 *Quorum; Vote Required for Action.*   At all meetings of the board of directors a majority of the whole board shall constitute a quorum for the transaction of business. Except in cases in which the certificate of incorporation or these bylaws otherwise provide, the vote of a majority of the directors present at a meeting at which a quorum is present shall be the act of the board of directors.

Section 2.7 *Organization.*   Meetings of the board of directors shall be presided over by the chairman of the board, if any, or in his absence by the vice-chairman of the board, if any, or in his absence by the president, or in his absence by a chairman chosen at the meeting. The secretary shall act as secretary of the meeting, and in his absence the chairman of the meeting may appoint a secretary to act for the meeting.

Section 2.8 *Informal Action by Directors.*   Unless otherwise restricted by the certificate of incorporation or these bylaws, any action required or permitted to be taken at any meeting of the board of directors, or any committee thereof, may be taken without a meeting if all members of the board or such committee, as the case may be, consent thereto in writing, and the writing or writings be filed with the minutes of proceedings of the board of directors or such committee.

ARTICLE III
Committees

Section 3.1 *Committees.*   The board of directors may, by resolution passed by a majority of the whole board, designate one or more committees, each committee to consist of one or more directors of the corporation. The board may designate one or more members as alternates of any committee to replace any absent or disqualified member of such committee. In the absence or disqualification of a member of a committee, the members present at any meeting may unanimously appoint another member to the committee whether or not they constitute a quorum to act at said meeting.

Section 3.2 *Committee Rules.*   Unless the board of directors otherwise provides, each committee designated by the board may make, alter, and repeal rules for the conduct of its business. In the absence of such rules each committee shall conduct its business in the same manner as the board of directors conducts its business pursuant to Article III of these bylaws.

ARTICLE IV
Officers

Section 4.1 *Executive Officers; Election; Qualifications; Term of Office; Resignations; Removal; Vacancies.* The board of directors shall elect a president and a secretary, and it may if it desires elect a chairman of the board and a vice-chairman of the board, from among the board members. The board may also elect one or more vice-presidents, assistant secretary and a treasurer and assistant treasurer. Each such officer shall hold office until the first meeting of the board of directors after the annual stockholders meeting next succeeding his election, and until his successor is elected and qualified or until his earlier resignation or removal. Any officer may resign at any time upon written notice to the corporation. The board of directors may remove any officer with or without cause at any time, but such removal shall be without prejudice to the contractual rights of such officer, if any, with the corporation. Any number of offices may be held by the same person. Any vacancy occurring in any office of the corporation by death, resignation, removal, or otherwise may be filled for the unexpired portion of the term by the board of directors at any regular or special meeting.

Section 4.2 *Powers and Duties of Executive Officers.* The officers of the corporation shall have such powers and duties in the management of the corporation as may be prescribed the board of directors and to the extent not provided, as generally pertain to their respective offices, subject to the control of the board of directors. The board may require any officer, agent, or employee to give security for the faithful performance of his or her duties.

ARTICLE V
Stock

Section 5.1 *Certificates.* Every holder of stock shall be entitled to have a certificate signed by or in the name of the corporation by the chairman or vice-chairman of the board of directors, if any, or the president or a vice-president, and by the treasurer or an assistant treasurer, or the secretary or assistant secretary of the corporation, certifying the number of shares owned and type of shares owned in the corporation. Any or all of the signatures may be a facsimile. In case any officer, transfer agent, or registrar who has signed or whose facsimile signature has been placed upon a certificate shall have ceased to be such officer, transfer agent, or registrar before such certificate is issued, it may be issued by the corporation with the same effect as if he were such officer, transfer agent, or registrar at the date of issue.

Section 5.2 *Lost, Stolen, or Destroyed Stock Certificates.* The corporation may issue a new certificate of stock in the place of any certificate theretofore issued by it, alleged to have been lost, stolen, or destroyed, and the corporation may require the owner of the lost, stolen, or destroyed certificate, or his legal representative, to give the corporation a bond sufficient to indemnify it against any claim that may be made against it on account of the alleged loss, theft, or destruction of any such certificate or the issuance of such new certificate.

ARTICLE VI
Indemnification

Section 6.1 *Right to Indemnification.* The corporation shall indemnify and hold harmless, to the fullest extent permitted by applicable law as it presently exists or may hereafter be amended, any person who was or is made or is threatened to be made a party or is otherwise involved in any action, suit, or proceeding, whether civil, criminal, administrative, or investigative by reason of the fact that he, or a person for whom he is the legal representative, is or was a director, officer, employee, or agent of the corporation or is or was serving at the request of another corporation or of a partnership joint venture, trust, enterprise, or non-profit entity, including service with respect to employee benefit plans, against all liability and loss suffered and expenses reasonably incurred by such person. The corporation shall be required to indemnify a person only if the preceding was authorized by the board of directors of the corporation.

Section 6.2 *Prepayment of Expenses.* The corporation shall pay the expenses incurred in defending any proceeding in advance of its final disposition, provided, however, that the payment of these expenses incurred by a director or officer in advance of the final disposition. The proceeding shall be made only upon receipt of an undertaking by the director or officer to repay all amounts advanced if it should be ultimately determined that the director or officer is not entitled to be indemnified under this article or otherwise.

Section 6.3 *Claims.* If a claim for indemnification or payment of expenses under this article is not paid in full within sixty days after a written claim has been received by the corporation, the claimant may file suit to recover the unpaid amount of such claim and, if successful in whole or in part, shall be entitled to be paid the expense of presecuting the claim. In any such action, the corporation shall have the burden of proving the claimant was not entitled to the requested indemnification or payment of expenses under applicable law.

Section 6.4 *Non-Exclusivity of Rights.* The rights conferred on any person by this article shall not be exclusive of any other rights which such person may have or hereafter acquire under any statute, provision of the certificate of incorporation, these bylaws, agreement, vote of stockholders or disinterested directors, or otherwise.

Section 6.5 *Other Indemnification.* The corporation's obligation, if any, to indemnify any person who was or is serving at its request as a director, officer, employee, or agent of another corporation, partnership, joint venture, trust, enterprise, or non-profit entity shall be reduced by any amount such person may collect as indemnification from such other corporation, partnership, trust, joint venture, enterprise, or non-profit enterprise.

Section 6.6 *Amendment or Repeal.* Any repeal or modification of the foregoing provisions of this article shall adversely affect any right or protection hereunder of any person in respect of any act or omission occurring prior to the time of such repeal or modification.

ARTICLE VII
Miscellaneous

Section 7.1 *Fiscal Year.* The fiscal year of the corporation shall be determined by resolution of the board of directors.

Section 7.2 *Seal.* The corporation seal shall have the name of the corporation inscribed thereon and shall be in such form as may be approved from time to time by the board of directors.

Section 7.3 *Waiver of Notice of Meetings of Stockholders, Directors, and Committees.* Any written waiver of notice, signed by the person entitled to notice, whether before or after the time stated therein, shall be deemed an equivalent to notice. Attendance of a person at a meeting shall constitute waiver of notice of such meeting, except when attending the meeting solely for the purpose of objecting, at the beginning of the matter, to the transaction of any business because the meeting was not lawfully called or convened. Neither the business to be transacted at, nor the purpose of any regular or special meeting of the stockholders, directors, or members of a committee of directors need be specified in writing.

Section 7.4   *Interested Directors; Quorum.*   No contract or transaction between the corporation and one or more of its officers or directors, or between the corporation and any other person, corporation, association, or other organization in which one or more of its directors or officers have a financial interest shall be void or voidable solely for this reason, or solely because the director or officer is present at or participates in the meeting of the board, or committee thereof, which authorizes the contract or transaction, or solely because his, her, or their votes are counted for such purpose, if: (1) the material facts as to his, her, or their relationship or interest and as to the contract or transaction are disclosed or are known to the board or the committee, and the board or committee in good faith authorizes the contract or transaction by the affirmative votes of a majority of the disinterested directors, even though the disinterested directors constitute less than a quorum; or (2) the material facts as to his, her, or their relationship or interest and as to the contract or transaction are disclosed or are known to the stockholders entitled to vote thereon, and the contract or transaction is specifically approved in good faith by vote of the stockholders; or (3) the contract or transaction is fair as to the corporation as of the time it is authorized, approved, or ratified by the board, a committee thereof, or the stockholders. Common or interested directors may be counted in determining the presence of a quorum at a meeting of the board or committee which authorizes the contract or transaction.

Section 7.5   *Form of Records.*   Any records maintained by the corporation in the regular course of its business, including its stock ledger, books of account, and minute books, may be kept on, or be in the form of, punch cards, magnetic tape, photographs, microphotographs, or any other information storage device, provided that the records so kept can be converted into clearly legible form within a reasonable time. The corporation shall so convert any records so kept upon the request of any person entitled to inspect same.

Section 7.6   *Amendment of Bylaws.*   The bylaws may be altered or repealed and new bylaws made, by the board of directors, but the stockholders may make additional bylaws and may alter and repeal any bylaws whether adopted by them or otherwise.

FORM FOR A CLOSE CORPORATION AGREEMENT
A/K/A (also known as) STOCKHOLDERS AGREEMENT

AGREEMENT made this   day of   , 20   , by and between JOE ACCOUNTANT, residing at 123 Book Street, Good Town, Minnesota, hereinafter referred to as "JOE"; FRED MARKETING, residing at 5657 Market Street, Chicago, Illinois, hereinafter referred to as "FRED"; TOM SALES, residing at 987 Sales Street, Portsmouth, Maine, hereinafter referred to as "TOM"; JOHN INSURANCE, residing at 468 Prudential Lane, Boston, Massachusetts, hereinafter referred to as "JOHN"; and MARIE EXECUTIVE, residing at 456 Executive Blvd., Scarsdale, New York, hereinafter referred to as "MARIE".

WHEREAS "JOE" represents that he is an accountant with twelve years experience and is a senior partner in the accountantcy firm of Books, Pencil, and Eraser, and

WHEREAS "FRED" represents he is marketing vice-president with the firm of Marketing and Marketing, and has been with the firm for nine years, and

WHEREAS "TOM" represents that he is a senior partner in Sales Galore, a sales company with offices in fifteen states and two foreign countries, and that he is a founder of the firm which was started thirteen years ago, and

WHEREAS "JOHN" represents that he is an independent insurance broker with offices in five cities and is the sole owner of the business, and

WHEREAS "MARIE" represents that she is an executive vice president with ABC Corp., a Fortune 500 company. She has been with the company twelve years, and

WHEREAS The parties have formed a corporation known as Best Friends, Inc., and desire said corporation to be a close corporation.

WITNESSETH:

NOW, THEREFORE, the parties agree as follows:

FIRST: The corporation known as Best Friends, Inc., was duly chartered in the state of New York on the   day of   , 20   , with a capitalization of 250 of no par common stock. The stockholders in this corporation all signatories to this agreement, shall be as follows:

Joe Accountant	Address as above	Two Shares, no par common stock.
Fred Marketing	Address as above	Two Shares, no par common stock.
Tom Sales	Address as above	Two Shares, no par common stock.
John Insurance	Address as above	Two Shares, no par common stock.
Marie Executive	Address as above	Two Shares, no par common stock.

Each stockholder shall purchase their stock interest from the corporation for an original issue purchase price of seventy-five thousand dollars ($75,000.00) per share; one hundred and fifty thousand dollars ($150,000.00) for the two shares.

SECOND: The names of the members of the board of directors of the corporation shall be as follows:

JOE ACCOUNTANT
FRED MARKETING
TOM SALES
JOHN INSURANCE
MARIE EXECUTIVE

It is herein agreed that all of the stockholders of this corporation shall, at all times hereinafter, vote their entire stock interest for the above-named parties as directors of the corporation. No other parties may be nominated for director or be elected as a director unless there is unanimous written consent, of all the stockholders of the corporation to nominate and elect a party not named herein. It is further agreed that all of the above directors will at all times vote to elect Marie Executive, as chairperson of the board and Tom Sales as vice-chairman of the board. Any change herein requires the unanimous written consent of all of the stockholders.

THIRD: The officers of the corporation shall be as follows:

Marie Executive	President
Fred Marketing	Vice President, Marketing
Tom Sales	Vice President, Sales
Joe Accountant	Treasurer
John Insurance	Secretary

It is herein agreed that all of the directors of this corporation, above named, shall at all times hereinafter, vote for the above-named parties to be and remain as these officers of the corporation. No other party may be nominated or elected respectfully to these offices without the written unanimous consent of all the stockholders of the corporation.

FOURTH: The duties of each officer shall be as spelled out in the bylaws of the corporation. Each officer shall receive a yearly salary of fifty-five thousand dollars ($55,000.00). It is agreed that at the end of the second year, these salaries will be reviewed with an interest to increasing them to a rate consistent with their job duties in this industry. It is also understood and agreed that the president, marketing vice president, and sales vice president will be entitled to a bonus each year after the second year based upon profits achieved. The industry standards shall be the guide to use for these bonuses. These bonuses are in recognition of the additional hours and travel that these positions normally entail.

FIFTH: It is agreed that as soon as a value is set for the corporation, to be used if a stockholder tenders stock, pursuant to this agreement, on death, disability or desire to sell, then, in any of these events, the purchase price down payment will be funded through the purchase of an insurance policy. As soon as the corporate value is set (as discussed in detail later herein), the corporation shall purchase an appropriate policy and pay the premiums to cover said policy or policies. It is further agreed herein that as soon as the corporation is profitable, a policy will be obtained and paid for by the corporation to fund the entire purchase price. The object being to guarantee the purchase by the corporation, rather than by strangers and to guarantee the selling stockholder a buyer at a fair price.

The corporation shall within one year, or sooner if financially feasible, obtain a medical coverage policy for all employees and stockholders. At first the cost can be split between the corporation and stockholder or employee, but as soon as feasible, the corporation will pay the full premium.

It is the intention of the parties hereto that the corporation offer life insurance to its employees, as soon as financially practicable. Officers will receive two weeks vacation the first year, three weeks the second and third years, and four weeks thereafter. It is the intention of the parties hereto to be a very good employer and to take care of its employees in as many ways as possible and financially feasible.

As soon as practicable, the corporation shall purchase vehicles for the use of officers.

SIXTH: In the event one of the signers to this agreement becomes sick or mentally or physically disabled for a prolonged period of time and unable to perform the normal daily duties assigned, the party will receive full salary for the first two months of disability, half salary for the next four months, and one-quarter salary for the following four months. Thereafter, the party will receive no salary for the next four months; if still unable to return to full-time work, the stock interest of the party will be deemed tendered for sale pursuant to section "Eighth" herein. We are referring here to continuous disability, not cumulative.

SEVENTH: Every year, on the first Tuesday after the start of the fiscal year, the parties hereto will agree to setting a value on the corporation. This value will then be placed in a document to be known as "Certificate of Agreed Value," and recorded with the secretary of the corporation. The Certificate of Agreed Value shall be in force for a period of one year from its date, or until a new certificate of agreed value is issued in its place and stead. The Certificate of Agreed Value and the value stated therein shall be the conclusive value of the corporation. That value cannot be changed or modified without the unanimous consent of the signers of the certificate.

The Certificate of Agreed Value shall also contain the method of paying the seller of a stock interest, as follows: for example, let us assume that the value of the corporation is set at $1,000,000 in a certificate of agreed value. Assume that there are five equal stockholders. Assume one stockholder passes away. The selling price of that stockholder's interest as set in the certificate shall be $200,000, plus any monies owed the deceased by the corporation. The payment shall be 10 percent down, paid in cash upon the date of the sale, to the spouse of the deceased. In the event there is no spouse, it is paid then to the executor of the estate of the deceased. This payment shall in no event be longer than sixty days from the date of death of the deceased, and no less than twenty-one days from the date of death of the deceased. The remaining $180,000 plus one-fifth of any monies owed the deceased by the corporation, shall be paid the executor of the estate over a five-year period, the first payment being made one year after the date of the down payment. The remaining payments after the down payment shall be made in equal installments, including interest, which shall be the prime rate plus one percent on the date of death of the deceased. The stock interest of the deceased shall be retained by the spouse or estate until fully paid, at which time the certificate or certificates will be transferred to the corporation. Until fully paid, the spouse or estate shall vote the shares of the deceased. These terms can be modified each time a certificate of agreed value is executed by all stockholders, if unanimously desired and agreed to.

If for any reason, the corporation is unwilling or unable for any reason whatsoever to buy the shares of the deceased, then, the shares shall automatically be offered to all surviving stockholders in equal amounts at the above price and terms. If all of the stockholders, for any reason whatsoever, do not wish to purchase the interest of the deceased, then, the stock shall automatically be offered to the remaining stockholders or any one or group that wishes to purchase in equal shares, upon the same terms as stated above. If no stockholder wishes to purchase, then, the corporation shall be dissolved.

In the event any stockholder wishes to sell his, her, or its interest, the procedure shall be to tender the stock to the corporation for sale, the selling price and method of payment shall be the same as above for a deceased stockholder.

In the event a stockholder is disabled, physically or mentally, pursuant to paragraph "SIXTH" herein, then, the stock interest tendered shall be purchased pursuant to the terms of this section as if deceased.

In the event a stockholder is adjudicated incompetent or insane by a court of competent jurisdiction, then, the interest of that stockholder shall be deemed tendered to the corporation. The purchase price and terms of sale shall be pursuant to paragraph "SEVENTH" hereof as if deceased.

EIGHTH: In the event, for any reason whatsoever, there is no Certificate of Agreed Value that is recorded with the secretary of the corporation, or if the certificate recorded has for any reason whatsoever, been declared void by a court of competent jurisdiction, or otherwise, then, in any of these events, the purchase price shall be arrived at as follows: The corporation's Certified Public Accountant (CPA), or if no Certified Public Account is at that time being used by the corporation, then the last Certified Public Account used by the corporation, or if the corporation never used a Certified Public Account, then, the last accountant or bookkeeper used by the corporation, shall hire the closest of the top seven Certified Public Accountants in the country to set a value on the corporation. This shall be done by an inventory of all assets of the corporation. The price set shall either be current market value or the price paid for the asset, whichever is larger. All accounts receivable shall be considered and the accounts payable deducted from the accounts receivable. No provision shall be made for outstanding loans owed by the corporation and no provision shall be made for goodwill. Both loans owed and goodwill shall be valued at zero. Loans owed the corporation shall be valued at the full remaining balance owed. The cost of this shall be borne by the corporation. As soon as a value is set, the sale shall continue as outlined in paragraph "SEVENTH" herein.

NINTH: In the event the corporation requires additional capital, upon the unanimous consent of the board of directors, the chairman or president shall be impowered to negotiate a loan with a local bank or lending institution subject to the approval of the complete board. In the event a bank or lending institution is not willing to negotiate a favorable loan, then, the board may impower the chairman, or the president, to negotiate a loan on favorable terms with an individual or group of investors, subject to the approval of the board of directors.

In the event a loan cannot be negotiated with a bank, lending institution, private investor, or group of investors, then, the board can assess each member a sum of dollars, either as a capital contribution or as a loan to the corporation, as decided by the board.

TENTH: Dissolution of the corporation can be accomplished as follows: pursuant to paragraph "SEVENTH" herein, if the board votes to dissolve, oppressive actions by the board can be grounds for dissolution. If the board is continuously deadlocked on an issue, it may be grounds for dissolution.

In the event of dissolution, the assets of the corporation shall be sold, the creditors paid, the loans of stockholders to the corporation repaid, and the remaining monies divided among the stockholders on a pro rata basis determined by their stock holdings. Payment to the stockholders can be in cash, or in kind if agreeable by the stockholders.

ELEVENTH: Any dispute by the parties hereto with reference to this agreement shall be submitted to the American Arbitration Association for arbitration pursuant to its rules. The losing party shall pay all arbitration costs. The award of the arbitrator shall be binding with the same force and effect as a court order and may not be appealed.

TWELFTH: This agreement shall be construed in accordance with the laws of the state of New York.

THIRTEENTH: This agreement shall be binding on the parties hereto, their heirs, successors, and assigns, and cannot be modified or amended except in writing with the same formality as this agreement. A legend shall be placed on all stock certificates of the corporation as issued that they are held subject to the terms of this agreement.

WHEREUPON, the parties have hereunto set their hands and seals the day and year first above written.

_____	_____
Joe Accountant	Fred Marketing
_____	_____
Tom Sales	John Insurance
_____	
Marie Executive	

CERTIFICATE OF AGREED VALUE
OF
BEST FRIENDS, INC.

The parties hereto are all of the stockholders of Best Friends, Inc.

It is hereby stipulated and agreed that the value of this corporation is hereby set at one million dollars ($1,000,000).

That this price shall be pro rata according to the stock ownership of the selling party. The payment of same shall be pursuant to paragraph "SEVENTH" of the close corporation agreement dated   entered into between the parties hereto.

That this certificate shall remain in effect for a period of one year from the date the hereof or until a new certificate is executed by the parties and recorded by the secretary of the corporation.

This certificate shall be recorded by the secretary of the corporation. Signed and sealed this   day of   , 20   .

Joe Accountant	Fred Marketing
Tom Sales	John Insurance
Marie Executive	

Appendix F
FORM FOR A PROXY

PROXY FOR ABC CORPORATION
MEETING MAY 5, 2000

To: John Jones   0145 0000 18630 07
234 Main Street
Anywhere, USA 12345

Please mark your votes as in this example.   ⊠

This proxy when executed will be voted as you specify below. If you do not specify otherwise, the proxy will be voted FOR election of directors, and FOR items 1 through 3.

	For	Withheld	
1. Election of Directors	☐	☐	

	For	Against	Abstain
2. Appointment of Independent Public Accountant.	☐	☐	☐

	For	Against	Abstain
3. Amendment of Performance Based Compensation Plans.	☐	☐	☐

The undersigned, whose signature appears at the bottom of this page, hereby appoint John Smith, Fred Klutz, and Abe Honest, jointly and severally, proxies with full power of substitution to vote all shares of common stock the undersigned is entitled to vote at the Annual Meeting of Stockholders of ABC CORPORATION, on May 5, 20   , or adjournments thereof, on items 1 through 3 as specified herein and on such other matters as may properly come before the meeting.

Nominees for director: Thomas Two, John Three, Fred Four, Peter Five, and Mickey Six. You are encouraged to specify your choices by marking the appropriate boxes, but you need not mark any box if you wish to vote in accordance with the board of directors recommendations.

_____   Date, _____ 20__
Signature

GLOSSARY

absorb   To acquire or take in, as in a merger.

abstention   To abstain from voting (not vote).

acquisitions   Assets that are bought or acquired.

action   A legal proceeding commenced by the service of a summons or petition.

administrative   Executive or ministerial action.

adverse claims   Claims by various parties, all claiming the same rights.

affidavit   A written document sworn to before a notary public or someone authorized to administer oaths.

alien corporation   A corporation chartered in another country.

ambiguities   Not definite and certain; unclear.

appraisal rights   Rights granted by statute to determine the price of property by a third party expert.

assents   Agreement to do something; consent.

assets   All property, real, personal, tangible, intangible, legal, or equitable, that can be used to pay debts.

authorized stock   Amount of stock a corporation is authorized to issue or sell.

bankruptcy definition   Equitable definition—not paying bills on time; bankruptcy court definition—having more debts than assets.

bearer endorsement   A negotiable instrument made payable to the bearer. An instrument endorsed in blank.

bequest   A gift by will of personal property.

best efforts   All efforts that can be done to complete a transaction or contract.

bind   To make one liable for their actions; to obligate.

blank endorsement   A negotiable instrument signed in blank or made payable to the bearer.

blue sky laws   Laws intended to stop the sale of fraudulent stocks or stock by fly-by-night companies.

bona fide purchaser   Someone who purchases for value without notice of any defects.

bonds   Contracts to pay a certain sum of money at a particular date with interest at various times, as stated in the contract.

breach of contract   When a party to a contract fails to perform its obligations under the contract.

breached   When a party to a contract has failed to perform pursuant to the terms of the contract.

broker   Anyone engaged in the transaction or business of securities for the account of another.

business entity   A vehicle used to conduct business, such as a corporation, partnership, or joint venture.

business judgment rule   Allows corporate directors to make sound decisions based on knowledge and inquiry without personal liability.

C corporation   A corporation that is taxed as a corporation.

call   An option to buy a set number of shares at a set price within an agreed period of time. The opposite of a put.

callable bonds   Bonds that are redeemable by the issuer on certain conditions as stated in the bond.

capital surplus   Entire surplus of a corporation other than earned surplus. Excess paid over par value; from a higher reappraisal of assets; allocation from par value stock.

cash for assets   Use of cash to purchase assets of a corporation. A method of taking over a corporation.

cash for stock   Use of cash to purchase at least a majority of stock outstanding to take over a corporation.

certificate of agreed value   A certificate executed by parties, usually in a close corporation, to evaluate the corporation on a yearly basis.

certificate of authority   Authorization to function as a corporation, sometimes called a charter or a certificate of incorporation.

certificated security   A stock certificate.

chartered   Authorized by a state to function as a corporation.

classes of stock   Common, preferred, and various series stock can be issued.

close corporation   A small group may sign a close corporation agreement to restrict sale of stock.

comity   Each state must grant comity, or full recognition to the legal orders and statutes of another state.

commingling   The corporate accounts, or debts, cannot be mixed with the personal accounts or debts of stockholders.

commingling funds   Not keeping monies separate. Corporate monies cannot be mixed with the monies of shareholders in one account.

common fund theory   Plaintiff wins a derivative action and the monies are placed in a common fund under direction of the court for use by all for costs, and so forth.

common law   Stare Decisis; case law.

common stock   Usually has voting rights and often pays dividends. Different series have different rights.

consolidation transferor   In a consolidation, a new name emerges and stocks have to be transferred.

constructive trust   If a director uses inside knowledge to make money, the court can place that money earned in a constructive trust for the benefit of the corporation.

contingency fee   A fee based on something else occurring first. For example, if you win a case, you receive a percentage of the win.

controlling   One who is in a position that allows directing management and controlling the company direction and actions.

corporate address   The address of the main office of the corporation.

corporate opportunity   When the corporation has the opportunity to contract, buy, or sell something, a director or officer cannot take the deal away from the corporation.

corporation   An artificial person who is chartered by a state and permitted to function in that state. Corporations can be domestic, foreign, or alien.

crown jewels   The major assets of a corporation.

cumulative voting   Multiply the number of shares a stockholder has by the number of positions on the board to be filled, and that is the number of votes the stockholder has.

de facto corporation   A corporation that has not properly completed its paperwork with the state to be chartered.

de jure corporation   A corporation that is chartered and has completed its paperwork with the state properly.

deadlock   When the same amount of people vote yes and the same amount vote no. Usually the bylaws allow the chairman to have an extra vote to break the deadlock.

dealer   A person who makes successive sales as a business.

debentures   Security for a loan to a public company, usually issued in a series; states the terms of the loan.

debt securities   Bonds issued by a corporation to raise funds.

deceased   A person that has expired (died).

deceptive   Intent to deceive.

defraud   To cheat, trick, deceive and/or mislead intentionally.

deposition   Testimony of a witness that is reduced to writing, not in open court, but on notice to all parties, to be used as testimony in a court.

derivative action   Action by a party on behalf of another party. All benefit from the action accrues to the other party who benefits from the action.

derivative stockholders   An action by a stockholder on behalf of the corporation. All benefits of the action go to the corporation.

devise   A gift of real property by the last will and testament of the donor.

direct action   An action by a party for the benefit of the party bringing the action.

directors   Persons elected or appointed to manage and/or direct the affairs of a corporation.

dissolution   Dissolution can be either voluntary or involuntary. *See also* voluntary dissolution; involuntary dissolution.

distributions   Can be cash, property, or stock distributions (dividends); or distributions after dissolution of stock, cash, or assets that are left after payment of all debts.

diversity of citizenship   When one party to a lawsuit resides and works in a different state than the other party to the lawsuit, raising jurisdiction questions.

dividend   Can be cash, stock, or property, distributed to shareholders when declared by the board of directors.

document   Any form of writing.

domestic corporation   A corporation doing business in the state of incorporation.

due care   Care that a reasonable, prudent person would exercise under similar circumstances.

duty of diligence   A director must act with reasonable care and skill and make decisions only after properly obtaining all information necessary for an informed decision.

earned surplus   Undistributed net profits, income, gains, and losses.

enabling   Legislation that permits something to be done is called enabling legislation.

endorsement   The act of a holder of a negotiable instrument in signing the instrument on the reverse side.

equitable ownership   When one has ownership but has given another the right of possession and voting, as in a voting trust.

equity   Justice administered that is fair and just, rather than through the strictly formulated rules of common law.

equity capital   Capital earned by a corporation through its sale of stock interests.

equity securities   Stock certificates sold by the corporation to raise capital.

exceptions   Items that are excepted (not covered) by certain legislation.

exclusive statute   The statute is the only basis to obtain indemnification. No other indemnification is allowed.

execute   The act of signing a document.

exemption   Items not covered by the legislation. They are exempted.

fiduciary   Someone who has rights and powers to be exercised for the benefit of another; a director or trustee.

fiduciary duties   A fiduciary cannot take advantage of the trust placed in the fiduciary and must proceed as a normal, reasonable prudent person would under similar circumstances.

firm underwriting   An underwriting that is firm, not subject to any conditions limiting the sale of the stock. The issuer is guaranteed to receive the full amount of the underwriting.

foreign corporation   A corporation doing business in a state other than where it is chartered.

freeze-outs   A majority shareholder prevents a minority shareholder from participating in the decision making process.

general partnership   Two or more persons or entities carrying on a business for profit as co-owners.

heirs   A legal right, regulated by law, stating who the heirs of an ancestor are. For example, siblings are heirs of their parents.

hypothecate   To pledge something without delivering title of it to the pledgee; as in hypothecating securities with a bank for a loan.

impairing   To weaken or diminish. The bankruptcy court can impair a contract.

in kind   In the distribution of assets after dissolution, the assets can be sold and the cash distributed, or some can receive cash and others in-kind, meaning they would receive some asset equal to the cash they would have received.

income bonds   The interest rate on the bond would be stated, and that percentage would be paid on the income earned by a named asset in the bond.

incompetent   Evidence that cannot be used in court; lack of ability to discharge the required duty.

incorporation   Abbreviated by Inc.; means a corporation.

indemnification   Paying someone back after they have paid another person's debt.

indentures   An agreement, a contract. Very often used with bonds and states the entire contract of the loan.

independent committee   Usually appointed from directors serving on the board and used to determine if another director took a corporate opportunity from the corporation.

indispensable party   A necessary party to a legal proceeding.

infinite   Continuing forever.

insider interest   The interest of an insider. A person who has knowledge about the corporation that the general public does not have.

interested director   A director who has a personal, financial, or otherwise interest in a corporate transaction, other than the interest of the corporation.

interrogatories   Written questions that must be answered as sworn testimony; used to prepare for a trial.

intrinsic fairness   Absolute fairness.

involuntary dissolution   Dissolution by court order, creditors, bankruptcy, or administratively by the state.

issue   Point in a contract, arbitration, or court litigation.

issued   Corporate stock that has been issued and is outstanding.

issued stock   *See* issued.

issuer   The corporation that issued the stock.

issues   Points in a contract, usually submitted to a court or arbitrator as questions to be decided.

judgment   A decision by the court. With a person, it means the opinion of the person.

judicial   Proceeding from a court or judge.

judiciously   Done in a judicial manner.

junk bonds   A bond with a high risk of default, usually used in an LBO.

LBO   Another name for a leveraged buyout.

legal entity   An entity that can buy and sell real estate and enter into contracts in its own name.

legend   A notice, as a legend on a stock certificate, advising of restrictions on the sale or otherwise of the certificate.

liability   Something for which one must pay or make good.

limited partnership   One or more general partners and one or more limited partners. It is formal, must comply with the statute, and must be in writing.

litigation   A lawsuit to enforce a right through the courts.

lock-up   When one broker or dealer has full control of selling a new issue or a series of bonds in corporation law. Occurs when a favored bidder is given a good deal on the purchase of assets or stock to ward off a raider.

loss causation   A loss that must be as a result of the wrongs of the insider.

lost certificate   A stock certificate that is lost, misplaced, or destroyed. Each corporation transfer agent has a timely procedure you must follow before being issued a replacement certificate.

majority   Fifty percent of the vote plus one more vote.

manipulative   Use of trickery.

market efficiency   All information available to investors is quickly reflected in the price. For example, stock splits and dividends.

market out clause   Gives the underwriter a chance to cancel the contract on any change in circumstances of the issuer.

maturing   The date when an obligation becomes due.

merger   When two or more corporations come together and one of them is the survivor.

misnomer   An incorrect name in a pleading or document.

net assets   The total assets of a business or person, minus the total debts of the business or person.

nimble dividends   Dividends paid out of current profits.

no par value   Stock that is sold without having a par value.

nonassessable   Stock sold that is fully paid for and cannot be assessed any additional monies.

nonexclusive statute   For example, indemnification can be obtained through the statute plus the bylaws of the corporation. In an exclusive statute, only the statute, not the bylaws, govern.

original issue   The first sale of stock by the corporation. The selling price goes to the corporation.

outstanding stock   Stock that has been issued and is held by investors or others. Not held by the corporation.

overissue   When the corporation sells more stock than it is authorized to sell in the certificate of incorporation.

par value   An arbitrary figure set by the board of directors for the initial original issue sale, which must be at least at par value.

parent   When another corporation owns the majority of stock of a corporation, the other corporation becomes a subsidiary; the owner of a subsidiary.

participating bonds   Where a bondholder participates in the net profits of the corporation, usually by receiving a percentage of the gains in the form of interest.

perpetuate   To cause to last indefinitely, as in a corporation.

perpetuating   Lasting forever.

personal property   Everything that is not real property. Real property is land and anything firmly attached that cannot be removed without damage to the item or the land.

piercing the corporate veil   When someone attempts to defraud with a corporation to avoid paying debts. The court can order personal liability on the stockholders.

plurality   The person having the largest amount of votes; preemptive rights.

preemptive rights principal   When a stockholder has preemptive rights, the stockholder can buy the same percentage interest in another issue by the corporation to maintain the same percentage interest in ownership.

preferred stock   Stock that pays dividends before common stock gets paid dividends.

principal office   The main office of a corporation.

private action   An action for the sole benefit of a person instead of bringing a derivative action where the benefit goes to a corporation and costs may have to be deposited.

private attorney general   This is a theory to aid private parties in bringing a derivative lawsuit where they will receive costs for the action.

pro rata   Proportionately; according to a certain rate, percentage, or proportion.

promissory note   A written promise to pay a stated sum of money at a stated time.

property dividend   Payment by a corporation of some property as a dividend; for example, a case of corn flakes for each 500 shares owned of the corn flakes company. It can also have a cash dividend or other kind of dividend with it.

prospectus   A document setting forth the nature and objects of an issue of shares, bonds, or securities, inviting the public to subscribe and participate in purchasing the same.

proximate   Closest in casual connection; nearness; as in proximate cause, the cause of the action.

proxy   A written authorization permitting someone to vote shares of stock other than the true owner.

public corp   A corporation that is traded on an exchange.

punitive damages   Damages that are in addition to compensation damages to punish a civil wrong that was intentional.

quorum   The number of directors or stockholders necessary to be present at a meeting to legally carry on the business of the meeting.

raider   Party who is attempting to take over a corporation.

redeem   When a corporation buys up its shares or bonds.

redemption   A corporation can sell bonds and/or stocks with redemption rights in the corporation so that the corporation can redeem the securities pursuant to the agreement.

registration   If you sell stocks or bonds to the public, they have to be registered with the SEC unless you claim an exemption.

registration statement   The registration statement requires full disclosure. Violation thereof can result in criminal and civil sanctions.

regulatory   The SEC is the regulatory agency for the federal government. State governments also have regulatory agencies for securities.

reorganization   Reorganization sometimes leads to a merger or take over. Other times it is used to settle debts.

resident agent   One who is in the state where the corporation does business to accept process on behalf of the corporation. Every corporation needs a resident agent.

resolution   When the board of directors agrees on something, they pass a resolution to carry out the agreement.

reverse triangular merger   Method of merger without tax. A minimum of 80 percent of stock must be transferred.

right to dissent   When a stockholders' vote is necessary, any stockholder can dissent; sometimes this gives the dissenter the right of appraisal to determine the value of the holdings of the dissenter so the corporation can purchase the dissenter's interest.

RMBCA   Revised Model Business Corporation Act.

Rule 10b-5   Insider prohibitions concerning buying and selling of securities.

S corporation   When a small group are the stockholders; on petition to the Internal Revenue Service, you can become an S corporation and be taxed as a general partnership instead of as a corporation.

scienter   Having the intent to injure someone or cause losses to someone; a willful, intentional, knowing act to cause damage.

secondary market   After the original issue, the stock of many public corporations is traded on the secondary market or exchanges.

Section 10(b)   Anti-fraud provision.

secured bonds   Bonds that are secured by some asset of the corporation.

security   Collateral given for a loan, bond, or note.

security for costs   Some states require security for costs prior to commencing a derivative stockholders action to prevent unnecessary suits.

series of stock   A group of stock that is sold, possibly a series with a special right to vote on a particular issue.

service of process   When a person is served with a subpoena, summons, petition, or other legal document.

settlement objection   When one objects to a settlement. Sometimes they are entitled to appraisal rights and sale of their interest instead of the settlement.

share exchange   Majority of shareholders agree to share exchange. All shareholders thereafter must accept the exchange.

shareholder   A person who owns stock in a corporation.

short form mergers   The parent of a subsidiary merges the subsidiary into the parent. Needs approval of both boards. No appraisal rights if any dissenters.

short swing profits   Profits made by buying and selling a security within a 6-month period.

signatories   The parties that sign a document.

sole liability   The only person having liability.

sole proprietorship   A business owned by one person and not incorporated.

sovereignty   States and the federal government are sovereigns. A sovereign cannot be sued without its permission, or legislation permitting the lawsuit against the sovereign.

standards of conduct   How one should perform in a given situation.

standards of review   The court decides whether there is liability and whether to issue a judgment or other order.

standstill   Management agrees with a favored stockholder to buy more stock and not sell to the raider without first offering to the target.

stated capital   All of the monies a corporation received for its stock, except for the amount allocated to capital surplus; also includes amount transferred to cover a dividend payout.

statute   On the federal and state side statutes: county, city, town, or village ordinances. Administrative agencies: rules and regulations.

statutes   *See* statute.

statutory intent   The intent of the legislators in passing the legislation.

statutory mergers   The boards of all corporations merging approve the merger. Many states do not require shareholder approval.

stock dividend   A dividend in stock instead of cash or property.

stock for assets   When stock is used to purchase assets of a corporation for take over purposes; a method of merger.

stock for stock   A method of merger. Exchange stock in one company for stock in another.

stock interest   A person who owns stock has a stock interest or equity interest in the corporation.

stock options   The right to buy stock at a stated price some time in the future with condition for purchase.

stock rights   A right to buy additional shares if issued.

stock splits   When a corporation splits its stock, two for one or any other split.

stockholder   One who owns an interest in the corporation through stock ownership.

stockholders agreement   A closed corporation agreement, or just an agreement between shareholders in a small corporation defining the rights of all parties.

stop order   An order by the SEC to stop all sales in a security pending investigation by the SEC.

straight preferred stock   The usual kind of stock issued. Fixed dividend, paid quarterly; dividends must be paid before common can be paid. Rights on dissolution.

strict liability   Any unauthorized acts by the corporation will cause strict liability to the persons committing the acts in certain jurisdictions.

strict underwriting   Underwriter agrees to sell the entire issue.

subscribe   When one subscribes (agrees) to purchase a stated amount of securities at a stated price on certain conditions.

subsidiary   A division of the corporation, controlled or fully owned by the parent.

suppletory   When an act is suppletory it covers only those areas where a private agreement does not govern.

surplus   The amount by which the net capital of a corporation exceeds its assets.

survivor   The corporation that survives in a merger.

target   The company being taken over.

tax aspects   The various tax consequences of a transaction.

tender   A tender is an offer of delivery.

tender offer   An offer to buy a stated amount of securities at a stated price for a stated time.

transaction causation   When plaintiff sues to recover for violation of the rule. There must be a relationship between defendant's violation of Rule 10b-5 and plaintiff's purchase or sale.

transactional disclosure   Disclosure only concerning a public issue.

transferee   The buyer.

treasury stock   When a corporation redeems its stock, it becomes treasury stock.

triangular merger   A method of effecting a merger without the liabilities of the corporation to be merged.

Truth in Securities Act   The 1933 Securities and Exchange Act.

"Type A"   Statutory merger for tax purposes.

"Type B"   Stock for stock merger; no cash. For tax purposes.

"Type C"   Stock for stock merger; can be cash involved. For tax reasons.

ultra vires act   An act that is unauthorized by the certificate of incorporation.

unanimous   The unanimous vote of those voting; all vote the same.

uncertificated security   A stock issued by a document rather than a certificate of stock.

underwriter   Any one group, or entity offering the sale of securities.

unified intent   Where the legislature does not make a special act or section to cover a subject, but modifies various other statutes to include these problems.

unsecured bonds   Bonds that have no specific collateral other than the general assets of the company.

vehicle   The method used to go into business; for example, corporation or general partnership.

vesting   A point in time when the property belongs to the vestee.

voluntary dissolution   The board of directors with the consent of the shareholders agrees to dissolve, or when the articles of incorporation state dissolution is to be on a certain date.

voting group   An agreement by a group that one person will vote on their behalf as agreed by the group or that all in the group will vote in the same manner on certain issues.

warrants   Usually traded on an exchange; warrants are similar to options.

white knight   A favorite to take over a corporation.

with cause   Having good legal reason to do something; for example, to discipline or terminate an employee with just cause.

without cause   Without legal reason to do something; for example, to terminate or suspend an employee unlawfully.

INDEX